# The Scrolls and Christian Origins

# The Scrolls and Christian Origins

Studies in the Jewish Background of the New Testament

*by*

## MATTHEW BLACK

**St Mary's College
The University of St Andrews**

Charles Scribner's Sons, New York

Dead Sea scrolls
Qumran community
Christianity - origin

# Preface

The basis of this book was a course of lectures delivered in May, 1956, under the Morse Lectureship Foundation, in Union Theological Seminary, New York. It seemed advisable, at the time, to postpone publication until more of the texts of the scrolls were available, and the result has been a more copious use of the Qumran material now accessible to scholars. Not all these texts are yet published or accessible, but any further delay in the publication of these studies would have seemed a discourtesy to the sponsors of the Morse Lectureship and the Seminary which did me the honour of inviting me to deliver the lectures.

In any case, while important texts may still be forthcoming (though we may well have had the best of Qumran), there is already an abundance of original material for the most part in Hebrew, available, not to mention a veritable flood of Qumran studies; and there has already emerged, in the course of the prolonged Qumran debate, a number of well-grounded working hypotheses (such as the identity of the Qumran sect with the ancient Essenes) which furnish the New Testament scholar with ample material for comparison and judgment.

The importance of this new material for the problems of Christian origins is widely acknowledged. The distinguished American orientalist W. F. Albright wrote (*BASOR*, Supplementary Studies, Nos. 10-12 (1951), p. 58): 'The new evidence with regard to the beliefs and practices of Jewish sectarians of the last two centuries B.C. bids fair to revolutionize our approach to the beginnings of Christianity . . . , and it is safe to say that nothing written on the sectarian movements of the last three centuries of the Second Temple can escape thorough revision in the light of the evidence now available. . . .' In the same vein M. Dupont-Sommer, who pioneered the Essene hypothesis, wrote: 'All the problems relative to primitive Christianity henceforth find themselves placed in a new light, which forces us to reconsider them completely' (*The Jewish Sect of Qumran and the Essenes*, p. 152). These opinions were given in the first flush of discovery, and subsequent studies have led to more temperate statements, but the view is nevertheless crystallizing among scholars that it is from this side of Judaism that Christianity took its origins.

It is certainly becoming increasingly recognized in historical scholarship on the New Testament documents that one of the few approaches still left to us to the complex issues of Christian beginnings is to seek to 'wring truth relevant to the history of Jesus from the increasing stock of remains of the Judaism of his time' (D. E. Nineham, in *JTS*, October, 1960, p. 260). That stock has been enormously enriched by the Qumran discoveries.

It was not possible to deal with the central problems without at the same time attempting some reassessment, in the light of the scrolls, of the Greek and patristic evidence for ancient Judaism, and, in addition to so doing, I have included in the book an appendix with a new English translation of the main reports of Josephus and Philo on the Essenes.

Several parts of the book have appeared, usually in earlier drafts, in several learned periodicals, and I am grateful to their editors for permission to reproduce them. The patristic accounts of Jewish sects formed the subject of a lecture given in Manchester which has appeared in the *Bulletin of the John Rylands Library*, 41, March, 1959. I am grateful to the editors of 'The Background of the New Testament and its Eschatology' for permission to reprint in the form of an appendix my study of the Josephan and Hippolytean reports about the Essenes. Appendix B appeared as part of an article entitled 'The Recovery of the Language of Jesus' in *New Testament Studies*, 3, 305ff., and Appendix D is a shortened form of a contribution to *New Testament Essays*, published as a memorial volume for T. W. Manson (Manchester University Press, 1958).

Emeritus Professor H. H. Rowley of Manchester very kindly read an early draft of the lectures and made a number of helpful suggestions. And I owe a special debt of gratitude to Professor James Muilenburg of Union Theological Seminary, New York, and a former Director of the American Schools of Oriental Research in Jerusalem, for hospitality and help during my first visit to Jerusalem and Qumran and for early encouragement and stimulus in these studies. Père Roland de Vaux, Director of the École Biblique, has also given me every facility for a first-hand acquaintance with the scrolls and the Qumran excavations.

I am indebted to Miss Gillian Unwin, a former secretary in St Mary's College, for help with my first draft, and to her successor, Miss Mary Blackwood, for the completion of the final draft of the typescript. The Rev. J. P. Robinson, of Stockton, California, a post-graduate student in St Mary's, has kindly assisted me in the preparation of the indexes.

It remains for me to thank the publishers for their patience in waiting for my manuscript and for their skill and co-operation in the printing of it.

M.B.

St Mary's College
University of St Andrews
December, 1960

# Contents

# List of Plates

# Abbreviations

## (1) Abbreviations for Qumran texts
### (as in Barthélemy-Milik, *Discoveries in the Judaean Desert, Qumran Cave I*, p. 46ff.)

| | |
|---|---|
| 1 QS | *Manual of Discipline* |
| 1 QSa | Appendix to 1 QS (*Serekh ha'edhah* or *Rule of the Congregation*) |
| 1 QSb | Collection of *Benedictions* |
| 1 QM | *War of the Sons of Light with the Sons of Darkness* |
| 1 QH | *Hymns of Thanksgiving* |
| CD | *Damascus Document* (Fragments of a Zadokite Work) |
| 4 QEx<sup>a</sup> | *Exodus* fragment from Cave 4 |
| 1 Qp.Hab | *Habakkuk Commentary* |

## (2) Other Abbreviations

| | |
|---|---|
| *BASOR* | *Bulletin of the American Schools of Oriental Research* |
| *CSEL* | *Corpus Scriptorum Ecclesiasticorum Latinorum* |
| *ET* | *Expository Times* |
| *HTR* | *Harvard Theological Review* |
| *JBL* | *Journal of Biblical Literature* |
| *JJS* | *Journal of Jewish Studies* |
| *JTS* | *Journal of Theological Studies* |
| *NTS* | *New Testament Studies* |
| *RB* | *Revue Biblique* |
| *REJ* | *Revue des Études Juives* |
| *RHPR* | *Revue d'Histoire et de Philosophie religieuses* |
| *RHR* | *Revue de l'Histoire des Religions* |
| *VT* | *Vetus Testamentum* |
| *ZATW* | *Zeitschrift für die Alttestamentliche Wissenschaft* |
| *ZNTW* | *Zeitschrift für die Neutestamentliche Wissenschaft* |
| *ZRG* | *Zeitschrift für Religions—und Geistesgeschichte* |

# Part I: HISTORICAL

KANSAS CENTER
for
**PUBLIC** EDUCATION RELIGION STUDIES
1300 Oread
Lawrance, Kansas 66045

CHAPTER I

# The Qumran Essenes

I

### THE QUMRAN 'ESSENES' AND THEIR LIBRARY

It is now more than twelve years since the chance discovery
by a Bedouin Arab of a hoard of hidden Hebrew documents,
written on parchment, in a cave overlooking the northern
shores of the Dead Sea.  Since then almost every cave, in an
area honeycombed with caves, has been explored and an
entire library—or the debris of a library—brought to light.
The first discoveries consisted of both Biblical and non-
Biblical documents, two scrolls of Isaiah, a commentary on
the text of Habakkuk of a very peculiar type, a document
which was proved to be the rule of a Jewish sect and has been
given the name *The Manual of Discipline*, a collection of
ancient Hebrew psalms or 'hymns', and a scroll describing a
kind of Armageddon, and given the title by its first editor
'The War of the Sons of Light with the Sons of Darkness'.

A second harvest of manuscripts was yielded by later
exploration, and numerous fragments of documents are at
present deposited, for the most part, in the Palestine
Museum; they cover most of the books of the Hebrew canon,
and include other commentaries of the same type as the
Habakkuk commentary, with, in addition, Hebrew and
Aramaic fragments of the inter-testamental Apocrypha and
Pseudepigrapha (Enoch, Jubilees, Tobit, the Testaments of
the Twelve Patriarchs) and similar writings, together with
a fragment of the Greek Old Testament.  A copper scroll,
containing what appears to be an inventory of Temple
treasure, has also been discovered.[1]

[1] An up-to-date account of the scrolls at the time of writing will be found in
J. T. Milik, *Ten Years of Discovery in the Wilderness of Judaea* (S.C.M., London,
1957), or in Millar Burrows, *The Dead Sea Scrolls* (1955) and *More Light on the
Dead Sea Scrolls* (1958).
  In addition to the Qumran texts, Hebrew documents have been found at other

3

These remarkable finds at Qumran had a dramatic sequel. They gave an impetus to archaeologists to excavate some ancient ruins in the neighbourhood of the caves and a nearby cemetery with more than a thousand graves: the main ruin is known as Khirbet Qumran, and is situated less than a mile south of the first cave, on a terrace of marl overlooking the ravine of Wadi Qumran and about the same distance from the shores of the Dead Sea. A second ruin, more recently excavated, lies some three miles to the south at 'Ain Feshka, where a spring of fresh water terminates a cultivable strip of coastal plain, stretching from within a few hundred yards of the Khirbeh itself.[1]

The prevailing theory is that these ancient ruins represent the remains of the famous Essene settlement located in this area by the Elder Pliny[2]; and that the scrolls belong to the library of the sect, hidden away for safety in the nearby caves at some time during the first Jewish Revolt (A.D. 64-70), possibly even hurriedly deposited in the caves at a single *moment critique* during the war, when the Roman legions approached the Dead Sea in the summer campaign of Vespasian to Jericho in A.D. 68.[3]

The view that the people of the scrolls were Essenes now enjoys a wide consensus of scholarly opinion.[4] It may, indeed, be regarded as one of the best established positions about the scrolls so far reached. So much in the scrolls themselves chimes in with the reports of the Essene sect in the ancient historians, the Elder Pliny, Josephus, and Philo Judaeus of Alexandria.[5] The geographical location alone at Qumran on the northwestern escarpment of the Dead Sea

sites in the Judaean desert, all of them, however, of a later vintage than the Qumran scrolls; they are all certainly post-Christian, and include a letter from the famous Jewish insurgent Bar-Cochba, from the second century A.D. (Milik, op. cit., p. 14f.).

[1] The excavations were conducted mainly by Père Roland de Vaux of the École Biblique et Archéologique Française (Jordan). Reports appeared in *RB*, 56 (1949), 60 (1953), 61 (1954), 63 (1956), 65 (1958), Milik, op. cit. p. 45f., and F. M. Cross, *The Ancient Library of Qumran and Modern Biblical Studies* (New York, 1958), p. 10f.

[2] Cf. *Historia Naturalis*, v.15. See infra, p. 9ff.

[3] The theory was first propounded by de Vaux, *RB*, 61, 1954, 232f.; cf. Milik, op. cit. p. 54f., Cross, op. cit. p. 45f.

[4] Cf. Cross, op. cit. p. 37.

[5] Cf., e.g., M. Burrows, 'The Discipline Manual of the Judaean Covenanters', in *Oudtestamentische Studiën*, Vol. 8, Leiden, 1950, pp. 156-92.

above 'Ain Geddi and some nine miles south of Jericho, and the settlement of Essenes reported in this same area by Pliny creates a strong presumption in favour of the identity of the two groups.[1]

Nevertheless, there are differences between the Essenes of the ancient Greek historians and the Qumran sect, and it may not be possible to account for all of these by the well-known idealizing tendencies of the Jewish-Greek authors, or by the hellenistic dress into which they at times have forced their subjects. Some of the more striking of these differences are discussed fully in a later chapter.[2] Meantime, however, if we are to see the Qumran sect in proper perspective, something must be said about the general character of Jewish 'sects' and 'sectarianism' in the conditions immediately prior to the year A.D. 70.

In his famous introduction to his discussion of Jewish 'sects',[3] Josephus describes the three main branches of the Jewish religion of the day, the three Jewish 'philosophies', Pharisees, Sadducees, and Essenes, by the term αἱρεσεῖς, a word which is usually rendered by 'sects' and which has given us the term 'heresy'. Both in its customary English equivalent, however, 'sects', and in its later derived sense of 'heresies', the expression αἱρεσεῖς can be extremely mis-leading, when applied to forms of Judaism at the beginning of the Christian era. For Josephus and his period it was a convenient term to denote opposing 'schools of thought', holding different and frequently conflicting tenets and beliefs. Pharisees and Sadducees, the custodians of the official Judaism of the period, centred on Jerusalem, are classed as αἱρεσεῖς side by side with the Essenes, an unofficial, marginal group of their co-religionists with whom they were frequently in conflict. The pejorative use of the term is a later Christian development, as catholic orthodoxy began to define itself over against opposing forms of belief.

Apart from its basic tenet of monotheism there never was any officially defined or recognized type of 'orthodoxy' in ancient Judaism before A.D. 70. On the contrary, there

---

[1] See further infra, p. 9.
[2] Infra, p. 26f.
[3] *Bellum Judaicum*, II.viii.2.

appears to have been the greatest latitude in matters of religious belief and speculation.  To regard, therefore, diverging groups within pre-Christian Judaism as 'sects' or 'heresies' in the later ecclesiological sense is to form a quite untrue picture of the situation.

But there always have been in the Jewish religion official standards of religious *orthopraxis*, the proper application of the Law (implying its correct interpretation), the correct observance of the annual festivals at the officially appointed seasons, the correct performance of rites and customs in Synagogue and Temple.   In ancient Judaism these were laid down by the religious party or parties in power, which, in the time of Christ, were represented by an uneasy coalition (under Rome) between Pharisees and Sadducees, and which, in practice, was predominantly the party of the Pharisees. Deviation from this official religion, centring on the Temple and Torah of Jerusalem was 'sectarianism'.

Jewish sectarianism in its pre-Christian forms can only be usefully defined, or, indeed, defined at all, as non-Pharisaic religious movements related to the Judaism of the Second Temple.

There were many such movements in pre-Christian Judaism.  According to the rabbis, it was this divisive tendency within the body of Judaism, and the proliferation of 'sects', each with its own special form of heteropraxis, which was one of the main causes of the catastrophe of A.D. 70.[1] Certainly, in the first three centuries of the Christian era the entire area of Judaea, and in particular Trans-Jordan and the Dead Sea (Arabia, in the wider Pauline sense), was the haunt and habitat of numerous 'sects', Christian as well as Jewish; it was in Trans-Jordan Josephus consorted with the baptizer Banus; it was here the Elkasites and the Sampsians, the Ebionites and the Nazorenes were located.   Christianity simply intensified a fissiparous process within Judaism that had already been going on for centuries, ever since the split between the northern and the southern kingdoms.  Samaria, with a tradition reaching back beyond the reorganization of

---

[1] See H. J. Schoeps, *Theologie und Geschichte des Judenchristentums*, Tübingen, 1949, p. 388.

Judaism under Ezra, was a nest of 'sectarianism' in the first century B.C., hostile to Jerusalem, and with the same baptizing rites as in the southern sects in Judaea.[1] In the vicinity of Jerusalem itself, as the Qumran literature has now confirmed, a vigorous form of sectarianism had established itself on the Dead Sea.

Even before the discovery of the Qumran library, there was evidence for the widely diffused existence and ramifications of this marginal type of Judaism throughout Palestine at the beginning of the Christian era. Moreover, these do not appear to have been isolated pockets of religious heteropraxis, but interrelated and affiliated groups, to be found wherever Judaism, or by-forms of Judaism flourished.

The studies of the older scholar Wilhelm Brandt[2] and (more recently) the work of Père Joseph Thomas[3] point to the ramifications of a widespread *mouvement baptiste* in the first century B.C.—a movement of Jewish non-conformity, as it were, opposed to the official Pharisaic religion of Torah and Temple in Jerusalem, for the most part ascetic or encratite, and, in some cases, apparently monastic or semi-monastic in character, cultivating the simple life of the ancient Israelite desert faith in opposition to the 'Canaanite' practices of the cities.

Josephus has been guilty of an over-simplification of the real situation, no doubt in the interests of his own literary presentation of Judaism. Even within his 'third philosophy' of the Essenes, he himself notes two distinct groupings, a monastic sect and another group which permitted marriage[4]; the number of Essene groups rises to three in Hippolytus who includes the Zealots among the Essenes.[5] Josephus's occasional reports of other groups, such as his 'fourth philosophy' (possibly a group of militant Pharisees), his Zealots, his Galilaeans, Herodians, etc. suggest a much more complex and variegated pattern of sectarianism than his simple threefold classification would seem to imply.

---

[1] Cf. J. A. Montgomery, *The Samaritans*, Philadelphia, 1907, pp. 252f., 265.
[2] W. Brandt, *Die jüdischen Baptismen, Beihefte zur Z.A.W. 18*, Giessen, 1910.
[3] *Le Mouvement Baptiste en Palestine et Syrie*, Gembloux, 1935. For a critical estimate of Thomas' work, see infra, p. 54ff.
[4] See infra, pp. 10, 27.     [5] *Refutatio omnium haeresium*, IX.26.

The actual situation in Judaism in the first century B.C. appears, in fact, to have been one of a widespread and dangerously proliferating and fissiparous heteropraxis, a kind of baptizing non-conformity, with many splinter-groups, extending from Judaea to Samaria and beyond into the Diaspora itself.[1]

Within this broad picture of Jewish sectarianism in New Testament times, the sect of the scrolls belongs. We can safely set aside all question of identity with Pharisaism, in spite of much that the scrolls can be shown to have in common with Pharisaic tradition (the Qumran sect, as we shall see, became, at some time in its development, even more fanatical legalists than the Pharisees themselves): this common ground can be best accounted for as a shared inheritance of the basic stock of ancient Judaism.

The reasons which Solomon Schechter gave in his *editio princeps* of the *Damascus Document*[2] for distinguishing our sect from Pharisaism have, if anything, been strengthened by the

---

[1] There is nothing inherently improbable in the widespread diffusion of marginal Judaism in the Diaspora, in particular, perhaps, in Asia Minor, where a form of Jewish Gnosticism is attested by the Epistle to the Colossians.

The penetrating influence of Judaism within the Roman Empire is a well-known and well-attested fact. In his *Contra Apion*, a patent but skilfully argued apology for Judaism, Josephus speaks of the widespread adoption of the Jewish religion in the Graeco-Roman world; among other claims he maintains that there was not a single nation where the Jewish Sabbath had not been introduced (2.40; cf. *Antiq.* III.viii.9). This might be deemed a typical exaggeration, did it not receive confirmation from less biased observers of the same period; Seneca is reported as saying that the way of life (*consuetudo*) of these 'most criminal people' (*sceleratissimae gentis*) had so prevailed as to have come to be accepted through all lands; the vanquished had given laws to the victors (cited in St Augustine's *De Civitate Dei, CSEL* 40.1.298, cf. Tertullian, *Ad nationes*, 1.13, *Commodiani Instr.* 1.24.v.11ff., *CSEL* 15.31). The other testimonies are to a similar effect; this privileged *religio licita* had come in the Roman Empire to enjoy a place of unparalleled influence.

It seems likely that these sectarian groups were to be found chiefly among the 'semi-proselytes' or adherents to the Jewish religion in the Diaspora. These formed an obviously numerous and well-defined class; they received a name that is attested in pagan writers, on tombstones and in the New Testament itself; they are the 'God-fearers', the *Sebomenoi* or *Metuentes,* from which the Christian Church was itself mainly recruited. These *Sébomenoi* formed autonomous religious groups of their own known as *Deicolae* or *Cultores Dei* and are reported in different sources; cf. J. Juster, *Les Juifs dans l'empire romaine,* Vol. 1, pp. 274 (6), 288 (2). There were also sectarian groups known by other names, which may have been similar, for example, the Hypsistarians and the Choreutae, not to mention the Gnostic sects of Ophites, Cainites, Sethites and Melchizedekites; some later groups such as the Euphemites and the Messalians included Christianity in their syncretism. It is not suggested that all such groups of this pagano-Jewish type belonged to the same type as the Palestinian sects, but the phenomena are the same.

[2] *Documents of Jewish Sectaries,* Vol. I, Cambridge, 1910, p. xxviii. Only the last statement about the messianism of the sect requires to be modified in the light of new knowledge. See further infra, p. 145ff.

new discoveries: 'For whatever difficulties the present un-
satisfactory state of our MS may place in the way of the
student, and whatever doubts may prevail as to the meaning
of this or that passage, one thing is certain, that we have to
do here with a Sect decidedly hostile to the bulk of the Jews
as represented by the Pharisees. It is a Sect equipped with
additional sacred books of its own, a calendar of its own, and
a set of laws of its own, bearing upon various commandments
of the Scriptures. It is at variance with the nation at large in
its interpretation of the past, abusing its heroes, as in the case
of David . . . nor does it share its hopes and aspirations for
the future, the Messiah expected by the Sect being an off-
spring of Aaron.'

The sect of the scrolls has sprung out of the broad non-
conformist movement of sectarian Judaism.

It clearly belongs to the southern branch of this widely
ramified Jewish (or para-Jewish) sectarianism. As we have
seen, the geographical evidence is one of the strongest
arguments for an identification with the Essenes of the
Elder Pliny.[1]

As this constitutes one of our most valuable pieces of
evidence, it is worth re-examining it in the light of the new
discoveries.

> *Ab occidente litora Esseni fugiunt usque qua nocent, gens sola
> et in toto orbe praeter ceteras mira, sine ulla femina, omni venere
> abdicata, sine pecunia, socia palmarum. in diem ex aequo convenarum
> turba renascitur large frequentantibus quos vita fessos ad mores
> eorum fortuna fluctibus agitat. ita per seculorum milia (incredibile
> dictu) gens aeterna est in qua nemo nascitur: tam fecunda illis
> aliorum vitae paenitentia est.*
>
> *Infra hos Engada oppidum fuit, secundum ab Hierosolymis
> fertilitate palmetorumque nemoribus, nunc alterum bustum. inde
> Masada castellum in rupe et ipsum haut procul Asphaltite. et hac-
> tenus Iudaea est.* [H.N. v.15]

---

[1] Cf. M. Burrows, *The Dead Sea Scrolls*, p. 280: 'For myself I must say that the
geographical connection remains the strongest reason for regarding the Qumran
sectarians as Essenes. If they were not the same, there was hardly room for both
Essenes and covenanters in the vicinity of Wadi Qumran.' The whole area occupies
little more than a few square miles, and Pliny's location of the Essenes points to the
site at Qumran. He tells us that below them (*infra hos*) lay 'Ain Geddi. The phrase
can only mean in the context 'south of them'; and 'Ain Geddi lies just south of Qumran.

(On the west side [of the Dead Sea], but inshore to avoid the unhealthy region of the seashore itself, dwell the Essenes, a solitary people, and the most extraordinary in the world, since there are no women (they renounce all sexual desire), they have no money, and they enjoy only the society of the palm-trees. From day to day the large crowd of new recruits keeps up their numbers, since they are frequently visited by people weary of life and cast up among them by the tides of fortune, which drives them to adopt this manner of life. Thus through thousands of ages—incredible to tell—a people among whom no one is born lives on for ever—so prolific for them is the repentance which others feel for their lives.

Lying south of the Essenes there used to be the town of Engada ['Ain Geddi] second only to Jerusalem [? Jericho[1]] in the fertility of the country and its groves of palm-trees, but now like it reduced to ashes. Next comes Masada, a rock fortress, itself not far from the Dead Sea. And this is the limit of Judaea.)

Are we to recognize 'the penitents of Israel' (as the Qumran sect can describe itself[2] in the *vita fessi* of the Roman historian? It seems very probable. Pliny's statement about the *seculorum milia* (*incredibile dictu*) of this ancient monastic community is patent exaggeration; nevertheless, a cemetery with more than a thousand graves proves at least many generations of occupation at Qumran. The fact that female skeletons were found in some of the graves does not necessarily invalidate the general statement of Pliny (and the other ancient historians) about the celibacy of the Essenes; we know from Josephus that there was one group among them which permitted marriage.[3]

There is one point of special importance in Pliny's account. If we take the report at its face value, the Essene community at Qumran appears to have been in still flourishing existence after the destruction of Jerusalem and the end of the First Revolt. The Roman historian (or his source) is clearly describing conditions as he knew them (or as they had been reported to him) after the war.[4] Pliny may, of course, be using earlier material and himself writing after

---

[1] Cf. Milik, op. cit. p. 44. The fertility of the soil and the palm-groves apply more fittingly to Jericho.
[2] *CD* vi.1, viii.6, ix.24; cf. ii.3, ix.41.
[3] *B.J.* II.viii.13. See further infra, p. 27.
[4] Milik, loc. cit.

A.D. 70; elsewhere he appears to combine anachronistic information with contemporary history.[1] On the other hand, the report may be an accurate one: the Qumran Essenes may have been dispersed during the Revolt, but may have returned to their monastery as soon as conditions allowed.

We cannot then be so certain about the date of the deposit in the caves *before* A.D. 70; and there are other indications that the deposit in the caves may not have been so early.

The connection of the scrolls with the Karaite Jews is now a well-established fact. This important medieval sect (known to the rabbis as the Saddoukim[2]) took on a new lease of life in the ninth and tenth centuries A.D., undoubtedly as the result of the rediscovery of ancient Hebrew manuscripts in a cave in the Qumran area.[3] From the Karaites medieval Arabic historians were informed about the 'Cave-people' (*Maghariya*), and it is evident that they are describing the Qumran Essenes; the tenth-century Karaite Kirkisani, in a treatise on ancient religious sects, enumerates, after the Samaritans, Pharisees, and Sadducees, but before the Nazorenes (Christians), the Maghariya, the name being explained from the discovery of the books of the sect in caves. (Evidently Kirkisani had not been told of any name for the sect, an indication that it had long been defunct.)

Among the writings of these people are said to have been the books of 'the Alexandrian', undoubtedly Philo Judaeus, 'whose work'—according to Kirkisani—'known everywhere, is the best among the books of the Maghariya'.[4]

There is nothing to cause surprise in this statement. It has, in fact, been argued that the Essenes were Greek-speaking Jews whose inspiration was derived mainly from Alexandrian Judaism.[5] But it seems unlikely that Philo's works found their way into an Essene library in Palestine before A.D. 70. Philo went out of circulation in Judaism when

[1] Milik, loc. cit.
[2] Cf. S. Poznánski, 'Anan et ses écrits', *REJ*, 44, 168ff.
[3] Cf. P. Kahle, *The Cairo Geniza*[2], p. 24ff.
[4] Poznánski, 'Philon dans l'ancienne Littérature Judéo-Arabe' *REJ*, 50, 14. R. de Vaux (*RB*, 57, 1950, 425) hesitates to identify 'the Alexandrian' with Philo.
[5] By M. Friedländer in his article 'Les Esséniens' in *REJ*, 14, 184. The discovery of an extensive Hebrew (and Aramaic) library disposes of Friedländer's theory of a Greek-speaking community.

he was being taken up by Christians and virtually enrolled among the fathers of the Church. It seems more probable that his works, preserved in just such Jewish circles as we find at Qumran, came into the possession of the Qumran Essenes at some time in the early Christian centuries.

All this would at least reinforce the theory that the hidden library at Qumran owes its existence to a solemn communal interment, possibly at some time in the late first or early second century when the sect was dying out.[1] Such a burial of the books may have been among the last solemn duties of the remanent Essenes at Qumran, when the sect had either been swallowed up in Palestinian forms of Christianity or was disappearing owing to the constant pressure and hostility of rabbinical Judaism. It seems unlikely that Essenism survived the Bar-Cochba Revolt—when Qumran appears again to have been occupied[2]—since there is no literature from Qumran belonging to this later period.

There are other issues still to be settled. Not all the documents need be pre-Christian, if a later date for the deposit is accepted; and even if the library is Essene, it does not follow that its contents are all Essene documents.[3] Most libraries of any size (and the Qumran collection appears to have been an extensive one) include volumes of different

---

[1] Cf. Kahle, op. cit. p. 15ff.: 'The careful way in which the MSS were deposited in the cave [Cave 1] tells against the surmise [concealment for protection in the Jewish war]; they were obviously put there with the intention of preserving them as long as possible. The logical conclusion is that temporary war measures were not responsible, but that it was a case of a solemn final concealment of the communal library. This could only have taken place when the community was on the point of dying out. When that happened, however, we do not know. We have no account of Jewish history for the period after Josephus. But we know for certain that at the time when Josephus wrote his *Antiquities* and Pliny reported about the Essenes, the religious order was in a vigorous condition and could have had no reason to store its books carefully in a hidden and inaccessible place. Interesting directions for the solemn preservation of a library are to be found in the so-called *Assumption of Moses*, a pseudepigraphical Apocalypse from about the beginning of our era. It reads (i, 16-18; Charles, II, 415): "And receive thou the writing that thou mayst know how to preserve the books which I shall deliver unto thee, and thou shalt set these in order and anoint them with oil of cedar and put them away in earthen vessels in the place which He made from the beginning of the creation of the world, that His name should be called upon until the day of repentance in the visitation wherewith the Lord will visit them in the consummation of the end of the days."'

[2] Milik, op. cit. p. 55ff.

[3] Cf. H. D. F. Sparks, 'The Books of the Qumran Community', *JTS*, N.S., 6, Part 2, 226. One other important consequence (as Sparks points out) is that books which can now be shown to have been part of this library, e.g. Ecclesiasticus, Enoch, Tobit, etc., are not on that account necessarily 'Essene'. See especially his remarks on p. 228.

dates, authorship and origin, and there is no reason to regard the Qumran library as exceptional. The *Damascus Document* or *Fragments of a Zadokite Work*[1] is a document of later vintage than the *Manual of Discipline*; the recensions of it which have survived have been preserved by the Karaite Jews. It may reflect a much later type of doctrine and organization. The *Manual of Discipline* shows signs of being a much older work. The *War* scroll probably dates to the Roman period. The historical background of the *Habakkuk* scroll is far from certain; it may be Hasmonaean or belong to Roman times.

Until the labour of fixing the date of the contents of the scrolls as well as of the manuscripts themselves reaches firmer conclusions, the safest assumption to make is that we have to do with wide limits of composition, the period between Daniel and Bar-Cochba (second century B.C.-second century A.D.) representing the outer limits of possibility.

It is the period of maximum interest to the student of the New Testament and of Christian origins.

II

THE ORIGINS OF ESSENISM

An immense amount of erudition has been expended on the name 'Essene', without any generally agreed explanation emerging from the numerous etymologies proposed.[2] It occurs in four variant forms, two of which, 'Εσσαῖοι and 'Εσσηνοί, are found side by side in Josephus (e.g., *B.J.* II.vii.3, viii.2). The first of these is favoured by Philo, Pliny prefers *Esseni*. The two other forms are variations of 'Εσσαῖοι, 'Οσσαῖοι, and 'Ιεσσαῖοι, both in Epiphanius (e.g., *Panarion* 19.1, 29.1); the second appears to be the result of a false derivation from Jesse, the father of David.

A wide consensus of scholarly opinion takes the word to

---

[1] Though fragments only have been found in the caves, this document can now be confidently included in the Qumran literature. The most recent edition is that of Chaim Rabin, *The Zadokite Documents*, Oxford, 1954.

[2] Cf. J. B. Lightfoot, *Colossians*, p. 347ff.

be a graecizing of a Semitic term, the most favoured view
deriving it from Syriac *ḥasayya* (plural of *ḥasya*), the 'pious
or holy ones'. This explanation has been recently revived
by J. T. Milik, along with the still older theory that the name
is the Aramaic equivalent of the Hebrew Hasidim, the pious
devotees of the Law in Maccabaean times.[1]   The equation
with *ḥasayya*, 'the pious or holy ones', agrees with Philo's
explanation that the word is a synonym of ὅσιοι.[2]

The main objection to this theory is that *ḥasya*, *ḥasayya*
is a Syriac word which is nowhere attested in any West
Aramaic dialect.   Its isolated occurrence in a Palmyrene inscription (as a verb) does not entirely remove the difficulty.[3]
It may be relevant to recall, however, that the Syriac word
itself is possibly Greek in origin (*ḥasya* = ὅσιος),[4] and a
cognate term from the same Greek word has found its way
into Jewish Palestinian Aramaic.[5]   This at least increases
the probability that the word, in this special and distinctive
use as an originally Greek description of the Hasidim, was
found in West Aramaic: it could then be explained as a
re-graecizing of an originally Greek borrowing in Aramaic
(ὅσιοι = *ḥasayya*) which had become so firmly embedded in
Semitic speech that its Greek origin became lost in centuries
of usage.   The development would then be חסידים = ὅσιοι =
חסיא = 'Εσσαῖοι ('Οσσαῖοι) = 'Εσσηνοί.   This might also
account for the fact that the term never occurs in the Qumran
literature; it was probably a popular designation by which the
later sect (and the earlier Hasidim) became known, especially in the Greek-speaking world.   In that case Philo's
explanation is not so wide of the mark, and he may, indeed,
have seriously meant the name to be derived from ὅσιοι.[6]
We are also able then to explain the variation in the first
syllable in Epiphanius's 'Οσσαῖοι = ὅσιοι (the endings in

---

[1] op. cit., p. 80.   For a discussion of recent, mostly abortive, attempts at an
etymology, see Cross, op. cit. p. 37.

[2] *Quod omnis probus liber*, XII (457), ed. Loeb, p. 54.

[3] Milik, loc. cit.

[4] P. A. de Lagarde, *Reliquiae Juris Ecclesiastici*, Vindobonae, 1856, Gr. xxiv.

[5] *ḥas*, 'far be it from' (lit. 'holy!'), See J. Levy, *Chald. Wört.*, p. 270.

[6] Philo, loc. cit., λέγονται . . . 'Εσσαῖοι . . . οὐκ ἀκριβεῖ τύπῳ διαλέκτου Ἑλληνικῆς
—παρώνυμοι ὁσιότητος: 'they are called 'Εσσαῖοι—by an inaccurate reproduction of the
Greek language—derived from ὁσιότης.'   This assumes the word to be a foreign
borrowing from Greek.   The *spiritus asper* would fall away in Aramaic, where the
gutturals tended to be slurred or not pronounced at all.

'Εσσαῖοι and 'Εσσηνοί are familiar Greek nominal (or adjec-
tival) terminations).

Much more important than the precise etymology of the
name is the clue this explanation supplies to the origins of
the sect.

The theory that the Essenes, like the Pharisees, are
descended from the ancient Hasidim has a long and respectable history behind it.

So far as the Qumran Essenes are concerned it receives
ample confirmation from their literature.

Before we come to this question, however, there is an
even older root in Essenism to be considered.

The Hasidim did not themselves suddenly emerge as an
entirely new thing in Judaism, at the time of the Seleucid
persecutions[1]; and the basic elements in hasidic Judaism
which eventually crystallized into the sect or order of the
Essenes go very far back indeed into Israel's religious past.
I refer to their asceticism which is undoubtedly to be traced
to an ultimate origin in the ancient tribal asceticism of Israel,
in particular that of the Rechabites or Kenites.[2]

We know very little about the ultimate fate of these
ancient Israelite orders, including the life-long Nazirate, in
post-exilic Judaism. Apart from a few scattered references
to individuals and families at Neh. iii.14 and I Chron. ii.55,
Jer. xxxv contains the last mention of the institution of
Rechabites. No provision is made for the life-long Nazirate
in the Pentateuch; Num. vi deals with the temporary vow
only. I Macc. iii.49 mentions Nazirites who could not be
released from their vows till the temple was restored, and
the temporary Nazirate appears to have been a popular form
of private asceticism in later times.[3] According to the
Mishnah both forms of the institution survived the Exile[4]:
but there appears, in fact, to be no evidence for the permanent
Nazirate after the Exile.[5] It would seem to have disappeared

---

[1] Lightfoot, op. cit. p. 353.
[2] See A. Hilgenfeld, *Die Ketzergeschichte des Urchristenthums*, Leipzig, 1884,
pp. 87ff., 139ff., and H. J. Schoeps, *Theologie und Geschichte des Judenchristentums*,
Tübingen, 1949, p. 252ff.
[3] Cf. Josephus, *Antiq.*, XIX.vi.1; Acts xxi.23.
[4] Strack-Billerbeck, II, p. 80ff.; Danby, *Mishnah*, Nazir, p. 280ff.
[5] Cf. G. B. Gray, 'The Nazirate', *JTS*, 1, 1900, 201ff.

in the reorganization of post-exilic Judaism—except in so far as it survived (or was revived) among the Hasidim, and perpetuated in later ascetic sects like the Essenes.

The asceticism of the Qumran Essenes has also (as we shall see) a direct priestly background and origin,[1] but their Hasidaean ancestors undoubtedly included Nazirites, as I Macc. iii.49 shows. The fact that abstention from wine is not certainly attested for the Essene sect (it is usual to explain this alleged characteristic as a misrepresentation of St Jerome[2]) is not conclusive against such a Nazirite element in Essenism; it is well attested for the Egyptian 'Essenes' of Philo, the Therapeutae, and for other affiliated groups in Palestine.[3] It seems less likely, however, that the Hasidim developed directly out of the Nazirate itself[4] than that they owed their ascetic tabus to the complete consecration of the earliest Hasidim to the Law, in particular the priestly code, and to their devotion of themselves as warriors in a holy war, a devotion of the individual as complete, and accompanied by the same forms of abstemiousness and Levitical purifications, as the Nazirate itself.[5]

The conception of the Hasidaeans (or even of a group among them) as in some sense pietistic pacifists, passively submitting to violence and wrong, rests on a modern misunderstanding of the motives which led a group of them to allow themselves to be massacred on the Sabbath rather than infringe its commandments by seeking to defend themselves (I Macc. ii.36). It was their entire devotion to the Law which brought about this early Hasidaean debacle, but they were quick to learn their lesson. I Macc. ii.42 is much more important evidence for their essential character: they were warrior-saints utterly devoted to the Law,[6] ἰσχυροὶ δυνάμει,

---

[1] See further infra, p. 29f.
[2] Cf. Schürer, *History of the Jewish People*, II.ii, p. 201.     [3] Infra, pp. 47, 70.
[4] So Graetz, *Geschichte der Juden*, II.ii, pp. 240, 273. Tosephta, *Ned*. 1, Bab. Talmud, *Ned*. 10a.
[5] For the close connection of the warrior's self-dedication with the Nazirate, cf. J. Pedersen, *Israel*, Vol. III, p. 264ff., p. 10, p. 36: 'He [Samson] was a *nazir*, which means that his soul was cleansed and sanctified. He was to be constantly in a similar state to that in which warriors found themselves, while under the law of war.' See further Pedersen's *Der Eid bei den Semiten*, p. 119ff.
[6] ἐκουσιάζεσθαι renders *hithnaddebh* (hithpael) in the LXX Judges v.2; the Hebrew verb is regular in 1 QS for the voluntary devotion of the Qumran saints. Cf. Cross, op. cit. p. 98, n. 43.

*gibbore ḥail*, like the Israelite warriors of I Chron. vii.27. A parallel is provided by the Knights Templars and similar orders of the Church Militant in the Middle Ages, described by Jacques de Vitry as 'rudes guerriers en campagne, moines et eremites à l'Eglise'.[1] The historical perspective of II Macc. vii.13, which identifies the entire Maccabaean army with the Hasidaeans, is more correct than some modern interpretations, even if the writer has mistaken the part for the whole; the Hasidaeans were the *corps élite* of the Maccabaean resistance.

This is one of the most important features of the whole hasidic tradition, and it is not surprising to find in the Qumran library a document concerned exclusively with the waging of a holy war. It may also help us to understand the sexual tabus of the Essenes; Essene 'monasticism' has very possibly its roots not only in the priestly character of the whole movement, but also in the Hasidaean warrior's abstention from sexual relations, the revival or perpetuation of an ancient Israelite custom.[2]

The immediate ancestors of the Essenes were the Hasidim; and it is from the period of the Hasidim the Qumran scrolls begin to date.

One of the few historical names which are neither reconstructed by the palaeographer nor concealed behind vague Biblical allusions or soubriquets is that of Antiochus Epiphanes, the Seleucid ruler who made the first direct attempt to hellenize Judaism.[3] The *War* Scroll, which appears to come from Roman times, opens with a historical survey with unmistakable references to the Hasmonaean age and the struggle with the Seleucids. Similarly, the *Habakkuk* scroll, while its script points to the first century A.D. (and its composition to the Roman period), describes situations which may best fit the second century B.C. rather than the first century A.D.[4]

The most important historical references, however, occur

---

[1] Cf. Abel, *Les Livres des Maccabées*, p. 43.

[2] See further infra, p. 29f., and cf. Pedersen, *Israel*, Vol. III, p. 10ff.

[3] 4QpNah, published by J. M. Allegro in his article 'Further Light on the History of the Qumran Sect' in *JBL*, 75, 1956, 93f.

[4] Cf. Milik, op. cit. p. 64f.

in the opening verses of the *Damascus Document* in a passage
containing the first explicit mention of an individual as
founder of the movement.

1   *And now, hear ye all ye that know righteousness,*
2       *and consider the works of God,*
    *For He hath a controversy with all flesh, and will execute judgment*
        *on all who reject Him;*
3   *For when they acted wickedly by forsaking Him,*
4   *He hid His face from Israel and from His Sanctuary,*
    *And gave them over to the sword.*
    *But when He remembered the Covenant with the forefathers,*
5   *He left a remnant for Israel, and did not give them over to*
        *destruction.*
6   *But at the end of the period of wrath [three hundred and ninety*
        *years after He had surrendered them into the power of*
        *Nebuchadnezzar, King of Babylon],*
7   *He visited them, and caused to spring up from Israel and from*
        *Aaron*
8   *A root of planting to possess His land and to become prosperous in*
        *His good soil.*
9   *They reflected on their wickedness, and knew that they were guilty*
        *men;*
    *And they were like blind men and like those groping for a way for*
        *twenty years:*
10  *But God considered their works, for with a perfect heart they*
        *sought Him.*
11  *And He raised up for them a true Doctor [of the Law],*
12  *To guide them in the way of His heart.*
    *And He made known to the latest generations, what He would do*
        *in the latest generation with the assembly of renegades.*

This first part of the *Damascus Document* (Rabin's A,
'The Admonition') consists for the most part of a fairly
extensive collection of prophecies, set out in poetic form, but
with a number of later prose interpolations and additions.[1]
The bracketed words above, giving an apparently precise
date for the origins of the 'sect', clearly belong to the work
of such a glossator. Though the words are secondary, however, and later than the original text, they possess a certain

---

[1] Cf. R. A. Soloff, 'Towards Uncovering Original Texts in the Zadokite Documents', in *NTS*, 5, 62ff.

*Plate 1* A general view of Wadi Qumran, looking northeast, with the adjacent escarpment and terrace of marl, and the Qumran excavations (centre) ; in the background the Dead Sea and the mountains of Moab. The Buqei'a or wilderness of Judaea stretches westwards in the direction of Jerusalem; Jericho lies some nine miles to the northwest, 'Ain Feshka about three miles and 'Ain Geddi about twenty miles to the south. See pp. 4 and 10. (*Sabine Weiss/Rapho, Paris*)

*Plate 2* The ruins of the Qumran monastery, facing northeast. The building covered an area of approximately 260 square feet and formed a rectangular enclosure with a tower in the northwest corner. A canal leading from an aqueduct from the foot of the waterfall in the Wadi fed the seven large cisterns. See p. 95 and Plates 10 and 11. (*Sabine Weiss/Rapho, Paris*)

value, for they give the sect's own version of the period of its origins.

Precise chronology is not something we generally find in Jewish literature, so that the tendency has been to treat this figure of 390 years since the Exile as possessing no more than a schematic value.[1] It may well have arisen, however, as a hasidic correction of the Hebrew text of Ezek. iv.5 (LXX correctly 190, MT 390)[2]; in that case the exact figure was meant to be taken seriously. But even if no more than schematic value is attached to it, a period of roughly four hundred years after the Exile brings us to the threshold of the Hasmonaean Age (586–400 = 186 B.C.). There seems little doubt that 'the root of planting' refers to the rise of the Hasidim.[3]

It seems to be generally assumed that the twenty years of groping were antecedent to the emergence of the leader or founder (if the figure 390 is a literal one, 586–390 = 196 + 20 = 216 B.C.).[4] But the twenty years may have followed 196, bringing us to the year 176 B.C., as near as makes no difference to the year of accession of Antiochus Epiphanes (175 B.C.). The emergence of the Hasidim under its founder would then be dated precisely by the event which precipitated organized resistance to Seleucid hellenization.

Whichever explanation of the twenty years is preferred, it gives us a date for the rise not only of the party but of its leader or founder, the Teacher of Righteousness (or the true Doctor of the Law) not later than the middle of the second century B.C., and this would rule out the many theories which identify the Teacher with individuals in the second half of that century or even later in the Roman period.[5] Even with no more than a schematic value, the figure would still refer more naturally to the first half of the second century B.C.

---

[1] Cf. H. H. Rowley, *The Zadokite Fragments and the Dead Sea Scrolls*, Oxford, 1952, p. 62ff.

[2] Cf. R. H. Charles, *Apocrypha and Pseudepigrapha of the Old Testament*, Oxford, 1913, p. 800, n. 5.

[3] Charles, loc. cit.

[4] R. H. Charles is not consistent. On p. 792 he says, 'When God visited his people about 196 B.C. there *ensued* a period of spiritual unrest which lasted for 20 years . . .', but at p. 800, n. 5 he assumes that the period of groping *preceded* 196 B.C.: ' . . . for "twenty years" already [before 196 B.C.] the faithful in Israel had been groping for the way . . .'.

[5] Cf. Cross, op. cit. p. 95ff.; Milik, op. cit. p. 62ff.

The identity of the so-called 'Teacher of Righteousness' has been a subject of heated controversy, on which no two scholars agree. The title itself appears to mean the 'true (legitimate) teacher', in contradistinction to a 'false teacher'. While the reference is clearly to a single, historical individual in the period of origins, the title could apply to a succession of teachers or to an office, perhaps that of the Head of the Community.

If ca. 176 B.C. marked the emergence of the Hasidim in the sense of their organization and consolidation under a leader, then the most likely individual to be their leader and founder is the High Priest Onias III.[1] As a Zadokite, he seems the most probable person to have founded a priestly sect which named its members, or at least its priestly members, Bene Zadok. The identification of the 'man of the lie', who 'rejected the law among all peoples', with Antiochus Epiphanes; the sect's condemnation of marriage with a niece, and the *cause célèbre* of the Tobiad Joseph's illicit union with his niece: these and other converging lines of argument seem to point to the deposed High Priest Onias III as the Teacher.[2] To all other theories it may be objected that the Founder of a movement so famous and influential as that of the Hasidim must have left some trace on our known historical records, and in no single case except that of Onias can this be reasonably claimed. The deposition of Onias, which created a great sensation at the time, is almost certainly reflected at Dan. ix.25f., possibly at Zech. xii.10 and xiii.6 and at I Enoch xc.8, and actually described at II Macc. iv. 30-38. At II Macc. xv Onias is represented along with Jeremiah as a celestial champion of his people like a Jewish Thomas à Becket or a Stanislaus.[3]

---

[1] Cf. E. R. Bevan, *Jerusalem under the High Priests*, London, 1952, p. 72.

[2] Cf. H. H. Rowley, 'The Internal Dating of the Dead Sea Scrolls', *Analecta Lovaniensia Biblica et Orientalia*, Ser. II, Fasc. 30, p. 265ff.

[3] Cf. A. P. Stanley, *The Jewish Church*, London, 1906, Vol. III, p. 252. One objection to this view is that there is no evidence for the martyrdom of the Teacher, whereas, according to II Macc. iv.34, Onias III was assassinated (cf. Cross, op. cit. p. 117). There is just as little real evidence, however, for the actual martyrdom of Onias III: there is no doubt about his persecution and exile (and this would fit the Teacher), but the account of his martyrdom is confined to II Macc. iv.34, and the omission of any mention of it in our more reputable sources has led to the justifiable suspicion that it is largely unsubstantiated legend; either Onias III has been substituted for the son of Seleucus or for the high-priest Alkimos (cf. Wellhausen, *Nachrichten d. Göttingen Gesellschaft d. Wiss.*, 1905, p. 125ff.).

Other passages in the *Damascus Document* reflect the same situation in the early pre-Hasmonaean period, when the forces of the nation, both religious and political, were slowly gathering strength for revolt. The withdrawal of the Bene Zadok to Damascus under their 'Lawgiver', their entering there into a New Covenant or Covenant of Repentance, to return to a new, spiritual obedience to the Law, point to an exodus from Jerusalem led by their spiritual leaders, the Zadokite priesthood, to take refuge in some retreat beyond Jordan—or possibly no further than the Wilderness of Judaea. In this respect the *Damascus Document* records the same events (as Eduard Meyer recognized[1]) as are told at I Macc. ii.42, vii.13-17 about the rise of the Hasidim.

Another important clue to the birth of this community of the pious is to be found at *CD* vi.11f. which Dr Kahle quotes and elucidates as follows:

And all those who have made the resolution not to enter the Temple any more nor to kindle the fire on the altar in vain, who 'have closed the door', by so doing have fulfilled what God has said (Mal. i.10): 'Oh, that there were some amongst you who would close the door so that no fire may be kindled on my altar in vain.'

Only the priests were entrusted with kindling fire in the Temple so these words apply to priests who had resolved not to enter the Temple and not to kindle fire in vain on the altar. They are called *closers of the door* whom the Prophet Malachi had prophesied. These priests had evidently taken their duties in the Temple very seriously, but had at this time made up their minds to renounce their privileges, withdraw from the Temple and search for a place where they and their followers could live according to their ideals. Their withdrawal must have taken place at the time when the Bnē Ṣadok lost their dominant position in the Temple at Jerusalem, i.e. the time of Antiochus Epiphanes.[2]

Such origins help us to understand and appreciate better the nature and value of the discoveries at Qumran: we have already seen that it is somewhat naïve to assume that the library represented by these discoveries was entirely Essene. The later Essene sects were no doubt the descendants of the

---

[1] Cf. *Die Gemeinde des Neuen Bundes im Lande Damaskus. Eine jüdische Schrift aus der Seleukidenzeit*, Berlin, 1919. Cf. also Kahle, op. cit. p. 19ff.   [2] op. cit. p. 19.

Hasidim, but the precious Hebrew documents they have preserved represent a large part of the surviving literature of
the ancient Hasidim—in particular the literature of the
priestly tradition of Israel.  Since no literature in the original
has survived of Sadducaean authorship—thanks to the hostility of the Pharisees to any tradition other than an oral one
—the value of these priestly writings is all the greater.[1]
Pharisaic and rabbinical antagonism may even supply a
further motive for the concealment of these writings in
inaccessible caves in the Judaean desert.

This view of the origins of the sect of the scrolls in the
Hasidaean movement is now widely accepted.  J. T. Milik
writes: 'When one tries to give a name to these "Proto-
Essenes" one thinks immediately of the Asidaeans (Hasidim)
of the Maccabaean period.'  Milik goes on, however, to say:
'Rather than identify Asidaeans and Essenes, it seems more
plausible to assume that within the vast Asidaean movement
a certain group of more precise tendencies crystallized, and,
at a point of time which we will try to determine more
exactly, the Essene group may be said to have emerged.'[2]
Milik traces the emergence of this Essene group, as a sect
or order, to the critical phase in post-exilic Judaism when the
non-Aaronite Hasmonaean family took over the high-
priesthood.  This brought the ruling house immediately
into conflict with the Hasidim, and since the latter failed to
obtain the political support it needed, 'the Asidaeans are
eliminated at this period as serious candidates for political
power, and part of them, whom we may now call the Essenes,
abandoned Jerusalem for an exile at Qumran'.[3]

The details in Milik's reconstruction of the history of the
Essenes are far from certain, but in general both the archaeo-

[1] Cf. Kahle, op. cit. p. 23ff.: 'The great significance of the books found in the
caves obviously lies in the fact that they belonged for the most part to the priestly
literature.  The religious community, in whose possession the books had been, was
formed by the followers of those priests who, under protest, had severed their ties
with the Temple in Jerusalem.  In the new community they retained their dominant
influence.  We can well understand that the library consisted largely of books which
derived from priestly circles and carried on the priestly traditions.  Through concealment in inaccessible caves these books were preserved from the Rabbis who managed
to destroy the whole literature, in its original language, which dealt with priestly
traditions.  Parts of it have survived in translations.  Often the Christians revised
these for Christian purposes and, as Apocrypha and Pseudepigrapha, they have played
their part and have had their influence in Christian circles.'    [2] p. 80.    [3] p. 82.

logical and the literary evidence support the idea of the emergence of the Essenes, as a distinctive party or sect, out of the older Hasidaean movement at some point in the Hasmonaean period; Essenes are first mentioned by Josephus during the reign of Jonathan (160-142 B.C.) (*Antiquities* XIII.v.9), and the main phase of occupation at Qumran dates roughly from this period.[1]

No doubt the usurpation of high-priestly power by a non-Aaronite family was an important factor in the transformation of the Hasidim or some among them into a sect, but it was one aspect only of a more general type of non-priestly influence and movement within Judaism which began in the Exile, but which only appears to have achieved ascendancy in the reign of John Hyrcanus. This was the rise of lay interpreters of the Law and their final consolidation under the Hasmonaean rulers as a powerful democratic movement or political party known as the Pharisees. Almost certainly it was the successful lay challenge of the Pharisees to their ancient prerogatives of legal interpretation which drove the priestly Hasidim a second time into the desert to become the sect of the Essenes.

Pharisaism is itself frequently declared to be descended from the Hasidim, and this is in so far correct that lay scribes, who had existed as a class since the Exile, may also have joined the ranks of the Hasidim during the Seleucid persecutions.[2] The Pharisees would then be descended from this branch of the Hasidaean movement. The Pharisaic Party,

---

[1] Cf. Milik, op. cit. p. 83ff. The Jerusalem Talmud (Ber. 7, ed. Schwab, p. 130) supplies us with the following piece of interesting information, the historicity of which we have no reason to question. At the time of R. Simeon b. Shetah 300 Nazirites came to Jerusalem. 'In the case of 150 R. Simeon found reasons for annulling their vows, but in the case of the others he found none. He went to his brother-in-law King Jannai (Alexander Jannaeus, 103-76 B.C.) and said to him: There are 300 Nazirites who need 900 sacrificial animals; you give one half and I will give the other half; so the king sent 450 animals.' The order at Qumran may have been reinforced and recruited from these surplus Nazirites.

[2] It appears to be generally assumed that the 'synagogue' or company of scribes of I Macc. vii.12 belonged to the Hasidim, and that we are to look on this group as the ancestors of the Pharisees. Cf., e.g., L. Rabinowitz, 'The First Essenes', in *The Journal of Semitic Studies*, 4, no. 4, p. 358ff. (Rabinowitz argues that the ancestors of the Essenes were the group who refused to defend themselves on the Sabbath.) Verse 12, however, may mean that the 'company of scribes' went over to the side of Alkimos against the loyal Jews (ἐπισυνήχθησαν, cf. ii.42, συνήχθησαν), and were made use of as a go-between to try to decide the issue on legal grounds (ἐκζητῆσαι δίκαια). They may still have been the ancestors of the Pharisees, but they would hardly then qualify as Hasidim.

which consisted for the most part of laymen concerned with
an oral tradition of the Law opposed to the priestly writings,
eventually came to power in the Jewish State. Just when
and how they successfully ousted the priestly caste from its
ancient position is not known: the struggle had been going
on even before the Greek period and was continued with the
Sadducees long into New Testament times. At some time
in the reign of Hyrcanus, however, the ranks of any remanent
Hasidaeans at Qumran appear to have been increased by a
fresh influx of recruits, as a result of Pharisaic pressure and
persecution; at any rate, it was then that the priestly wing
of the Hasidim (and their adherents) appears to have become
the sect of the 'pious ones', and begun to be called by their
Graeco-Aramaic name *hasayya*, Essaioi or Essenes, and to
acquire other characteristics and customs about which we read
in the Greek historians.

No one has seen this important factor in the emergence
of Essenism proper more clearly than Dr Kahle:[1]

The opponents of these priests who had withdrawn [from the
Temple] are described as people who built a wall and covered it
with unmixed mortar; who built a hedge around the law. Solomon
Schechter and Israel Lévi instantly identified them as Pharisees.
I think it is worth while to recall the following words which the
discoverer and first editor of the *Damascus Document* writes on
page xxviii of his introduction:

The general impression we receive from the Rabbinic literature,
which remains, after all, the only authoritative source for the
teachings of the Pharisees, is that they had a deep aversion to
all 'external writings'. . . . Hence it is not likely that they
would have indulged in the production of a literature towards
which they all maintained a more or less hostile attitude. And
this impression is now confirmed by our Text. . . . One thing
is certain, that we have to deal here with a Sect decidedly
hostile to the bulk of the Jews as represented by the Pharisees'.[2]

By the middle of the first century B.C. this priestly wing
of the Hasidaeans had become a religious order of desert
ascetics, under constant pressure and opposition from the
Pharisees and the Temple hierarchy.

[1] op. cit. p. 20ff.                    [2] Cf. supra, p. 9.

# CHAPTER II

# The Reports of the Greek Historians

Next to the Qumran documents themselves our two main contemporary sources are the accounts of the Essenes in Josephus and the Alexandrian philosopher Philo Judaeus. The fullest and best-known account is that of Josephus in his *Bellum Judaicum*, II.viii.2-13; two shorter accounts appear in the *Antiquities*, XIII.v.9 and XVIII.i.5. (A third is said to have been contained in the second of his two lost treatises Πρὸς Ἕλληνας.[1]) In addition, a number of incidental references to Essenes are to be found in his two main works.[2]

The two main reports about the Essenes in Philo are in his *Quod omnis probus liber sit*, XII-XIII, a work of his earlier years, and his *Hypothetica* (11.1-18). Philo's *De vita contemplativa* is entirely given over to an even fuller and more detailed account of the closely related Jewish sect of the Therapeutae, characterized by Philo as the 'contemplative' Essenes as distinct from the 'practical' Essenes of Palestine.[3]

Since both Philo and Josephus are writing for Greek readers in the Roman Empire—and both presenting a case for Judaism—some allowance must be made for idealizing tendencies and the need to accommodate Jewish thought or customs to Greek ideas and institutions. Idealization is most evident in the *Quod omnis probus*, the thesis of which, that virtue alone guarantees freedom, is based entirely on the ideal lives of the Egyptian Therapeutae. These 'contemplative Essenes' are classed with the Seven Greek Sages, the Persian Magi, and the Indian theosophists as the ideal moral philosophers. The same tendencies to idealization and accommodation to familiar Greek models appear in the work of Josephus who compares the Essenes with the Dacian ascetics, just as the Pharisees are said to resemble the Stoics

---

[1] Cf. Porphyry, *De abstinentia*, iv.11.

[2] *B.J.* I.iii.5 (*Antiq.* XIII.xi.2) (Judas, the Essene prophet); II.xx.4; III.ii.1 (John the Essene, in command of northwestern Judaea in the Roman War).

[3] Philo is quoted at length by Eusebius, *Praeparatio Evangelica*, viii.12. See further, infra, p. 45ff.

(*Antiq.* XVIII.i.5, *Vita*, 2). We cannot, therefore, be certain that the Greek historians present us with an entirely reliable picture.

Closely related to this question of the reliability of these two historians is the problem of sources, written or oral. It has been suggested that Josephus draws at times on Philo.[1] It is also possible that both historians are deriving their material from a common source, the history of Nicolas of Damascus. We can certainly confidently name this writer as an important source for the *Bellum*.[2] Very little is known about Nicolas except that he appears in history as an amanuensis of Herod the Great, but it is believed that Nicolas's work had a first-class value for the period, his narrative giving an exact and detailed account of contemporary events in the Herodian period.[3] There does not appear to be much substance in Josephus's own claim that he himself had served a period of training among the Essenes.[4]

It will be convenient to begin by examining the three best-known characteristics of Essenism according to the ancient Greek historians, namely (A) Essene asceticism, in particular their monastic (or semi-monastic) ideal; (B) their communism; and (C) their rejection of animal sacrifice.

These were all characteristic features of Essenism as portrayed by the ancient historians. Does the picture remain unchanged in the light of the new discoveries? And do other features mentioned less prominently or even entirely ignored by the hellenistic authors come to assume a much greater importance?

---

[1] Cf. Schürer, *History of the Jewish People*, II. ii, p. 192, n. 12.

[2] Cf. H. St John Thackeray, Loeb, *Josephus*, Vol. II, Introd., p. xxii.

[3] Cf. Th. Reinach, ed., *Josèphe*, V, p. 156. Thackeray and G. F. Moore are agreed that Josephus's main section on the Essenes (*B.J.* II.viii.2-13) is derived from Nicolas's lost history; Hölscher (Pauly-Wissowa, *Josephus*) traced it to a Jewish source (Thackeray, loc. cit.; Moore, 'Fate and Freewill in the Jewish Philosophies according to Josephus', *HTR*, 23, 1929, 383; Hölscher, followed by Thackeray and Moore, was inclined to trace the second Josephan account (*Antiq.* XVIII.v.9) to some other written source (agreeing with later rabbinical tradition in its portrayal of the Pharisees)). The historical details about individual Essenes were traced by Reinach to Essene Haggada (op. cit., loc. cit.).

[4] Cf. *Vita* 2. See further, Appendix A, p. 173. He tells us that he passed through (διῆλθον) the three sects (Pharisees, Sadducees, and Essenes), as well as spending three years with the eremite Baptist Banus, between the ages of 16 and 19. (Josephus was a younger contemporary of St Paul, born ca. A.D. 37, 38; *B.J.* was published in Rome 75-79, *Antiq.* A.D. 93-94.)

## A. ASCETICISM

The position as stated by Schürer with regard to the attitude of the Essenes to marriage and the opposite sex is still generally assumed to be an accurate one:

They entirely condemned marriage. Josephus indeed knew of a branch of Essenes who permitted marriage. But these must at all events have formed a small minority. For Philo says expressly: Ἐσσαίων οὐδεὶς ἄγεται γυναῖκα. (*Hyp.* 11.14)

It is Philo who thus states unequivocally the universal negative, admitting of no exception. The context of his words, however, in the *Hypothetica*, where woman and her ways are being violently repudiated, rouses our suspicions. Though Josephus has not much more to say in favour of women, he still makes it clear that, while holding marriage in little esteem, *Essenes do not in principle condemn wedlock.*[1] His statement that there was another order of Essenes which permitted marriage[2] does seem to imply, however, a definite group (or order) which did not marry, though the main reason which Josephus gives (avoidance of and abstention from pleasure) has a Greek rather than a Hebrew ring about it.

When we turn from this familiar position to the scrolls, we find that this important and indeed central characteristic of this order—its rigid ascetic monasticism—is nowhere expressly attested or even implied in any of the texts so far published and where we would most expect it to be men-

---

[1] *B.J.* II.viii.2: 'They shun pleasures as a vice and regard temperance and the control of the passions as a special virtue. Marriage they disdain, but they adopt other men's children, while yet pliable and docile, and regard them as their kin and mould them in accordance with their own principles. They do not, indeed, on principle, condemn wedlock and the propagation thereby of the race, but they wish to protect themselves against women's wantonness, being persuaded that none of the sex keeps her plighted troth to one man' [trans. Loeb].

[2] *B.J.* II.viii.13: 'There is yet another order of Essenes, which, while at one with the rest in its mode of life, customs, and regulations, differs from them in its views on marriage. They think that those who decline to marry cut off the chief function of life, the propagation of the race, and, what is more, that, were all to adopt the same view, the whole race would very quickly die out. They give their wives, however, a three years' probation, and only marry them after they have by three periods of purification given proof of fecundity. They have no intercourse with them during pregnancy, thus showing that their motive in marrying is not self-indulgence but the procreation of children. In the bath the women wear a dress, the men a loincloth. Such are the usages of this order.'

tioned. Its total absence from the *Manual of Discipline* in particular is unexpectedly strange. In the Appendix to the *Manual*, the so-called *Rule of the Congregation*, marriage and family life are contemplated as the norm, as in every other Jewish community; certainly the *Rule of the Congregation* assumes that there will be families in the community of 'the last days', and the *Damascus Document* thinks in terms of a community of married men with families.[1]

One obvious inference and explanation is that we have to do in Josephus and the scrolls with two quite different groups. But there may be alternative explanations.

There is a passage in the *Rule of the Congregation* which seems important for this discussion:

1 *QSa*              (*Rule of the Congregation*)              *Col. I*

6    And this is the Order for all the hosts of the congregation, for every native born [Israelite] in Israel [cf. Lev. xxiii.42].

7    From his youth he shall be taught in the Book of Hagu [?], and according to his age he shall be instructed in the ordinances of the Covenant, receiving his education in their command-

8    ments for ten years. . . . At the age of twenty years, he shall

9    pass before the examiners to be elected by ballot, in the midst

10   of his clan, to join the holy congregation. *And he shall not approach a woman to have sexual relations with her, unless he has reached his maturity of twenty years, so as [to be able] to*

11   *know good and evil.*

Here there is no question of the forswearing of marriage or the prohibition of marriage. Sexual relations (by which is clearly meant marriage) are assumed to be the norm *at the time of full moral maturity* when the young 'Israelite' is

---

[1] Cf. M. Burrows, *Dead Sea Scrolls*, p. 233: 'The *Damascus Document* . . . clearly contemplates a group of married men with families, and the additional columns from the *Manual of Discipline* or a closely related document, which were acquired by the Palestine Museum, mention explicitly women and children. Skeletons of women were found in some of the graves in the cemetery of Qumran. Probably the sect included both communities of celibates and settlements of families. It is possible also that a few women of eminent saintliness were buried in the cemetery of the order even if no women were admitted as members'; and *More Light on the Dead Sea Scrolls*, p. 383: 'Not much that is new concerning the daily life of the sect has come out since DSS was published. The fact that marriage and family life are contemplated as normal in the *Rule of the Congregation* was noted in DSS. It is not yet possible to go beyond the tentative conclusion suggested there, that the sect probably included both communities of celibates and settlements of families. At any rate, the *Rule of the Congregation* assumes that there will be families in the community of "the last days".'

admitted as a full member to the community, that is, at twenty years of age.

For Judaism this was a most irregular, if not totally unheard of, postponement of marriage. In rabbinical Judaism, marriage was based (as it still is in the East) on physical puberty, not, as here, on considerations of full moral maturity and the reaching of an age of discretion.[1]

Was it such an abnormal postponement of marriage which gave rise to the idea in Josephus that the Essenes despised and repudiated marriage?

This would not, however, explain altogether the statement that there were Essenes who did not marry, and the probability is that, alongside this regular family life, there were also groups of professional *renuntiantes*.[2] The strangely un-Jewish character of this ideal has given rise to speculation about the influence of Pythagoreanism, where celibacy, if not required, was at least highly esteemed.[3] The most probable explanation is that given by Schürer: since everything connected with sexual functions and relations was unclean, total renunciation alone meant complete holiness, especially in a priestly sect.[4]

There may also have been some connection with the ancient sexual tabus of the Israelite warrior and of the holy war. It is clear that the Hasidaean ancestors of the Qumran Essenes were consecrated warriors; and it is reasonable to

[1] Cf. *Discoveries in the Judaean Desert*, I. p. 113: 'Vingt ans accomplis constituent un âge minimum très tardif pour le mariage. Selon les chronologies royales, Amon aurait engendré Josias à l'âge de 16 ans; au même âge Josias aurait engendré Joachez; quant à Joiaqim c'est à 18 ans qu'il aurait engendré Joiaqin. Le Talmud estime le garçon bon à marier dès le début de sa 13e ou de sa 14e année. [Cf. Krauss, *Talmudische Archäologie*, t. ii, p. 23.] Mais le point le plus original ici est qu'on ne se fonde pas, comme dans le Talmud, sur la puberté physique mais sur la maturité du jugement moral. Le mariage est donc envisagé avec un sérieux réfléchi qu'il importe de souligner.'

[2] Cf. Burrows, *More Light*, loc. cit.

[3] Cf. Schürer, op. cit., II.ii, p. 217.

[4] Cf. Schürer, op. cit. p. 211: 'Their repudiation of marriage is indeed a matter quite heterogeneous to genuine Judaism. [He compares the *debitum tori*, *Jebamoth* vi.6: "No one must withdraw from the duty of propagation, unless he has children already, according to the school of Shammai two sons, according to that of Hillel at least a son and a daughter." Also *Kethuboth* v.6, 7; *Gittin* iv.5; *Edujoth* i.13, iv.10.] But even this may be explained from Jewish premises. For since the act of marriage as such made an individual unclean and necessitated a Levitical bath of purification, the effort to attain to the highest degree of purity might well lead to the entire repudiation of marriage. In all these points a surpassing of ordinary Judaism is apparent, and this is also the case in the strongly puritanical trait, by which the Essenian mode of life is characterized.'

suppose that the ancient sexual restrictions on the dedicated *gibbor hail* were revived in the Maccabaean period.[1]

It is not without significance that one of the longest of the non-Biblical texts from Qumran is the *War* scroll, a large part of which deals with the ritual for conducting a 'holy war'.[2]

The organization of the sect, as set out in the Appendices to the *Manual of Discipline*, is that of a military hierocracy, so that it is not surprising to find, among the conditions excluding admission to conventions or convocations of the sect 'impurity' (1 QSa II.3), a word in this context referring to sexual impurity. (The same reason is given as for the exclusion of such people at 1 QM 7.4-6, that 'holy angels are in their congregation' (1 QSa II.8ff.[3]).)

As was noted above, there is a close relationship between the early Nazirate and the state of dedication of the warrior.[4] There is an equally close connection between the regulations in the priestly code for the high-priest, for serving priests, and for Nazirites[5]: they are in fact identical, and the reason is that Nazir and priest (and warrior) are set apart as 'holy'. When the Zadokite priests seceded from Jerusalem and the service of the altar, they became, in practice, Nazirites. Only this was no temporary Nazirate; it was a life-long business. Moreover, their military organization puts them all into the category of 'warriors', under the warrior's vows of sexual abstinence during a campaign.[6]

No doubt originally the vows taken by the Hasidim in this connection were of a temporary nature: but with the continuance (or recurrence) of the conditions of the Maccabaean age, the period of consecration would be prolonged, eventually to become a devotion of the person for life, and calling for complete sexual abstinence and renunciation.

Even in all these circumstances the custom or practice

[1] Cf. supra, p. 17; G. von Rad, *Der heilige Krieg im alten Israel*, p. 83.
[2] Cf. 1 QM 7.4-6 which gives regulations for sexual 'purification'. Cf. Deut. xxiii.10-11.
[3] For this interesting parallel to I Cor. xi.10 see J. A. Fitzmyer, 'A Feature of Qumran Angelology and the Angels of I Cor. xi.10' in *NTS*, 4, 48ff.
[4] Supra, p. 16.
[5] Lev. x.8ff., xxi; cf. Ezek. xliv.21.
[6] The ἀξινίδιον of the Essenes (*B.J.* II.viii.9) corresponds to the instrument of Deut. xxiii.13, which was a weapon of war.

remains a thoroughly un-Hebraic one, and the completely celibate Essenes may have been an exception, or they may have consisted of a small group only. They may, indeed, have been confined, like the Therapeutae, to the very old who took such vows late in life, after their family life lay behind them.[1]   Or the practice may have been introduced, as Hilgenfeld suggested,[2] when the Essene order was being augmented by the large numbers of *vita fessi* about whom Pliny speaks. Nor can foreign influence be ruled out altogether; the Pythagoreans shared the same general attitude to sexual matters.[3]

At the same time, even if the celibate Essene may have been exceptional in this connection or represented a small minority only, the general trend of the Essene literature, including the scrolls, is in the direction of a strict and puritanical attitude in such matters. This was due, no doubt, partly at least, to a reaction to the sexual laxity of the period, in particular among the Sadducees and Pharisees. According to *CD* vi.11 Belial has three nets with which to entangle and snare mankind, 'fornication' (*zenuth* = πορνεία), riches[4] (*hon*), and the pollution of the sanctuary.

The words here attributed to Levi are not found in our *Testament of Levi*, but at ix.9 of that Testament the Sadducaean priests are accused of fornication and pollution of the holy place—two of the deadly sins mentioned here. In Charles's Aramaic and Greek fragments of an original source of the *Testament of Levi*, Col. b, 16, Levi and his sons are similarly warned against fornication and uncleanness (Charles, *Testament of the Twelve Patriarchs*, p. 229). Indeed, for the Testaments πορνεία appears as the one most deadly sin.[5] While it was no doubt the corrupt Temple priesthood against which these protests were made (cf. *CD* vii.8-18) occasionally it is against the Pharisees; thus vii.1-7 is directed against Pharisaic frequency of divorce and contains an inter-

[1] Infra, p. 47; Appendix A, p. 184 (Philo, *Hyp.* 11.3).
[2] *Die Ketzergeschichte des Urchristenthums*, p. 126.
[3] Cf. Clement of Alexandria, *Stromata*, III, 3. 24.
[4] Cf. Jubilees vii.20, where the list is fornication, uncleanness, and iniquity.
[5] Cf. Levi xiv.5-6, xvi.1; Reub. iv.7, 11; vi.1ff.; T. Sim. v.3; T. Jos. vii.1.   Cf. also Jub. vii.21, xx.3, 5, 6, xxiii.14, xxv.7, xxxiii.20.
*CD* iii.1ff. implies the same doctrine of the Fall as I Enoch; it was the legacy of the illicit union between the Watchers and the daughters of men.

esting use of Gen. i.27 parallel to Mk. x.6.[1]  No doubt sexual corruption was especially rife among the hellenizing priesthood, especially if Greek practices were being introduced into the Temple worship.

Such a situation would naturally bring into existence its opposite by way of protest and this goes a long way to explaining the Essene attitude.  Some would inevitably be or remain unmarried, and, as Justin Martyr declares in a similar connection,[2] εὔχομαι κατὰ πᾶν γένος ἀνθρώπων τοιούτους δεῖξαι (*Apology* I 15.6).

### B.  COMMUNITY OF POSSESSIONS

Essene community of possessions is attested by Josephus and Philo: thus Josephus writes (*B.J.* II.viii.3): 'They are despisers of wealth, and a thing to wonder at among them is their community of goods (τὸ κοινωνικόν); it is not possible to find anyone among them possessing more than another. They have a law that those who enter the sect should turn over their property for the public use of the order, the consequence being that among them all there does not appear either the degradation of poverty or an excess of wealth, the possessions of each individual being all put together to be the common property of all brethren. . . .  The overseers of their common property (οἱ τῶν κοινῶν ἐπιμεληταί) are elected and chosen by the whole body, each with regard to his special function.'  At *Antiq.* XVIII.1.5 we are informed that good men were elected as receivers of income (πρόσοδος) and agricultural produce.  According to Eusebius's version of Philo (*Praep. Evang.* VIII.11) the Essene hired out his labour, surrendering his wages to the steward elected as treasurer and from this the needs of all were met: 'none of them stoops to acquire any property of his own'; Pliny tells us they lived *sine pecunia* (supra, p. 10).

In this connection the close resemblance between the Essenes and the primitive Church in the Book of Acts is frequently noted: St Luke tells us that 'they had all things in common' (Acts ii.44, εἶχον ἅπαντα κοινά).

This community of possessions is said to be endorsed for

---

[1] See further infra, p. 123ff.          [2] Infra, p. 86.

the Qumran Essenes by the *Manual of Discipline*. Thus Dr Herbert Braun claims that the renunciation of all personal property (*persönliche Besitzlösigkeit*) and community of goods is the most striking regulation in the *Manual*.[1] It had so great a significance, he contends, that the community can be called 'a community (*yahadh*) in Torah and in property (*hon*)'.[2] On entering into the sect, the novice brings his entire property,[3] though not immediately: it is only at the beginning of the second year of his novitiate that he hands over to the appropriate official his property and his work (*mel'akha = Arbeitsdienst*), the former being registered and placed in an account temporarily 'frozen' (*Sperrkonto*) to his credit; only after the second year is the candidate's property added to the common property of the community.[4] At 1 QS vi.24 penalties are laid down for false declarations about property.

Dr Millar Burrows writes on this question[5]:

The general impression that the *Manual of Discipline* requires a complete sharing of property, thereby differing from the Damascus Document, is denied by Del Medico and Roth. Bringing everything into the order, as required by the *Manual of Discipline* (i.11-13), means only, Del Medico feels, making no wrong use of one's knowledge, strength and property. Roth here sees a fundamental difference between the Essenes and the sect of Qumran: property was not held in common, he says, at Qumran.

Burrows argues that money was used only at the headquarters of the community, as excavations indicate; many coins were found in the Qumran buildings, but none at all in the caves. All this seems to point to community of property.

In a recent important study, Professor Chaim Rabin has convincingly shown that the situation with regard to property in 1 QS is much more complicated and is not so simply explained.[6] There are, first of all, the well-known difficulties raised by the *Damascus Document* where it is obvious that the existence of the institution of private property is assumed;

---

[1] 'Spätjüdisch-häretischer und frühchristlicher Radikalismus I', *Beiträge zur historischen Theologie*, Tübingen, 1957, p. 35ff.
[2] 1 QS v.2.    [3] 1 QS i.12.    [4] vi.17, 19, 22; vii.6. Braun, loc. cit.
[5] *More Light*, p. 383.
[6] *Qumran Studies*, Chapter II, Private Property in the Qumran Community.

and there is no doubt about the possession of private property by members of the sect in this document; 'they could lose it (ix.14), it could be stolen (ix.11ff.), and they could quarrel over it'.[1]   In the *Manual* itself the ability of the sectarians to pay fines assumes the possession of private means.[2]   So also the business dealings of the sectarians with one another or with the community itself (vii.5, 6) can only be explained on the assumption that the sectarian still had property and business interests of his own.

A key expression in this connection in the *Manual* is the verb '*arabh* (noun, '*erubh*, e.g., vi.22), which means in Mishnaic Hebrew 'to mix'.[3]   According to several interpreters it connotes in 1 QS the 'communism' or 'intermingling' of the property of the sectarians.[4]   The expression in this sense has been equated with Josephus's use of ἀναμίγνυσθαι as applied to the property of the community,[5] where he informs us that each sectarian's possessions are 'intermingled' with those of everyone else.[6]   Rabin has conclusively shown, however, that this interpretation rests on a misunderstanding of the meaning of the term, which is used in 1 QS in its classical Hebrew meaning 'to transact business with', 'to have dealings with', or 'to be in contact with'.[7]

What the 'intermingling' of property really meant for the community is best illustrated by a passage which forbids such 'intermingling' with the property of outsiders.   Thus 1 QS ix.8-9 reads, 'Let their property not "intermingle" with the property of the men of deceit whose ways have not been purified.'   (The latter may refer to Gentiles or out-

---

[1] op. cit. p. 23.                              [2] ibid. p. 24ff.

[3] *M. Yoma*, 5.7; *M. Middoth*, 3.2; see Rabin, op. cit. p. 27ff.

[4] For example, Dupont-Sommer, *The Jewish Sect of Qumran and the Essenes*, p. 65: 'Community of goods is total, at least for the fully initiated members.   This is rendered by the root '*rb*, meaning "to mix".   In addition to the surrender of inheritances, it included handing over their daily wages into the hands of the Treasurer of the Community.   It thus formed a common capital, "the goods of the Community" (*hôn hayyaḥad*).   All damage caused to the goods "of the Community", and, above all, all frauds connected with the handing over of goods or wages, are strictly punished.'

[5] Dupont-Sommer, loc. cit.

[6] supra, p. 32.

[7] op. cit. p. 27ff.   Thus II Kings xviii.23 ( = Is. xxxvi.8), where the meaning of *hith'arebh* is 'to make a bargain with' rather than 'to make a wager with' (R.V.).   So also Prov. xx.19, xxiv.21; Prov. xiv.16, LXX.   At Ezra ix.2 and Ps. cvi.35 it is used in a wider sense = 'to have to do with'; Ps. cvi.35 is rendered by Briggs as 'have fellowship with'.   Cf. Rabin, loc. cit.

siders generally: if the reference is to members of the sect they can only have been members of a lower rank.) What is clear is that there is no question here of 'community of possessions'. There is to be no 'mixing' of possessions, that is, no business dealings, buying, selling, loans, etc. with outsiders; and the motive is fear of contamination with what is impure; at 1 QS v.20 it is said of such outsiders that 'all their deeds are uncleanness before Him, and *impurity is in all their property*'. Since property (*hon*) included all that belonged to one, such as land, livestock, houses, etc., as well as money, the prohibition is of *all commercial intercourse with non-sectarians*.

The opposite of this prohibition is found at 1 QS vi.22. At vi.17 we are told that the novice is not 'to mingle', that is, 'to have commerce with' the property of the Many till after his period of probation, but after two years he is to be enlisted for Torah and 'to mingle his property', that is to have business dealings with the members of the community. The reason for this is again clear from the context: neither the novice nor his property is 'pure' until he is tested and admitted: when this happens, he is then permitted to have business dealings with his brethren.[1]

Nothing could make it clearer that business was conducted within the community on the basis of the institution of private property.

A closer scrutiny of the passages which appear to support 'total community of possessions' reveals that they are all capable of this alternative interpretation. 1 QS i.11ff., it is true, lays down that the novice shall bring his property into the community, but it also goes on to state the reason, which, so far from implying that the owner surrenders all subsequent rights to it, states the conditions under which such rights are to be further exercised after admission.

All who dedicate themselves to His [God's] truth shall bring all their knowledge and strength and property into the community

---

[1] Wernberg-Møller renders: 'If the decision is made to bring him near to the community, he [the Inspector] shall enlist him in his definite place among his brethren, for Torah and for pooling of his property ...' The last expression (*le'erubh 'eth hono*) should be rendered for the *inclusion* of his property, i.e. within the system of property ownership and of buying and selling permitted in the community.

of God, to purify their knowledge by the truth of the statutes of God, and their strength, to employ [*letakken*] it according to the perfection of His ways, *and* [*to employ*] *all their property according to the counsel of His righteousness.*

It seems not unlikely that the description of the sect as a 'community in Torah and in property' is to be understood as the grammatical construction known as hendiadys, and that it means a community whose property is administered and regulated *according to the Torah*, as interpreted by the priests. The purpose of the registration of the property of the candidate for admission was no doubt to ensure that it could be returned intact in the event of an unsuccessful candidature: but it may also have been to decide later the initiate's status in the community as a property-owner and also as a test of how it was administered during the probationary period.[1]

1 QS i.11ff. also discloses the basis of Scriptural authority for this submission of all property to the rule of Torah as interpreted by the sect.

All who dedicate themselves to his [God's] truth shall bring *all* their knowledge and their strength and their property into the community of God.

These words are a sectarian interpretation of the *Shema* (Deut. vi.5ff.), the 'strength' of the Hebrew text being further interpreted by the word *hon* 'property'. It appears to have been a very ancient interpretation, for it is preserved in Onkelos and in the Palestinian Targums.[2]

How then are we to understand the phrase 'the property of the community', against which it was apparently possible for the sectarian member to perpetuate fraud ( 1 QS vii.6, 'if he commits fraud against the property of the community, causing it loss, he shall repay it in full')? Rabin suggests that there existed a central fund from which certain members of the community were maintained, and compares the economic basis of the Pharisaic *Haburah* which collected a central

---

[1] Cf. Rabin, op. cit. p. 31: 'The registration was designedly made one year before admission so that the supervisor could keep an eye on the use made of this property, whether it was being properly tithed, whether no *kil'ayim* was grown on it, and so on.'

[2] See further, infra, p. 123.

sustentation fund by tithes through which social services for the *Haburah* and certain members were maintained.

This is confirmed by the *Damascus Document* xviii. The community taxed its members for certain social services and this income went to their central fund; the minimum contribution of each individual consisted of two days' wages every month to be deposited with the Treasurer. And this agrees with Philo's statement that wages were paid into the treasury, except that Philo implies that *all* wages were surrendered in this way. In addition to such taxation (which was no doubt graded according to income), tithes on property would be the other main source of income; and it seems likely that it was the priests and levites who so benefited, being maintained entirely by the central resources of the community.

The *Damascus Document* also specifies the nature of the services which the community provided from taxation: they include provision for orphans, the poor and needy, the old, the homeless, the prisoner, the provision of dowries for young women without relatives, and help in other ways for the young unmarried woman, in general for the whole charitable work of the community.

The Qumran sect was, in fact, organized as a kind of welfare state.

It was also a hierocratic community: all its affairs, affecting the disposition of property no less than its purely 'spiritual' concerns, came within the jurisdiction of priests. This is stated a number of times in 1 QS but nowhere more clearly than in the two following passages:

v.2

They shall be a community in Torah and in property, *submitting response according to the sons of Zadok.*[1]

v.20-21

When he [the novice] enters into the covenant to act according to all these ordinances, they shall examine [him] . . . on the authority of the sons of Aaron.

The model and pattern for this community was the Temple hierarchy or the ancient hierocratic Israel; just as in

---

[1] i.e. the novice is to be interrogated in all such matters by the priests. See Wernberg-Møller, *The Manual of Discipline*, Brill, Leiden, 1957.

the latter priests and Levites were presumed to have no possessions or tribal territory (Numbers xviii.20, 23ff.; xxvi.62), so, among the Qumran Essenes, priests and Levites, the leaders of this priestly sect, would also have no landed or personal property: but they would also, like the ancient priesthood, be the recipients of fixed revenues in the form of tithes or through the collection of fines and penalties,[1] or from the tax on income of the members, and this would constitute their means of livelihood.

This picture of the economic structure of the life of the sect appears to be in such striking contrast to that in Josephus and Philo that it is not surprising to find some scholars inferring that we have to do with two quite different groups: the Essenes and the Qumran sect are not identical. Second thoughts, however, show that there is much in common between the two accounts: the sect's highest ranks, those of the priesthood, conform to the picture of the Essenes in Josephus, and it was no doubt from its priestly members the Greek or Roman observers formed their picture of the whole sect. The invaluable Qumran evidence shows us how unreal and even distorted this Greek picture of the sect was. In his application of the unusual Greek word ἀναμίγνυσθαι to the 'communism' of the sect Josephus (or his source) appears to be familiar with the Hebrew *hith'arebh*, but so far from understanding its meaning, he distorts it to mean something completely different, namely a total community of possessions, which had in fact no relation to the real situation. No doubt the Greek authors, in singling out this characteristic, saw in it an opportunity for idealizing their own race. By the time Pliny receives the report the sect is supposed to live entirely *sine pecunia*.

In the same connection it is possible that the 'communism' of the Primitive Church in Acts was of the same character as that at Qumran. It is true Luke tells us that 'they had all things in common' but this again may be a misrepresentation of the actual situation, where one observes the same concern about honest registration of property (Acts v.1) and the disbursing of public charity (Acts vi.1ff.). It may be, of

[1] Cf. *CD* x.7.

course, that the imminent expectation of the Parousia in the primitive Church led to a total community of property just as the non-fulfilment of this hope eventually led to the abandonment of the experiment. But there is no evidence for such a theory in Luke, whereas there is evidence for the Qumran pattern of economic life.[1]

## C. RELATION TO THE TEMPLE AND TO TEMPLE SACRIFICE

As Oscar Cullmann has recently reminded us, a critical attitude to the Temple and its sacrificial cultus together with a tendency to spiritualize the worship of the Temple is already making itself apparent in the ancient Hebrew prophets.[2] As is also now well known, this rejection of animal sacrifice and the substitute for it of a more spiritual form of worship reaches its climax in the speech of Stephen at Acts vii. It is well, however, to be reminded that its roots lie deeply buried in Israel's historical past: Stephen can cite Isaiah lxvi.1 in support of his attitude: 'Heaven is my throne, and earth is my footstool: what house will ye build me? saith the Lord. . . .'

It is not difficult to point to the kind of circles in pre-exilic times where such an attitude would be found and to the reasons for it. The elaborate cultus of the Temple in Jerusalem became inevitably associated with the evils and corruption of the great city. It would be chiefly in those places where the simple life of desert Yahwism was cultivated that such ideas would find a welcome—in particular among the Rechabites and the ascetic desert tribes.

Again it is Philo who presents us with the simple negative when he declares of the Essenes οὐ ζῷα καταθύοντες (*Quod omnis*, 75). The situation in Josephus (*Antiq.* XVIII.i.5) is much more complicated. The best supported text is that of Niese's edition (the bracketed negative is inserted in Naber's edition):

Εἰς δὲ τὸ ἱερὸν ἀναθήματα στέλλοντες θυσίας [οὐκ] ἐπιτελοῦσιν δια-

---

[1] 'All who believed were together and had all things in common; and they sold their possessions and goods and distributed them to all as they had need' (Acts ii.44).
[2] Cf. O. Cullmann, 'A New Approach to the Interpretation of the Fourth Gospel', in *ET*, 71, 2, p. 39.

φορότητι ἀγνειῶν ἃς νομίζοιεν, καὶ διὰ τοῦτο εἰργόμενοι τοῦ κοινοῦ
τεμενίσματος ἐφ᾽ αὑτῶν τὰς θυσίας ἐπιτελοῦσιν.

In the first place it must be emphasized that *no manuscript of
Josephus reads the negative*; it has been imported into that text
from a misunderstood Latin translation of the *Antiquities* of
the sixth-century Father Cassiodorus.[1]   The text (without
the negative) should be rendered: 'In sending gifts[2] to the
Temple, they render up [their] offerings[3] with superior purifications as they think.   And for this reason they are excluded
from the public precinct and give up their offerings by
themselves. . . .'

If this interpretation is adopted, the situation envisaged
is not that of a community which held itself completely aloof
from Temple worship and rejected animal sacrifice outright
and on principle, but of a group which avoided the ritual
contamination of its sacrifices (and Temple offerings generally) by contact with other sacrifices and in particular other
worshippers in the public precinct.   This view agrees with
the general policy of *apartheid* practised by the sect; and we
are then able to account for an Essene gate in the Temple[4]—
it was to enable them to have access to the Temple without
contaminating contact with others.

So far as the scrolls are concerned it seems obvious that,
in the early period of Seleucid hellenization, there must have
been a complete break with the Temple and its worship.
The *Damascus Document*, in fact, refers to those 'who have
made the resolution *not to enter* the Temple any more or to
kindle the fire on the altar in vain', who 'have closed the

---

[1] For a useful discussion and summary of the different views of the passage see
J. Thomas, *Le Mouvement Baptiste en Palestine et Syrie*, p. 12, n. 3.   Cassiodorus did
not in fact read a negative with ἐπιτελοῦσιν giving the absolute meaning 'they do not
render up sacrifices' (that is, to the Temple for slaughter).   His full text (ed. Migne,
*P.L.* LXX, col. 1133 c) reads: *in templo autem anathemata prohibent, sacrificia vel
hostias cum populo non celebrant*, which can only mean (so far as the negative is concerned) that they do not 'celebrate' sacrifices or offerings *with the people, but do so in
some other place or part of the Temple*, which is precisely what Josephus says: 'they
render up their sacrifices by themselves'.   (Does *prohibent* misunderstand στέλλοντες?)
[2] ἀναθήματα = gifts, the general word for all offerings.
[3] θυσίαι, generally, animals for sacrifice, but capable of being used more widely.
ἐπιτελεῖν must refer to the 'paying up' of the offering due in the circumstances: the
offering was accepted by the priests and (in the case of an animal sacrifice) slaughtered
on behalf of the worshipper.
[4] *B.J.* V.iv.2.

door', by so doing have fulfilled what God had said (Mal. i.10): 'Oh, that there were some amongst you who would close the door so that no fire may be kindled on my altar in vain.'[1]    A community of priests, however, could not carry on for long without a Temple or without developing some compensatory system of worship.    In fact, in the earliest period, a group of exiled Zadokites made their way to Egypt under the son of Onias III to found there the Temple at Leontopolis.    No doubt relations with the Jerusalem Temple were resumed as soon as conditions allowed, and this is, in fact, what we find in the *Damascus Document*—offerings from this priestly community are brought to the Temple.

This is implied in the following passage from *CD* xiv. 1-4.

Let no man send to the altar a burnt-offering or a grain-offering or frankincense or wood by the hand of any man affected with any of the types of uncleanness, thus empowering him to convey uncleanness to the altar; for it is written: 'The sacrifice of the wicked is an abomination, but the prayer of the righteous is like an offering of "delight".'[2]

It should be noted, however, that the person conveying the offering has to be free from impurity.    Is this what Josephus means by 'a superiority of purifications'?    No doubt the 'purity' of the offering was safeguarded and guaranteed in other ways as well, but this may well be the kind of 'superior purification' which the Jewish historian had in mind.

In his important book *Le Mouvement Baptiste en Palestine et Syrie* Père Joseph Thomas has persuasively argued that the Essenes developed in place of the Temple cultus (and in compensation for its loss) an elaborate system of baptismal rites together with a sacred meal.    Since Thomas takes the view that the sect severed all connection with the Temple, he is able to maintain that their entire cultus came to consist of such rites; it is to such rites Josephus is referring when he mentions the θυσίαι which the Essenes celebrate by themselves.[3]    In view of the interpretation which is adopted above of the disputed Josephan passage and the evidence of the

---

[1] Cf. P. Kahle, *The Cairo Geniza*[2], p. 19.   The translation is that of Kahle; the italics are mine.  See supra, p. 21.

[2] Cf. Chaim Rabin, op. cit. p. 58.            [3] Cf. Thomas, op. cit. p. 13ff.

scrolls it is unnecessary to take up this extreme position. There seems little doubt that the Essenes did continue their relationship with the Temple (there may have been other groups who took a more extreme position),[1] but it is also true to say that they compensated for the loss of a Temple of their own with a developed system of baptismal washings and a sacred meal. The evidence for this in the scrolls we shall discuss in a later chapter.[2]

This exiled priestly community seems responsible for the growth of a conception which was to play an important part in the New Testament, namely, that of the community itself as a spiritual Temple.[3]

There are three passages, where this idea is most fully developed, 1 QS v.6, ix.3 and viii.8.

The first passage reads:

They [the covenanters] shall lay a true foundation for Israel,[4] a community of an eternal covenant, for making atonement [and] for all those who devote themselves for a Sanctuary in Aaron and a House of truth in Israel, and for those who join them for a community.

The passage is not free from difficulties of interpretation and ambiguity: thus it is not perfectly clear whether the Sanctuary in Aaron refers to the whole community or to the 'devoted' saints within the community. But the central idea of the community (or a group within the community) as a spiritual Temple is not in doubt. As Wernberg-Møller comments: 'The idea is that of the pious forming a spiritual temple.'

The second passage reads:

When these things are carried out in Israel according to these regulations for a foundation of the holy spirit for eternal truth, they shall atone for the guilt of transgression and sinful wickedness and redeem[5] the land by means of the flesh of burnt-offerings and from the fat pieces of the sacrifice, by right offerings of

---

[1] Cf. infra, p. 66.                    [2] See further infra, p. 91ff.
[3] See also infra, p. 128ff.            [4] Cf. Is. xxviii.16.
[5] I have adopted Wernberg-Møller's emendation of *leraṣon* to *leraṣeth*. Wernberg-Møller renders 'to (pay off) (sin) for the earth'; I understand *'ereṣ* here of Israel.

the lips like a true sweet-smelling savour and a perfect way of life as a free-will offering pleasing [to God].  At that time [i.e. when this programme is fulfilled] the men of the community shall separate themselves as a sanctuary unto Aaron, and a house of Community unto Israel that walks perfectly.

Here at ix.3ff. the same expressions are applied to the sect: it is likened to a priestly sanctuary or a house (or it may be Temple) for Israel.  Different interpretations have been given of ix.4 where there is mention of animal sacrifices.[1] It seems likely that we are to understand the words in some such sense as ʿexpiation is assured through the flesh of holocausts and the fats of sacrificeʾ,[2] thus implying an approval of a sacrificial cultus.  But it is equally clear that this does not exclude the spiritual sacrifices appropriate in such a community.

The study of the reports of the ancient historians in the light of the Qumran writings themselves emphasizes differences as well as common ground.  But none of the differences is of a kind to oblige us to assume that we have to do with two different groups; and the amount held in common between the Essenes of Josephus and Philo and the Qumran sect is decisive for the question of their relationship.  Their common asceticism—in particular with regard to sexual matters—is something unique in Judaism.

While the study of the Qumran writings, therefore, confirms the identity of the group at Qumran with the ancient Essenes of the Greek historians, it at the same time corrects and fills out the picture, by supplying a great deal of detail, hitherto unknown.

We are presented in the scrolls with invaluable information about one of the most remarkable phenomena in the history of ancient Judaism—the life of a priestly (or monastic) sect or order of Torah, descendants and guardians of the tradition not only of the Hasidim of Maccabaean times but probably, beyond them, of the ancient asceticism of desert Yahwism, the orders of the Rechabites and Kenites or the

---

[1] Cf. the translation of M. Burrows, *The Dead Sea Scrolls*, p. 383.
[2] Cf. O. Cullmann, op. cit. p. 39.

permanent Nazirate; these were revived among the Hasidim and crystallized eventually into a religious order of priest-governed *renuntiantes*, themselves both lay and 'clerical', developing an extraordinary communal life of their own, with their peculiar rites of baptism and their 'welfare state'.

As we shall see in a later chapter, the further study of the scrolls brings out such essential features of Essenism as its legalism (a form of priestly Torah and Torah exposition). This fundamental characteristic of the life of this desert community is fully endorsed by the Greek historians (the devotion of the sect to Moses is singled out for special mention by Josephus[1]): but it is a feature of the sect's life which naturally stands out more prominently in their own documents.

The priestly character of the sect is also fully borne out by the Greek writers, but, again, it assumes still greater prominence in the Qumran writings themselves.[2]

The main and essential characteristics of the sect, however, are to be explained in terms of the priestly ascetic ideal which formed the original basis and inspiration of hasidic legalism. Whether full members of the order were life-long Nazirites, as has been claimed, or not,[3] the classic accounts of individual Essenes and of their communal life point to such a hierocratic ideal, embodied in a system designed to ensure the observance of the highest grade of Levitical purity, only to be found elsewhere among the Temple priesthood; they led a life of outward *apartheid*, with frequent ceremonial purifications accompanied by an increased holiness and consecration to Yahweh.

What is most remarkable about the Essene Order, however, was not just—as the Elder Pliny noted—the tenaciously conservative and centuries-old existence of this strange race of Jews, but the extraordinary development this form of Jewish pietistic asceticism underwent in the centuries immediately preceding and following the beginning of the

---

[1] *B.J.* II.viii.9.
[2] We need not, on this account, exclude an earlier connection with the prophetic tradition of Israel as well; and this might account for their special interest in prophesying. Cf. especially A. Hilgenfeld, *Die Ketzergeschichte des Urchristenthums*, p. 97ff.  [3] *Supra*, p. 16.

Christian era. By the first century B.C. it had become a closed and elaborately organized monastic (or semi-monastic) institution and community, so that, in New Testament times, the number of full members could be estimated in the region of 4,000.[1] If full initiates or *renuntiantes* of the highest grade were only less in numbers than the Pharisees themselves, we must reckon with a following of adherents (including women and children) which brought their numbers little short of 10,000 souls.[2] We are bound to conclude that this ideal of priestly ascetic monasticism, guarded and maintained by the most detailed prescriptions for *apartheid* from the world—in particular by the multiplication of rites of ceremonial lustration—had taken a very powerful hold on the religious life of first-century Judaism. They were a peripheral sect only in the sense that they were pursuing an unworldly life, but not in the extent of their penetrating influence on the religion of the period.

Their main centre must have been at Qumran, with, possibly, outside Palestine, a similar settlement of even stricter Jewish ascetics at Lake Mareotis in Egypt.[3] But the presence of Essene groups in every city of Palestine[4] is a further indication of the ramifications of the movement throughout the country. It was only, however, in the ideal surroundings of complete isolation from the world in the inaccessible area of the Dead Sea that the full life of sacerdotal consecration and perfection could be achieved, or organized, within the life of a monastic community.

Before we pass from the reports of the Greek historians, something must be said, however briefly, about the related Jewish sect of the Egyptian Therapeutae.

Who were these Jewish ascetics from Egypt? Since the time of Eusebius Philo's Therapeutae have been claimed as Christian monks, but since the brilliant work of F. C. Conybeare[5] the question has now been settled in favour of the view that the Therapeutae in Egypt, like their kinsmen the

---

[1] *Antiq.* xviii.i.5.
[2] Cf. the calculations of T. W. Manson, *The Servant Messiah*, p. 10ff.
[3] Infra.   *B.J.* II.viii.4.
[5] *Philo: About the Contemplative Life*, Oxford, 1895, especially p. 258ff.

Essenes in Palestine, were Jewish, not Christian, ascetics. The fact, however, that resemblances between these pre-Christian forms of Jewish monasticism and the early Church were so close that the Fathers went out of their way to claim Jewish ascetics as Christian raises again the old problem of the connection of the asceticism of the Therapeutae with primitive Christianity.

The problem takes on an even greater interest in view of the Qumran discoveries. Hitherto the latter have been related mainly to the sect of the Essenes, or to their Palestinian sectarian environment: but Jewish monasticism was probably basically the same, outside or inside Palestine, and the customs and practices of the Egyptian sect help us to understand better the significance of the Qumran literature.

In the introduction to his translation of Philo's *De vita contemplativa* F. H. Colson wrote (in 1941): '(The treatise does not seem to me to rank high among the works of Philo. . . .) Historically it is perhaps of some importance as giving an account of an institution with some of the marks of later monasticism for which we have no parallel either without or within the Judaism of the times. And the importance would be much greater if we could suppose that this Alexandrian community was of a type widespread through the world outside. The opening words of section 21 may at first suggest that this was so and the argument of Lucius who maintained that the treatise was spurious was primarily based on this assumption. The Therapeutae, he argued, are said by the author to have been found in many places; if it were so we must have heard of them from other sources, and as we do not hear of them the whole thing must be a fiction.'[1]

The discovery of the Qumran library disposes finally of the idea that pre-Christian Jewish monasticism was a fiction; and, as we shall see, the life of the Qumran sect bears some marked resemblance to the religious life of this Egyptian branch of the 'Essenes'.

Philo reports about this group of Jewish ascetics, that, unlike the Essenes, they were of a contemplative rather than a practical turn of mind. They had settled in the region of

[1] p. 104ff.

Lake Mareotis in Egypt, and much of Philo's account is concerned with their mode of celebrating the Jewish Festival of Pentecost, including a description of their sacred meal, which consisted of unleavened bread only.[1] They represent an even stricter order of asceticism than Essenism: they were rigidly abstemious (their food and drink consisted mainly of edible plants, bread, salt and water), and practised frequent fastings. Nothing is said about baptismal rites or their attitude to sacrifice, but as Philo is silent about the former in his account of the Essenes, the argument from silence is scarcely cogent; their abstention from animal sacrifice is not explicitly attested but seems probable.[2] Women also belonged to the order, the majority among them being 'aged virgins' (viii.67). The likelihood is that we have to do with a community of anchorites or semi-anchorites, possibly exiled from Palestine because of their heteropractic customs.

There seems little doubt that the ascetic ideal of the Therapeutae included a voluntarily imposed poverty and celibacy.[3] In both cases the state of renunciation appears to be one which was entered into late in life. The ideal of virginity (which Philo himself held in high esteem[4]) was a means to perfection and appears to have been a cardinal principle among them.[5] Philo emphasizes that the παρθένοι of the Therapeutae were quite unlike the Greek priestesses, since the latter kept their chastity by compulsion, the Therapeutrides 'of their own free-will in their ardent yearning for wisdom'.[6]

[1] See further infra, p. 106ff.
[2] Cf. Porphyry, De abstinentia, 4.6 and Conybeare, op. cit. p. 299.
[3] Cf. De vita, II.13 (trans. Loeb): ' . . . such is their longing for the deathless and blessed life that, thinking their mortal life already ended, they abandon their property to their sons and daughters or to other kinsfolk. . . .'
[4] Cf. Conybeare, op. cit. p. 317.
[5] VIII.68.
[6] loc. cit.

# CHAPTER III

# The Patristic Accounts of Jewish Sects

There is another source of evidence available to the student
of pre-Christian 'sects'—one cannot say always as valuable
—in the accounts of Jewish 'sects' or 'heresies' in the early
Fathers of the Church; and their reports can occasionally be
supplemented and supported by notices from rabbinical sources.

Among more recent discussions of this evidence is a paper
read at the Patristic Conference in Oxford in 1955, entitled
*Les Sectes juives d'après les témoignages patristiques*, by Professor M. Simon of Strasbourg.[1]  Professor Simon confines
himself for the most part to the second-century lists of Justin
Martyr and Hegesippus; the later lists and accounts of Jewish
'heresies' such as those in the *Apostolic Constitutions*, Ephrem
Syrus, Isodore of Seville, Epiphanius, and the Pseudo-Jerome,
are set aside as largely dependent on the second-century
catalogues, supplemented by information drawn from Josephus and the Gospels.  Justin and Hegesippus themselves
appear to get their material about the older pre-Christian
'sects', Pharisees, Sadducees, and Essenes, either from
Josephus or the Gospels (though it is surprising to find
Justin omitting the Essenes altogether).  When we subtract
these older and well-known groups (including the Samaritans), and suspend judgment on the Galilaeans and Meristai
(possibly a Gnostic group), what is left consists, for the most
part, of very general descriptions of tendencies within the
Judaism of Justin's own period, but not 'heresies' in the
strict ecclesiological sense of unorthodox bodies existing on
the margin of the Synagogue and under its ban; they are
only 'heresies' for the Fathers, who interpret *la réalité juive
à travers une optique chrétienne* (p. 538).

The passage in Justin's *Dialogue with Trypho* (lxxx)
opens with a question from Trypho whether all Christians
really believed in the Parousia.  Justin's reply is that all

[1] *Studia Patristica*, Vol. 1 (T.U. lxiii, Berlin, 1957), p. 526ff.

Christians do so believe, but that even among Christians there are godless and unbelieving heretics, ὥσπερ οὐδὲ Ἰουδαίους, ἄν τις ὀρθῶς ἐξετάσῃ, ὁμολογήσειεν εἶναι τοὺς Σαδδουκαίους ἢ τὰς ὁμοίας αἱρέσεις Γενιστῶν καὶ Μεριστῶν καὶ Γαλιλαίων καὶ Ἑλληνιανῶν καὶ Φαρισαίων [καὶ] Βαπτιστῶν (just as, if one were to look into the matter rightly, one would not acknowledge to be Jews those who are Saddoukaioi or similar sects of Genistai and Meristai and Galilaeans, and Hellenians and Pharisees [and] Baptists).

It is clear that Justin believed himself to be describing Jewish heretics; if his argument was to carry any weight with Jews (and that seems to have been its intention), it is unlikely that he would destroy his case by including respectable Jewish groups in such a list, even though he himself may have looked at all such groups *à travers une optique chrétienne*. There is also his general trustworthiness in this connection to be considered; Lukyn Williams writes of him: 'The more the *Dialogue* is studied, the deeper becomes the impression of the general accuracy of Justin's presentation of Judaism, as well as the width of his knowledge of it.'[1] M. Simon, moreover, favours the view that Justin's Genistai is simply a Greek translation of the Hebrew word Minim, a general term for all 'heretics'. He does not, however, mention the *Birkath ha-Minim* in Hadrian's time. The Minim were banned by the Synagogue in the early second century, and though the ban was especially directed against Jewish Christians, it was intended for all Jewish 'heretics'.

Such groups, however general the description applied to them, may well have all constituted dangerous 'heresies' or sects on the margin of the Synagogue and under its ban. (If Simon is correct in his explanation of the Meristai as Jewish Gnostics who 'divided' the person of the deity, then we have to do with an intolerable 'heresy' in Judaism, involving the denial of its central tenet of monotheism.)

The Galilaeans are not discussed, but a reference is made to the views of Père Milik that they were Jewish Christians.[2]

[1] Lukyn Williams, *Justin Martyr: The Dialogue with Trypho*, Translations of Greek Literature, Series I—Greek Texts, S.P.C.K., London, 1930, p. viii.

[2] J. T. Milik, 'Une inscription et une lettre en araméen christopalestinien', *R B*, 60, 4, 526ff.

The only evidence produced for this view is the statement in the recently discovered letter of Bar-Cochba that the Jews were to break off all relations with the Galilaeans, with whom they had apparently been previously allied in the war with the Romans. It is improbable in the extreme that Bar-Cochba would ever have contracted an alliance with Jewish Christians. We have no reason to doubt that they too were a Jewish schismatic group.

There does not seem to be much to add about the Galilaeans that is not already well known. Judas the Galilaean (or the Gaulonite) is reputed to have been the founder of the movement. At Acts v.37, Gamaliel mentions him as the leader of a popular revolt 'in the days of the enrolment' (conducted by Quirinius in A.D. 6 or 7), and which ended in his destruction and the dispersion of his followers. The movement appears to have been a considerable one to judge from the frequency of Josephus's references (*Antiq.* XVIII.i.1, 6; XX.v.2; *B.J.* II.viii.1; VII.viii.1). Josephus tells us it was from this group the Party of the Zealots arose, but Galilaeans appear to have had a reputation for violent action in even earlier times; a massacre of Galilaeans by Pilate is reported in the Gospels (Luke xiii.1). The movement deserves much more attention than is given to it in the recent discussion of *Maccabees, Zealots and Josephus* of W. R. Farmer (New York, 1956), especially in view of the Gospel evidence for the association of Jesus and his disciples with Galilee and Galilaeans.

I shall have something to say about the Hellenians and the Baptists presently: meantime there remain the Pharisees and the Sadducees.

The most extraordinary feature of the list, among other curious things, is not only Justin's omission of the Essenes, especially if he is dependent on Josephus, but his inclusion of the Pharisees in a list of Minim or heretics. The fact is all the more incomprehensible, not only (as Lukyn Williams pointed out[1]) because of the irreproachable orthodoxy of Pharisaism in post-Biblical sources, but in view of what Justin himself has to say later (cxxxvii.2), where the Phari-

[1] op. cit. p. 171.

*Plates 3 and 4* Two views of Cave 4 from the Wadi. This cave was one of the richest in manuscript finds; eight manuscripts of the original Aramaic Enoch have been identified among the numerous fragments. See Appendix C, p. 192, n.2. (*Pl. 3—Sabine Weiss/Rapho, Paris; Pl. 4—Professor B. Reicke, Basel*)

*Plate 5* The first cave to be discovered, where the *Manual of Discipline*, the two Isaiah scrolls and the *War* scrolls were found. There was evidence that it had been ransacked and some of its contents removed at an early period. See P. Kahle, *The Cairo Geniza*, 2nd edition, p. 16, and this volume, p. 11. (*Sabine Weiss/Rapho, Paris*)

sees are referred to as the 'chiefs of the synagogues', that is to say, as the pillars of orthodox Judaism.'

M. Simon meets this difficulty by the suggestion that the term is used in this connection ambiguously by Justin; it has the later sense of Christian heresy as well as the meaning of Jewish heresy or sect. 'Cette équivoque explique une curieuse contradiction de Justin. Il écrit d'un côté: "Un bon juge ne reconnaîtra pas pour Juifs des Sadducéens, ou ces hérésies similaires . . . des Pharisiens et des Baptistes." Mais comme il a tout de même quelque idée de la situation du judaïsme, il reconnaît un peu plus loin les Pharisiens pour ce qu'ils sont en réalité: "Les didascales pharisiens . . . les chefs des synagogues"' (op. cit. p. 530). In a context, however, where it was important not to misrepresent Judaism, it seems very unlikely that Justin would have brought in the Pharisees, the pillars of orthodox Judaism, just because he himself regarded them as 'heretical' from his Christian standpoint.

The simplest solution is to explain the Φαρισαίων (as Harnack did[1]) as the insertion of a copyist; it may well be a later gloss (it brings the number up to an even seven) added by a learned scribe familiar with the Gospels. The reading Φαρισαίων, however, would seem to be an integral element in Justin's original text. The same, however, cannot be claimed for καί before βαπτιστῶν; it is a purely conjectural insertion, the original text reading 'Pharisees, Baptists'. It is possible to take the two words closely together, the second in apposition to and qualifying the first; Justin's 'sect' may have been one of 'baptizing Pharisees'. Harnack admits this possibility, but is inclined to consider it an unlikely combination.[2] We are now, however, in a much better position to judge: recent investigations have shown that so extensive was the baptismal cult in Judaism in the first two Christian centuries, in particular in the Diaspora (possibly not uninfluenced by Christian practice and example), that it spread even among the orthodox and into the ranks of the Pharisaic teachers themselves. This situation is reflected for the

---

[1] *Judentum und Judenchristentum in Justins Dialog mit Trypho.* T.U. xxxix (1913), 57.
[2] loc. cit.

orthodox Judaism of the period in other passages in Justin's *Dialogue* (xiv.1, xix.2). Professor David Daube refers to it and cites instances of the practice among leading Hillelites, some of whom were even prepared to go so far as to accept proselyte baptism as alone that which constituted a convert a Jew: 'Joshua ben Hananiah claimed that baptism alone was sufficient to make even a male gentile Jewish. They did not go quite so far as Paul: they did not deny that it was the duty of a male convert to be circumcised. But they did consider him fully Jewish as soon as he was baptized. It is interesting that their argument was that baptism was the decisive rite in the case of a woman, so it should be the same in that of man.'[1]   Such views were almost bound to be pronounced heretical.[2]

It is not without significance that Justin finds it necessary to apologise at this point for what he has just said: 'pray do not be vexed with me as I say all I think' (Williams). He clearly felt it necessary to say this in view of his mention of Pharisees, even heretical Pharisees, in such disrespectable company as the other Minim listed.

What about the Sadducees?   The identification of Justin's εαδδουκαίοι with the ancient Sadducees, and their classification as 'heretics', raises problems as intractable as the presence of 'Pharisees' in such a list, for the ancient Sadducees almost certainly disappeared from the scene with the Temple. I would suggest that the possibility is worthy of serious consideration that what Justin really meant by his heretical 'Sadducees' were the Zadokites, the *Bene Zadok* or Qumran Essenes; so far from omitting the Essenes, they would then figure at the top of Justin's list. Obviously the identity of name was bound to lead to confusion, and something like this appears to have happened in rabbinical sources as well. When the Rabbis place Saddoukim among the Minim and equate them with the Qaraite Jews, they can only be referring to the Zadokite sect. Maimonides, for instance, tells us, in his Commentary on *Pirqe Aboth* I, that the Qaraites called

---

[1] *The New Testament and Rabbinic Judaism*, London, 1956, p. 109.
[2] In this same connection the conjecture should be mentioned that Justin's Ἑλληνιανῶν should be read as Ἑλληλιαλῶν (from Ἑλλήλ, Hillel); cf. Epiphanius, *Panarion*, 30.4 and J. C. T. Otto, *Justini Opera*, p. 280, n. 12.

themselves Saddoukim, and were known by this name to their rabbis.[1] Arabic sources of the tenth century make a clear distinction between the ancient Sadducees and the Zadokite sect.[2] This explanation has been given more than once for Ephrem's 'Sadducees', whom he connects with John the Baptist.[3] (There is no longer any reason for pronouncing Ephrem confused when he speaks of a Jewish sect of Ebionites, for *Ebhjonim* is now well attested as a name for the Qumran sectarians.[4])

We conclude then that there is more in Justin's list than a few generalizing descriptions of innocuous tendencies in second-century Judaism: Justin is describing, as he himself tells us, Jewish heretical or sectarian movements, some of them (like the Galilaeans) pre-Christian groups.

M. Simon is on firmer ground when he comes to deal with Hegesippus, yet in some respects Hegesippus's list is even more interesting than Justin's. It is quoted in Eusebius's *Ecclesiastical History*, iv. 22: ἦσαν δὲ γνῶμαι διάφοροι ἐν τῇ περιτομῇ, ἐν υἱοῖς Ἰσραήλ, τῶν κατὰ τῆς φυλῆς Ἰούδα καὶ τοῦ Χριστοῦ. αὗται Ἐσσαῖοι, Γαλιλαῖοι, Ἡμεροβαπτισταί, Μασβωθέοι, Σαμαρεῖται, Σαδδουκαῖοι, Φαρισαῖοι. As with Justin, M. Simon believes that what we have in Hegesippus is not a list of Jewish 'heresies', but one of the first patristic catalogues of heresies of the Church; and in this case he is probably right.

Professor Simon renders the text: 'Il y avait des opinions différentes dans la circoncision parmi les fils d'Israël, contre la tribu de Juda et contre le Christ.' The words may be construed (if the text is right[5]): 'There used to be [schools of] thought deviating in the Circumcision (I mean among Israelites) from the [school of thought] in the "tribe" of Judah and Christ, namely Essenes, Galilaeans, Hemerobaptists, Masbutheans, Samaritans, Sadducees, Pharisees.'

---

[1] The Qaraites are described as *istae sectae maledictae haereticorum, et vocabuntur in hisce terris, nempe in Aegypto, Karraei. Nomina autem ipsorum sunt, id est nominantur apud sapientes Tzaducaei et Bejetosae* (cited in Buxtorf, *Lex. Talm.* under *Qaraites*).

[2] Cf. S. Schechter, *Documents of Jewish Sectaries*, i, p. xviiiff.

[3] Cf. J. Thomas, *Le Mouvement Baptiste en Palestine et Syrie*, p. 118, n. 2.

[4] Cf. Thomas, op. cit. p. 2, n. 1.

[5] Several MSS (AT¹M) read Ισραηλ η των (for Ἰσραηλιτῶν). If we read αὐτῆς for αὗται (conj. Schwartz), we can render: 'There used to be in the Circumcision among Israelites, [schools of] thought differing from the [school of thought] throughout the tribe of Judah and Christ itself. Essenes, Galilaeans,' etc. The general result is the same.

The 'tribe' of Judah and [of] Christ might be understood to refer to Jews and Christians respectively. In that case Hegesippus is listing 'sects' differing in their tenets from orthodox Jews as well as from Christians. The words, however, probably belong together as the description of a single group, namely Hebrew Christians, possibly converts to Christianity from Judaism, to which Hegesippus himself belonged. The Christian Father is then describing, not Jewish 'sects', but Jewish groups *à travers une optique chrétienne*. It is not then surprising to find Pharisees and Sadducees in such company, especially as Hegesippus is describing Jewish sects in the past, not, like Justin, heretical Jewish groups in the present. He may well have got his Pharisees and Sadducees from the Gospels or from Josephus.

More important than any of these observations, however, is the interesting fact that a Hebrew Christian, probably a convert from Judaism, can include Samaritans in a list of Israelites. Whatever his source here, in listing the Samaritans as a Jewish 'sect', even though he does so from the point of view of a Christian heresiologist, he is taking us back into ancient history.

The one thing that we cannot do, in discussing Jewish 'sects' or 'heresies' in the Fathers, is to overlook the Samaritans; and to this point I shall return later.

A more positive assessment of the patristic evidence as a whole is to be found in the studies of Père Joseph Thomas, whose book, *Le Mouvement Baptiste en Palestine et Syrie* was published some ten or twelve years before the discovery of the Dead Sea Scrolls.[1] Thomas carried forward the patristic researches of Brandt and others into the special problem of the existence of a widespread Jewish *mouvement baptiste* in Palestine (and beyond) before A.D. 70.[2] It was a movement (Thomas thought) of baptizing non-conformity, as it were, in opposition and conflict with the Pharisaic authorities in Jerusalem, substituting baptizing rites for the observance of Temple sacrifice. With the help of the ancient historians and the testimony of the Fathers, Thomas concludes that such a sectarian movement existed in pockets or splinter-

[1] Gembloux, 1935.          [2] Cf. supra, p. 7.

groups from Samaria to Judaea, consisting of sects among the Samaritans—Dositheans, Sabaeans, Gorothenes—of Essenes, in Samaria as well as Judaea, Nasarenes, Masbuthaeans, etc.

So far as the ancient historians are concerned, the existence of a group of Essene sectarians who practised baptizing rites is not in doubt. What is still in question is whether, as Thomas maintains, the main characteristics of this group (or groups) were their baptizing rites as a substitute for Temple sacrifice.[1] The Qumran Essenes were undoubtedly a baptizing cult; and the large and prominent baptisteries in the excavated settlement at Qumran are impressive evidence for the importance of lustrations for the sect. The relation of the group to the Temple and the sacrificial cultus may still be a matter of debate (as is the conflicting testimony of Philo and Josephus on the point), but, in general, it is now widely recognized that the Qumran Essenes represented an opposition party to the established Pharisaic and Sadducaean authorities in Jerusalem; important evidence has now come to light in the Qumran texts which shows that, in the matter of the Festival Calendar, these Essenes were out of step with the official parties.[2] There is no evidence that they were heretics in the usual sense of the term (they did not, for example, reject the central tenet of Jewish monotheism), but they certainly indulged in a very large measure of heteropraxis.

The view that the Essenes were not an isolated pocket or 'resistance group' within Judaism, but existed in different and diverse but related splinter-groups throughout Palestine, rests mainly on the evidence of the Fathers. Josephus, it is true, tells us that the Essenes were to be found in every town of Palestine,[3] but the impression this statement gives is of the existence in different places of outposts of the same Essene sect. According to Thomas's interpretation of the Fathers, however, this *mouvement baptiste* existed in a whole complex of interrelated but different groups, practising, like the Judaean Essenes, their baptizing cult from Samaria to Judaea.

---

[1] Cf. supra, p. 41ff.      [2] Cf. infra, p. 60.      [3] *B.J.* II.viii.4.

*Prima facie* the garbled and disjointed reports of the later Fathers do not inspire confidence. The Samaritans were certainly a schismatic group, but there must be genuine doubt, so far as the patristic evidence takes us, about the separate existence of Samaritan sects in pre-Christian times. The Dositheans are probably the most important of the names, and I shall come back to them shortly. The Sabaeans and the Masbuthaeans are difficult to identify with any actual groups or 'sects', and they may have existed as such only in the minds of the Fathers; in both cases we know practically nothing but their names: both names may refer to baptism and the second certainly does, but, as Brandt pointed out, they may be no more than general terms to describe people who practised baptizing rites to excess, representing the Aramaic equivalent names for the Baptistai and Hemero-baptistai of Justin and Hegesippus.[1] Epiphanius's Goro-thenes (Γοροθηνοί) also looks like a generalizing name; I would derive it from the Hebrew *gere 'arayoth* (or its Aramaic equivalent), 'the proselytes of the lions', a name applied by the rabbis from II Kings xvii.25ff. to Samaritan proselytes to Judaism.[2] The Jewish Nasarenes of Epiphanius are gener-ally believed to be an entirely fictitious entity which the Christian Father has invented out of his Jewish-Christian sect of the Nazorenes.

We are thus left with two very broad groupings only, Essenes and Samaritans, as quite certainly pre-Christian schismatics or sectarians.

Do the Fathers add any information to what we already know about the Essenes? For our knowledge of the Samari-tans we are mainly dependent on patristic sources; and, in both cases, the star witness is the fourth-century Epiphanius, who has not generally enjoyed a high reputation for relia-bility.

According to Epiphanius the Essenes were a Samaritan sect, located in Samaria in times before the destruction of Jerusalem. He has no information about Judaean Essenes on the Dead Sea, a surprising fact if he is dependent on Josephus or Pliny. His Samaritan Essenes agreed, he tells

---

[1] *Die jüdischen Baptismen*, p. 113.    [2] T.B., *Yeb.* 24b, *Hull.* 3b.

us, in most fundamentals, with their Samaritan neighbours, the 'Dositheans', 'Sabaeans', 'Gorothenes', etc.; they disagreed with all of them, and even came to blows at one time with the Gorothenes, while the latter were on a pilgrimage to Jerusalem, on the subject of the dates of the festivals. The story of a fight with the Gorothenes supports the rabbinical evidence that these were Samaritan proselytes adhering to Judaism; and it has the ring of truth about it. If we could believe in Epiphanius's Samaritan Essenes as a pre-Christian sect, then these disputes about the calendar would be a link with Judaean heteropraxis; there would then be at least two closely related groups, Samaritan Essenes and Judaean Essenes, lined up against Samaritan proselytes and the Jerusalem Jews.

Epiphanius goes on to speak about another 'Jewish sect' called Ossenes, living in Trans-Jordan, south of his 'Jewish sect' of 'Nasarenes'. Thomas identifies Epiphanius's Ossenes with Essenes, and suggests that they represented the remnant of the Dead Sea Essenes, who had migrated to Trans-Jordan after the Jewish War. If this is correct, it would explain Epiphanius's ignorance about the Dead Sea Essenes; they no longer existed in his day at Qumran. But in that case he is simply reporting the existence of Jewish groups in his own time; he tells us further that the Ossenes were later merged in other Jewish sects. His reports about Samaritan Essenes may also be correct, but they too may hold only for his own period. Some of the Dead Sea Essenes may have found a refuge in Samaria as well as in Trans-Jordan. The Dositheans are another enigmatic group, though we are not dependent solely on Epiphanius for information about them.[1] We cannot, however, be certain that they were a pre-Christian group, and, in any case, their close resemblance to the Judaean Essenes suggests that they are the same group in Samaria[2]; their 'founder' Dositheus is a purely fictitious character, and it may perhaps be suggested that their name, like that of the Boethusians, is connected

[1] For literature on them, see H. H. Rowley, *The Zadokite Fragments and the Dead Sea Scrolls*, Oxford, 1952, p. 79. See further, infra, p. 60ff.
[2] J. Schousboe, *La Secte juive de l'Alliance nouvelle aux pays de Damas et le christianisme naissant*, Copenhagen, 1942, p. 52ff.

with the name Essenes (the name Boethusians has been explained as meaning *Beth Essaioi*). Some of their main features as reported by Epiphanius suggest that by the time he came to know them they had become even stricter ascetics than the ancient Essenes; they not only rejected marriage (or at least one group of them), but they were vegetarians —and they also believed in the resurrection.

Thomas's pre-Christian *mouvement baptiste* appears to be disappearing in the light of closer analysis: we are still not beyond the point of having two main schismatic groups only, the Samaritans and the Judaean Essenes, with no demonstrable connection between them.

The question might be left there were it not for two sets of important facts, some of them entirely new.

The origins of Essenism in the ancient tribal asceticism of Israel have already been discussed.[1] Hilgenfeld traced Essenes to their origin in a Rechabite clan; and this has been thought to have formed the basis of the later Essene order.[2] Patristic tradition supports the connection: the Abbot Nilus of Ancyra (ca. A.D. 400) takes it for well established that the Essenes were descendants of Jonadab ben Rechab.[3] If the Essenes had an ancient Israelite origin, there may be something after all in Epiphanius's tradition about pre-Christian Samaritan Essenes.

More striking evidence is the discovery of a Samaritan-type Pentateuch in old Hebrew, not Samaritan, script at Qumran; and this, together with accumulating evidence of affinities between the Qumran Essenes and the Samaritan schismatics—in language, religious tenets, customs, and practice—again points to the existence of a vital link in pre-Christian times between Qumran and Samaria, the Samaritans and the Essenes.

The most characteristic possession of the Samaritans was their special recension of the Pentateuch—the one and only form of Scripture the majority of Samaritans were prepared to accept. A Samaritan recension of the Book of Exodus has

---

[1] Supra, p. 15ff.    [2] Cf. Schoeps, p. 250.
[3] *De monastica exercitatione*, 3. The reader is further referred to the discussion on *Rechabiten-Essäer-Ebioniten* in H. J. Schoeps's *Theologie und Geschichte des Judenchristentums*, p. 247ff.

now been found at Qumran among the treasures of Cave 4 (4Q Ex.ᵃ).[1] It contains a substantial portion of the text of Exodus vi.25-xxxvii.15, extensive enough to show its essential characteristics; and it contains all the distinctive features of the much fuller Samaritan recension of the Pentateuch—its repetitious style (e.g. in the recounting of the Plague episodes at Exodus viii-ix), its borrowings from Deuteronomy —the Israelite document—(Deuteronomy i.9-18 in place of Exodus xviii.25 (?), Deuteronomy v.24 to follow Exodus xx.19, both as in the Samaritan Pentateuch), its transpositions and expansions (Exodus vii.18 followed by an expansion describing the fulfilment of Moses of a command at Exodus vii.16-18, viii.19, followed by a similar expansion fulfilling Exodus viii.16-19, etc., etc.). The scroll is not in the Samaritan script, but in an old Hebrew hand; and texts in this form of script were apparently being produced in the first and second centuries B.C.

No discovery could make plainer the affinities of the Qumran sectarians, for it is quite certain that no Pharisaic group ever possessed or used such a Pentateuch. If such texts were being written at Qumran for use in the first and second centuries B.C., then it was for circulation among Samaritan or affiliated sectarian groups, such as the Qumran Essenes. The fact that the document is written in palaeo-Hebrew points to use among Judaean sectarians.

There is other patristic evidence for the existence of such variant types of Pentateuch. The Nasaraean sect of Epiphanius (see further below, p. 66ff.) held that the Jewish form of Pentateuch was not that which Moses received, but a later fabrication; they themselves possessed the true Law. The same view is attributed by Epiphanius to his Ὀσσαῖοι; they renounced the Books (of Moses) [of the Jews] like the Νασαραῖοι.[2]

The greatest importance is to be attached to this difference in type of Pentateuch. It is a sign of the very great antiquity of the groups possessing such a book, for any fundamental differences in this connection must antedate the

[1] 'Exodus in the Samaritan Recension from Qumran', Patrick Skehan, in *JBL*, 74, 1955, 182ff.

[2] μόνον δὲ τῶ ἀπαγορεύειν τὰς βίβλους ὁμοίως τοῖς Νασαραῖοις (19.5).

work of Ezra. The Samaritan Pentateuch is in fact practically identical textually with that of the Jews; any different type of Pentateuch must come from a period before the Return.

In addition to the scrolls, recent studies of the Pseudo-Clementines have been underlining the same strong connection between the Samaritans and the Judaean Essenes.[1]

In the study and elucidation of the Qumran texts, Mlle A. Jaubert has drawn attention to similarities between the Qumran Calendar and that of the Samaritans[2]; in this respect, like the Samaritans, the Qumran sectarians were at odds with the Pharisees. As striking is the asceticism of these sects, their rejection of marriage (or the imposition of restrictions connected with it), the ritual bath, and their attitude to sacrifice and to the Temple. Such affinities do not oblige us to conclude that the Essenes were Samaritans, but they point to the same general movement of puritanical non-conformity. 'One thing is certain', as Schechter wrote in his *editio princeps* of the *Damascus Document* (and the scrolls further reinforce his conclusions), 'that we have here to do with a sect decidedly hostile to the bulk of the Jews as represented by the Pharisees. It is a sect equipped with additional sacred books of its own, a calendar of its own, and a set of laws of its own, bearing upon various commandments of the Scriptures. It is at variance with the nation at large in its interpretation of the past, abusing its heroes, as in the case of David. . . .'[3] That the Qumran sect looked for a Messiah of Israel points perhaps decisively to the place of its origin.

As we have already seen, the affinities between the Dositheans and the Judaean Essenes are so close that they seem to be the same sect at different periods in its history. That may still be correct, but, in the light of the new facts, we may require to revise our ideas about the relationship, for the explanation of the connection is not necessarily that a Judaean sect found its way into Samaria after the Roman War; a Samaritan sect of Essenes may have settled at an earlier period in Judaea; and in that case the Samaritan Essenes or Dositheans have a very long history indeed be-

[1] R. North, 'The Qumran Sadducees', *Catholic Biblical Quarterly*, 17, 164ff.
[2] Mlle A. Jaubert, *VT*, 3, 250ff., 258, and *RHR*, 146, 1954, 168.
[3] Cf. supra, pp. 8ff., 24.

hind them. Montgomery traced the influences producing
the Samaritan Dositheans to the Judaean Essenes[1]: we may
have to reverse this and look for the formative influences in
Judaean sectarianism in the ancient religion of Israel, or
rather in its remanent descendants in Samaria.

An objection to this hypothesis could be the alleged
hostility found in some of the scrolls between the Qumran
Sect and the Samaritans.[2] Père Milik detects a number of
references to 'the man of Ephraim and Manasseh' in the
*Commentaries on Nahum, Hosea and Psalm 37*, considered in
most cases as enemies of the sect and adds: 'In addition to
the general anti-Samaritan feeling of Judaeans, there may be
an allusion here to some specific conflict between them and
the Essenes: but, on this point our historical sources fail to
inform us'. The published evidence so far, however, contains two such allusions only, neither of which refers to any
conflict with the Essenes.[3] Until we are in a position to
study these other references, we must reserve judgment on
this issue. There may have been both affinity and conflict;
family feuds are often the most bitter; and, in any case, the
hypothesis proposed refers to origins only: what may have
happened at later stages in the history of these groups is a
different question.

It may also reasonably be asked how such a view of the
origins of these sects is to be reconciled with their derivation
from Hasidic Judaism. The answer quite simply is that,
while the Second Temple was renewed and reformed at the
time of the Restoration, its priesthood must have preserved,
with the conservative tenacity of a priestly institution, much
of the pre-Ezra type of indigenous Hebrew religion[4]; it
would then be this conservatism of the Zadokite exiled
priests which constituted the link with the descendants of the
Northern Kingdom.

These connections with Samaria and the North certainly
point to an origin for Essenism (and Palestinian sectarianism)
in the ancient religion of the Northern Kingdom, or, at any
rate, in what was left of Israelite religion after the Exile and

---

[1] *The Samaritans*, Philadelphia, 1907, p. 263.
[2] See J. T. Milik, *Ten Years Discovery*, p. 73.   [3] See *JBL*, 75, 1956, 93-95.
[4] Cf. Adam Welch, *Post-Exilic Judaism*, Edinburgh, 1935, esp. p. 280ff.

before the (supposedly) sweeping reforms of Ezra and Nehemiah.

It might be suggested, as a working hypothesis, that this first-century sectarianism is descended from a pre-Ezra type of Hebrew religion, pressed back into the peripheral areas by the Judaism, predominantly Pharisaic, of the Second Temple.

To come back to the patristic evidence: such considerations are important for our estimate of the testimony of the Fathers, and in particular Epiphanius. In his statements about pre-Christian Samaritan Essenes he may have drawn on a genuinely ancient tradition. In that case it may be worth looking again at some of his other statements about pre-Christian Jewish sects.

But first something more must be said about the Samaritans and their sectarianism.

The Samaritans are not included in Justin's catalogue in his *Dialogue with Trypho* (they are mentioned in that of Hegesippus); Justin did not regard them as a Jewish heresy, but elsewhere he leaves us in no doubt that he considered Samaritan sectarianism the arch-enemy of the early Church, in particular the form of heresy attributed to Simon Magus (Acts viii.5-24).[1] The vast amount of literature on this subject, both in the early Fathers and in modern authors, is an indication of the important rôle this 'heresy' played in the earliest Christian period; there is little doubt that it continued to persist, in different forms, and to exercise a widespread influence, especially in the marginal Judaism of the Diaspora.

It is not proposed here to enter into the complex problems raised by the subject. I wish simply to draw attention to three main points: 1. that, in its earliest discernible forms, it is to be classed with Jewish sectarianism as part of the *mouvement baptiste* of the period before the destruction of Jerusalem[2]; 2. it supplies us with the earliest evidence of a sectarianism which threatened the basic tenet of Jewish

---

[1] *Apol.* I, 26. Cf. A. Hilgenfeld, *Die Ketzergeschichte des Urchristentums*, Leipzig, 1884, pp. 21ff., 149ff.

[2] For the view that the Samaritans are Jews, though heterodox, cf. Schürer, *History of the Jewish People*, II, i, p. 5.

monotheism; 3. it may have been the *fons et origo* of the whole sectarian movement.

1. From the later heresiologists and others we learn that these Northern sectarians went under such different names as *Dositheans, Sabaeans* and *Gorothenes* (Epiphanius); a group of Essenes is included by Epiphanius in his Samaritan heresies.[1] We can dismiss the name *Gorothenes* as in the same category as Justin's *Genistai*: but the Dositheans, and possibly the Sabaeans, seem to have been genuine groups of baptizing sectarians.[2]

According to J. A. Montgomery,[3] these Samaritan heretics (or Gnostics), known mainly as *Dosithei*, are to be distinguished from another group, also pre-Christian, perhaps taking its rise in Egypt. The latter appears to have been a reforming group, standing under the influence of Judaism, insisting on Scriptural interpretation *au pied de la lettre*, and retaining the ancient Samaritan doctrine of Sheol and denying the Resurrection.

The first Dosithean group was very different in spirit and practice: it belongs to the enthusiastic cults, like the group around Simon Magus. Montgomery dates their rise around the beginning of our era, noting similarities and affinities with the Essene sectarians of Judaea. The Samaritan fourteenth-century historian Abulfath can describe the group as Zadokites (*bene Zadok*).[4] Montgomery writes (op. cit. p. 263):

It was ascetic and encratitic; the ritual bath was an accompaniment of all devotion; certain mystical books, among them those of 'the Sons of the Prophets', were included in their scriptures, while there was the Messianic devotion to the founder of their faith, along with the cult of a martyr of their sect. They were ardent resurrectionists of a very materialistic order of belief, and were awaiting the end of all things with millenarian expectations. We can probably even identify the influences producing the sect. Several points of practice connect them with the mysterious community of the Essenes, namely, not only their frequent baptisms,

---

[1] *Panarion*, 9.1ff.
[2] Cf. Brandt, op. cit. p. 113; supra, p. 56.
[3] *The Samaritans*, Philadelphia, 1907, p. 262.
[4] Cf. Marx, *Die vier Kanonischen Evangelien, Johannes*, p. 221ff. (*Exkurs über die samaritanische Gnosis*).

but also their scrupulousness in hiding their bodies when in the bath, which is to be compared with the Essene rule of wearing a loincloth when bathing, while further the fear of contact with others—amongst the Essenes even with those of a lower caste in the order—is common to both.  The vegetarianism of the Dositheans also agrees with Jerome's report of the like practice among the Essenes, although this notice is now generally invalidated by criticism.  Some element of truth therefore is found in Epiphanius's statement making the Essenes a Samaritan sect.  The rise of this body may then be placed about the beginning of our era, a date which would agree with the Patristic references collocating Dositheus with Simon . . .  This sect had evidently, from Origen's note, a short-lived existence, as it was already moribund in his day.  It doubtless was a product of the influences which induced the Samaritan adoption of the doctrine of the resurrection, and in this respect secured a triumph over its like-named rival.

2. The Samaritans might well have come in for the description *Meristai* applied by Justin to certain Jewish sects and possibly referring to their rejection or compromising of the fundamental tenet of all Jewish belief, monotheism (above, p. 49).

In the lengthy and learned discussions about pre-Christian Jewish Gnosticism, too little weight, it seems to me, has been given to the importance of the evidence of Acts viii.10.  It is true the Samaritans were not Jews, but their heresies represent a form of Judaism.  The type of sectarian belief behind Acts viii.10 (its early date here guaranteed) appears to be some form of Gnosticism.  Luke tells us that Simon's adherents called out, 'This is the δύναμις of God called great.' These words look editorial.  It seems historically probable that Simon was actually called ἡ μεγάλη δύναμις which amounted, in effect, to the claim to be divine or a divine being; the Aramaic (and also Hebrew) word *hēl* (*haîl*) stands for God in Samaritanism[1]; it appears in Greek form again at Mk. xiv.62, in the apocryphal *Gospel of Peter* v.19 and in the famous reply of James before his martyrdom.[2]

[1] Cf. Montgomery, op. cit. p. 215; cf. G. Dalman, *Words of Jesus*, p. 200ff. All that Dalman succeeded in proving was that the expression was rare in Judaism; cf. Lohmeyer, *Galiläa und Jerusalem* (Göttingen, 1936), p. 70.  It is clearly an Aramaism (or Samaritanism) peculiar to Northern Palestine.  See further, infra, p. 81ff.

[2] Infra, p. 81.

Certainly this is how Justin regarded the Samaritan heresy, for he tells us that Simon, in the reign of Claudius, had been considered even in Rome itself to be a god ($\theta\epsilon\acute{o}s$) and that there was even a statue to him erected on the banks of the Tiber, with the Latin inscription *Simoni Deo Sancto*.[1] The Hellenistic Gnosticism of the Ophites, Sethites, Cainites, etc., also appears to have consisted essentially in the belief in the manifestation of the Dynamis (in the Serpent, Seth, Cain, etc.). The clear and unmistakable continuity between the primitive Gnosticism of Simon Magus and that of these later sects is the best proof of Friedländer's well-known thesis of a pre-Christian Jewish Gnosticism.[2]

3. The origin of Samaritanism generally and of Samaritan sectarianism in particular is undoubtedly to be traced ultimately to the division of the Kingdom, and to the opposition which developed between Samaritans as the Northern 'descendants' of the ancient Israel, and the returning exiles during the period of the restoration of the Temple under Ezra and Nehemiah. It is not without significance that one of the main points of difference between Samaritans and Jews, going back to the times of Jeroboam, was connected with the question of the Calendar.[3] Indeed, one of the distinguishing marks of Palestinian heteropraxis, in addition to its ascetic tendencies and baptismal rites, and part too of its opposition to the Jerusalem authorities, was its acceptance of a festival calendar differing from the official calendar of Jerusalem. It is, in fact, not unlikely that the *fons et origo* of this whole movement of anti-Jerusalem sectarianism goes back ultimately to the ancient division in Israel and especially

---

[1] *Apol.* loc. cit. Epiphanius (*Panarion*, 19.1.10, 11) informs us that the Sampsaeans (whom he mentions in connection with his *Ossaeans*) made the same claim for their founder Elxai—he was $\dot{\eta}$ $\delta\acute{u}\nu\alpha\mu\iota s$ $\dot{\alpha}\pi o\kappa\epsilon\kappa\alpha\lambda\upsilon\mu\mu\acute{e}\nu\eta$, a derivation in which we can recognize both $\hbar el$ ($\delta\acute{u}\nu\alpha\mu\iota s$) and *kesa* ($\dot{\alpha}\pi o\kappa\epsilon\kappa\alpha\lambda\upsilon\mu\mu\acute{e}\nu\eta$).

[2] The reception given to Friedländer's main thesis is well known; it was rejected by Schürer (*Th. Lz.* 1899, col. 167ff.), but never completely disproved. Recent work is, if anything, supporting Friedländer; G. Quispel has been arguing recently, on the basis of new Coptic discoveries, for a connection between Gnosticism and sectarian Judaism (*The Jung Codex* (ed. F. L. Cross), London, 1955, p. 78; *Eranos Jahrbuch*, XXII (Zürich, 1954), p. 195ff., *ZRG*, 6, 1954, 302ff., *Evangel. Theologie*, 1954 (Christliche und jüdische Heterodoxie): see further H. J. Schoeps, *Urgemeinde, Judenchristentum, Gnosis*, Tübingen, 1946, p. 40, and H. Jonas, *Gnosis und spätantiker Geist*, Göttingen, 1954, Vol. I, p. 10). See further R. McL. Wilson, 'Simon, Dositheus and the Dead Sea Scrolls', *ZRG*, 9, 1957, 21ff.

[3] See the recent work of Mlle A. Jaubert, e.g. in *VT*, 3, 250ff.

to the forms it took at the time of the Restoration. Samaritans possessed the Law, regarded themselves as the true, ancient Israelites, and the returning Jews as foreigners and usurpers. The conflict persisted into New Testament times and was perpetuated with the utmost bitterness and savagery, as in the complete destruction of Samaria by John Hyrcanus. The Qumran sectarians have a number of features in common with the Samaritans; one of the most striking is their bitter opposition to 'Judah', and their attitude to the house of David. The princes of Judah are to be visited by the wrath of God, and among these princes David is also included; he is not only held in little esteem, but even declared to have been ignorant of the content of the Law.[1]

Affinities of this kind point not only to a close historical connection, but to the possible origin of this marginal Judaism and Samaritan sectarianism in the ancient feud between the North and the South.

Special interest attaches to Epiphanius's Jewish sect of the Nasarenes, located by him in the ancient Gilead and Bashan. They display some of the same characteristics as their neighbours, the Dositheans, and, like the Samaritans, had a variant, if not a different, form of Pentateuch from the Jewish Pentateuch; they declared that the Jewish Pentateuch was not the one received by Moses, but a later fabrication. The second main difference was their rejection of all animal sacrifice and abstention from eating the flesh of animals. Otherwise they were like all other Jews, practising circumcision, keeping the Sabbath and festivals. One other thing Epiphanius notes is that they rejected the doctrine of fate (εἱμαρμένη) and astrology.

The existence of such a sect is denied altogether by Schmidtke,[2] followed by Schoeps[3]: both regard this section

---

[1] Cf. S. Schechter, op. cit. I, pp. xiii, xviii.

[2] A. Schmidtke, *Neue Fragmente zu den Judenchristlichen Evangelien* (T.U. xxxvii, 1), p. 199ff. Schmidtke's conclusions and general estimate of the evidence of the Fathers for Jewish 'sects' appear to have been widely accepted. The most recent discussion of these problems by Georg Strecker, *Das Judenchristentum in den Pseudoklementinen* (Berlin, 1958, T.U. lxx), follows this line; Epiphanius is an untrustworthy witness. Yet Schmidtke did not receive much notice at the time of the appearance of his book; Holl (editor of the *Panarion* in *Griechische christliche Schriftsteller der ersten drei Jahrhunderte*), referring to Schmidtke's views on the Ebionites, gave as his opinion that 'die wilden Aufstellungen von A. Schmidtke (T.U. xxxvii) bleiben überall ausser Betracht' (Epiphanius, *Panarion*, i.337).    [3] op. cit. p. 14ff.

of Epiphanius's work as a parallel elaboration of his account of the Christian Nazorenes (ch. 29ff.); and, as, according to these scholars, all the reports of Epiphanius about the Nazorenes are secondary material 'woven together out of personal knowledge and groundless speculations', no importance at all can be attached to these later fabrications. A less sceptical estimate has been formed by other scholars, such as G. Hölscher[1] and H. Gressmann.[2] The debate has assumed importance in view of the claim that this reputed Jewish sect was connected with the description given to the primitive Church in Acts xxiv.5, as 'the sect of the Nazorenes'. Some idea of the extent of the literature on the subject may be obtained from a recent discussion of the name by Paul Winter.[3]

Epiphanius appears to be well informed about Nasarenes and Nazorenes; more than once he carefully distinguishes the Jewish sect, which he places before A.D. 70 (there were even survivors in his own day[4]) from the Christian Nazorenes.[5] The two presbyters at whose request he wrote his *Panarion* came from Coele-Syria where Christian Nazorenes are located and Epiphanius had himself been there.[6] The contentions of Schmidtke and Schoeps that the earlier Jewish Nasarenes are a fabrication of Epiphanius's imagination, and that his descriptions come from his information about the later Christian sect are not borne out by a comparison of the two passages. One of the main characteristics of the Jewish sect is their rejection of beliefs in fate and astrology (possibly directed, like similar Sadducaean doctrines, against the Pharisees). There appears to be nothing corresponding to this in Epiphanius's accounts of the Christian sects of Nazorenes, or Ebionites. It seems a little inconsistent to trace this feature of Epiphanius's account of the Nasarenes to the Pseudo-Clementines (Hom. iv.12), when there is again nothing corresponding in the parallel account of the Nazorenes, from which, *ex hypothesi*, the Nasarenes are derived

[1] *Urgemeinde und Spätjudentum*, Oslo, 1938.
[2] *ZATW* 43, 25.          [3] *NTS*, 3, 136ff.
[4] *Panarion*, 19, 3, 1-2. They are located in the upper Thebaid and 'further Arabia' (lit. beyond Arabia).
[5] ibid. 19, 5, 7; 29, 6, 1; 30, 1, 3.
[6] ibid. Introductory Letter, Vol. 1, p. 153.

(cf. Schmidtke, p. 202). The Christian Nazorenes recognized the Law and the Prophets; the Nasarenes accepted parts of the Pentateuch only. The geographical locations do not entirely agree. And their conformity to the general pattern of sectarianism argues further for their existence, thus accounting for much in the later Jewish Christian Palestinian sects.

Some importance must, no doubt, be assigned to the statement of the Elder Pliny (*H.N.* v.19) that there was a tetrarchy of Nazerini in Coele-Syria. If this is a reference to the same group, then it must have been a large one. Some recent evidence is contained in a Mandaean text to which attention has been drawn by Dr Rudolf Macuch.[1] Macuch, on the basis of a critical examination of the text, traces Mandaean origins to the emigration from Palestine about the year A.D. 37 of a Jewish sect of Nasoraeans, obviously baptizing sectarians; they were driven from Palestine by Jewish persecution. (The text mentions the number as 60,000.) Dr Macuch does not identify the sect further, and in view of the position of John the Baptist in Mandaeism, the Nasoraeans may have been adherents of the Baptism of John. But it is possible that we have to do with a movement of Christians,[2] emigrating from Palestine, though the date is curious.

How much value can we attach to this patristic evidence as a whole, and, granted such a sect existed, how did it originate?

It is to be regretted that the first use which ever appears to have been made of this passage in Epiphanius was to support the fantasies of the Christ-myth theory at the turn of the century.[3] The connection of the name Ναζωραῖος, Ναζαρηνός, in the Gospels and Acts with Ναζαρέθ was rejected as a 'myth within a myth', and explanations given which sought to explain the name (and the origins of Christianity) in terms of the ancient Jewish ascetic order of the Nazirites (Ναζιραῖοι). It was in support of this theory that Epiphanius's evidence was adduced.

In rejecting most of the fantasies of this school of thought

---

[1] 'Alter und Heimat des Mandäismus nach neuerschlossenen Quellen', *Th. Lz.*, 82.
[2] Cf. Kittel, *Th. W.* under Ναζωραῖος, p 881ff.
[3] See A. Schweitzer, *Geschichte der Leben-Jesu-Forschung*, Tübingen, 1913, pp. 465, 475, 533. (This discussion does not appear in the shortened English edition.)

Schweitzer concedes the relevance of this evidence of Epiphanius,[1] but agrees with the general and still widely held view,[2] that the 'sect' in Epiphanius has arisen through a confusion with the later heretical Christian sect of Nazorenes.[3] Schweitzer did not fail to note, however, how carefully Epiphanius distinguishes the Ναϲαραῖοι (sometimes spelled Ναζαραῖοι) from the Ναζωραῖοι, the later Christian sect. The Nazirites are also mentioned by him, for instance, in order to deny that this is the true etymology of Ναζωραῖοι to be explained correctly from Ναζαρέθ (*Pan.* 19.5, 6-7), but Schweitzer did not miss the fact that elsewhere in the *Panarion* (cf. 78.7) Epiphanius writes Ναζωραῖος and means Ναζιραῖος.[4] It should also be mentioned that when he speaks of the one or two survivors of the Jewish sect in the Thebaid and further Arabia, the form Ναϲαρηνοί is used (*Pan.* 20.3.2).[5]

If we accept Epiphanius's evidence at its face value, how are we to explain the character of these strange Jews from Trans-Jordan? Their Samaritan-type Pentateuch suggests some connection with Samaria. The name, in some of its forms, could be Aramaic, as M. Lidzbarski recognized, meaning 'the guardians' or 'the keepers'.[6] Now this is, of course, how the Samaritans have explained their name, deriving it, not from the name of the original owner of Samaria and his clan, Shemer (I Kings, xvi.24), but from *shamar*, 'to guard or keep'; and Samaritans explain that they are the guardians and keepers of the (true) Law.[7] When once the conflict arose between the Jews of the Return and the Samaritans, it would be natural for them later to adopt such an explanation of their name; they were the 'keepers' or 'guardians' of the true Law and inheritance of Israel.[8] The Aramaic equivalent of *Shomerim* is *Naṭarin* or *Naṭarayya*,

---

[1] ' . . . die formale Berechtigung jeder auf diese Notiz sich berufenden Hypothese (muss) zugegeben werden', p. 534.

[2] Cf. Kittel, *Th. W.* under Ναζωραῖος, p. 884.

[3] loc. cit.      [4] op. cit. p. 475, n. 1.

[5] It seems unlikely that the 'solitaries' of the Thebaid of Epiphanius's time would include Jewish-Christian Nazorenes, for there is nothing to suggest that this sect contained hermits. The Jewish sect, however, was probably an order of eremites.

[6] For various explanations and derivations, see my *Aramaic Approach to the Gospels and Acts*, 2nd edn., Oxford, 1954, p. 145, and P. Winter, *NTS, 3*, 136ff.

[7] Cf. J. A. Montgomery, *The Samaritans*, Philadelphia, 1907, p. 318.

[8] For a study of the position of the Samaritans at the Return, see especially Adam Welch, *Post-Exilic Judaism*, Edinburgh, 1935, p. 17ff.

and, since Samaria was Aramaic-speaking, it would not be surprising to find an Aramaic name either for Samaritans in general or for a sect or group of Samaritans.

As the usage in the Fourth Gospel shows (cf. Jn. viii.48), the word 'Samaritan' had become practically equivalent in meaning to 'schismatic' or 'heretic', and appears to have passed almost as a term of abuse. The same might be claimed for the word in its Aramaic form. If this explanation is sound, clearly the Nasarenes or Samaritans were sectarian in character, and belonged not only to the anti-Pharisaic fringe, but to those groups in the North most hostile to the hierarchy in Jerusalem.

An alternative explanation would be to associate the name with the ancient Nazirites. It seems obvious that the group were desert-dwellers, and, as they follow the Hemero-baptists in the list, they may also have been baptizing sectarians. They were plainly ascetics and their most striking custom is their abstention from flesh. Abstention from wine is not explicitly mentioned, but it was probably also included, since abstention from flesh implied an even stricter form of asceticism; the greater includes in that case the lesser.[1]

There is support for this view in the fourth-century heresiologist, Philaster of Brescia. Philaster's *Diversarum Haeresion Liber*[2] was mainly based, like the *Panarion* of Epiphanius, on the lost Syntagma of Hippolytus, a work on heresies composed in Rome towards the end of the second or the beginning of the third century A.D. Whether the Syntagma itself made use of Justin's list of heresies is not certain, but it undoubtedly contained ancient source material from the second century. In a list of no less than twenty-eight alleged pre-Christian Jewish heresies, the eighth, listed after the Pharisees, Sadducees, and Samaritans and before the Essenes is that of the Nazorei:

*Alia est heresis Iudaeorum qui dicuntur Nazorei, quae legem et prophetas accipit, carnaliter tamen uiuendum adfirmat, omnemque iustificationem in carnali obseruantia consistere suspicatur, crines etiam nutrientes capitis omnemque uirtutem iustitiae in eo putantes consistere,*

---

[1] Cf. W. Robertson-Smith, *The Religion of the Semites*, London, 1901, pp. 302, 306.
[2] ed. F. Marx, *CSEL*, 38, Vienna, 1898.

*quasi a Samson illo iudice sibi hoc praesumentes indicii quia Nazorei uocabantur: a quo postea pagani fortes uiros ex illius figura usurpantes Hercules nuncuparunt.*

Philaster is not simply reproducing the common source he used with Epiphanius, the Syntagma of Hippolytus, since the two descriptions are quite different.[1] Philaster's source has manifestly misunderstood the tradition, correctly reproduced in Epiphanius, that the Nasaraeans abstained from flesh, and turned it into something nearly its opposite, *carnaliter vivendum affirmat.* The presence of this revealing feature makes it unlikely that Philaster is simply inventing the explanation of the name by relating a tradition about Jewish *Nazorei* to the ancient Nazirate. It may well be a piece of ancient and genuine tradition about the essential nature of a sect of pre-Christian Jewish *abstinentes.*

The identification of Ναασαραῖοι with descendants of the ancient Nazirites would then supply us with some kind of foundation for Epiphanius's report about a pre-Christian Jewish sect in Trans-Jordan; and it meets one of the main difficulties in accepting his account at its face value, the absence of any other report about the existence of such a sect in the earlier Fathers. The derivation of the form of the name Ναασαραῖοι (or Ναζωραῖοι) from Hebrew *nezirim* does not present insuperable difficulties.[2]

In view of such a possibility, one turns with interest to the long account of the Christian Nazorenes in Chapter 34 of the *Panarion* in the hope that Epiphanius may have preserved there too some new facts or information. He goes out of his way to underline the derivation and connection of the name Ναζωραῖοι with Nazareth, denying expressly any connection or association with the Nazirites, although he recalls that John the Baptist was a Nazirite and tells us that so too was James, the Lord's brother (29.4):

Τοῦτο τὸ ὄνομα ἐπιτιθέασιν ἑαυτοῖς τοῦ καλεῖσθαι Ναζωραίους — οὐχὶ Ναζιραίους, τὸ ἑρμηνευόμενον ἡγιασμένους.

(29.5.6-7)

---

[1] Cf. A. Hilgenfeld, *Die Ketzergeschichte des Urchristenthums*, Leipzig, 1884, p. 14ff.

[2] The Old Latin version of I Macc. iii.49 has *nasaraei* for Nazirites.

There is one other passage of special interest where Epiphanius is again explaining the name Nazorene (*italics mine*).

The Nazorenes follow these [the Cerinthian heretics] next, being of the same period with them, either possibly before them or at the same time with them or following them, at any rate contemporary (for I am unable to explain more accurately who followed whom); for, as I said, they were contemporary with each other.

Now they [the Nazorenes] did not apply to themselves the name of Christ or the name of Jesus itself, but the name of Nazorenes.   And all Christians were at that time similarly called Nazorenes.   But it happened, for a short time, *they were also called* Ἰεσσαῖοι *before the disciples began to be called Christians at Antioch.* Now they were called Ἰεσσαῖοι on account of Jesse, I think, since David was the son of Jesse, and from the seed of David by succession Mary came, by the fulfilling of Holy Scripture, according to the Old Testament, the Lord saying to David 'From the fruit of thy loins shall I set one upon thy throne'.

(Pan. 29.1ff.)

After some further discussion of the Davidic descent of Christ through Mary (the main reason, no doubt, for this remarkable piece of etymology), the writer continues:

Much besides can be said about this, but since, however, I have come to the subject why Christians were called Ἰεσσαῖοι before those who believed in Christ were called Christians, it was on this account we stated that Jesse was the father of David, and either by the hypothesis of this [name] Jesse, or from the name of Jesus our Lord they were called Ἰεσσαῖοι, by beginning with [the name] Jesus (being his disciples), or on account of the etymology of the name of the Lord, for Jesus, according to the Hebrew dialect, is called θεραπευτής or ἰατρός or σωτήρ.   In accordance with this [meaning of the] name they received the name Ἰεσσαῖοι before they were called Christians.   But at Antioch, as we mentioned above (and as the true account tells) the disciples and the whole Church of God began to be called Christians.

(Pan. 29.4.9-10)

H. J. Schoeps regards the name Ἰεσσαῖοι for Christians as 'eine alte Bezeichnung', but adds that 'the derivation from Jesse, which Epiphanius suggests, is naturally wrong. We are to think of the name Jesus itself.'[1] Schoeps does not appear to have noted that Epiphanius does suggest the derivation of the name from Jesus in this same passage, but only in order to claim the *Essenes* as Christians. His next paragraph reveals the real reason for this derivation of the name from Jesus (in the sense of θεραπευτής), and no doubt also the motive for his original statement that Christians were at one time called Ἰεσσαῖοι.

You could find, O philologian, the explanation of these very matters if you read the Memoirs of Philo in his book which he wrote on the Ἰεσσαῖοι, how the man wrote about no other people than Christians when he described the ways and the festivals of these people, and their monasteries in the settlement by Lake Mareia. For when he was in their country (they call the place Mareotis), and lodged among them, he received help in the monasteries in this place. He was there during the days of the Passover [Easter] and saw their manner of life, and how some completed the observation of the holy week of Passover by fasting [lit. among themselves],[2] others eating after two days, others in the evening. All these things were recorded by the man with regard to the faith and the order of Christians.

(*Pan.* 29.5.1ff.)

It seems quite certain that Epiphanius's motive for linking the name Jesus with θεραπευτής is to enable him to claim the Egyptian 'Essenes' or Therapeutae as Christians; and the same reason may account for his earlier statement that Christians were at an early stage called 'Essenes'. But the connection is illuminating.

In conclusion, I would content myself now with the general point that there is more than meets the eye in these patristic accounts. They deserve as careful and exhaustive study as any of the other sources of information at our disposal. If we are prepared to accept their evidence, we are led to a conclusion very close to that of Père Thomas, and I would summarize my two main points briefly as follows:

1. There is credible patristic evidence for the existence

[1] op. cit. p. 10, n. 3.
[2] I have followed the interpretation of F. C. Conybeare in his *Philo: About the Contemplative Life*, p. 320.

in pre-70 Palestine and beyond of a widespread movement of Jewish or para-Jewish non-conformity, characterized by its ascetic or puritanical tendencies and manner of life and its baptizing cult, holding to a different canon of Scripture and different customs from the orthodoxy or orthopraxis of the official Pharisaic-dominated religion of Torah and Temple in Jerusalem. It was a sectarian movement in the proper sense of the term, though its deviation from normative Judaism in the period was probably more in the realm of heteropraxis rather than of heterodoxy.

2. This movement of 'Jewish' sectarianism may represent the survival into New Testament times of the old pre-Ezra type of Hebrew religion, with a strong ascetic element; and its puritanism may stem from the ancient asceticism of the religion of Israel. Its *fons et origo* was the Samaritan schism.

Epiphanius's pre-Christian sect of the 'Nasaraeans' is not to be dismissed as a patristic fiction[1]; it may represent, in sectarian form, the ancient Nazirate.

[1] Since this chapter was written, my attention has been drawn to Bertil Gärtner's monograph *Die rätselhaften Termini Nazoräer und Iskariot* (Uppsala, 1957). Dr Gärtner also is prepared to find more in the background of Ναζωραῖος than 'man of Nazareth', and to connect Epiphanius's Νασαραῖοι with the Mandaean Naṣorayya, rabbinical Noṣrim and the Qumran sect (cf. esp. p. 33).

# CHAPTER IV

# Sectarian Judaism
# and the Primitive Church

I

## QUMRAN AND THE 'HEBRAISTS' OF ACTS

A most important discussion of the problem of Qumran sectarianism and Christian origins is contained in the recent work of Oscar Cullmann.[1] Dr Cullmann has for many years defended the thesis that primitive Christianity took its origins, not in official Judaism, but in some more or less esoteric offshoot. From his study of the Pseudo-Clementine literature,[2] where ancient elements of primitive Jewish Christianity have been preserved, he came to the conclusion that there had existed, in pre-Christian times, on the edge of official Judaism, a form of Jewish Gnosticism which he argued, judged externally, must be considered the cradle of earliest Christianity.

Since this Jewish Gnosticism already shows Hellenistic influence, we must view the entire question of Hellenism *vs.* Judaism from a different perspective than has become habitual. In the past, as soon as Hellenistic influences could be shown in a New Testament writing, the immediate conclusion was: this must have been written very late. The Gospel of John is a case in point. Since Hellenistic elements are found in the Gospel, it was believed that a very late origin was proved. Behind this false conclusion stood a false, or at least too schematic, conception of the origin of Christianity, namely, the idea that at first Christianity was merely Jewish, and then later became Hellenistic.[3]

Dr Cullmann then goes on to argue that Qumran now

[1] 'The Significance of the Qumran Texts for Research into the Beginnings of Christianity', in *JBL* 74, Part iv, December, 1955, 213ff.; 'L'Opposition contre le Temple de Jerusalem, Motif Commun de la Théologie Johannique et du Monde Ambiant', in *NTS*, 5, no. 3, April, 1959, 157ff. See also 'A New Approach to the Interpretation of the Fourth Gospel', in *ET*, 71, 2 November, 1959.

[2] *Le Problème littéraire et historique du roman pseudo-clémentin. Étude sur le rapport entre le gnosticisme et le judéo-christianisme*, Paris, 1930.

[3] op. cit. *JBL*, 74, 213.

furnishes us with the evidence for this type of 'esoteric' or peripheral Judaism, within which the roots of primitive Christianity lie. New and striking similarities are shown to have existed between the beliefs, practices, and customs of the Qumran group and the primitive Church especially as we see it in the early chapters of Acts: the Jewish sect called itself among other things, the 'New Covenant' which in Greek is the καινὴ διαθήκη or 'New Testament'. The name *Ebhyonim*, 'the poor' has become almost a proper name for the group; the same term reappears in Galatians and Romans as a name for the first Christians, and was later applied to the remnant of the Jewish congregation, the Ebionites. The common meal of the Qumran sect, which has a purely sacred character and consists of bread and wine (or bread alone), exhibits much similarity to the Eucharist. The baptismal rites of the Essenes and Qumran Jews, their community of goods, their organization and their opposition to the Temple, make an impressive case for some historical connection between the two groups.

Cullmann's main thesis is that the bridge between this type of Judaism (of which Essenism and Qumran provide the most representative forms) and the early Christian Church is to be found in the group known as 'Hellenists' in the Book of Acts (vi.1, ix.29, xi.20). Like the Essenes and the Qumran group the Christian Hellenists rejected the worship of the Jerusalem Temple (their attitude is classically represented in the denunciation of the Temple in the speech of Stephen at Acts vii). The traditional explanation of the name Hellenists as 'Greek-speaking Jews of the Diaspora' is set aside in favour of the explanation of the name as meaning 'Jews who live according to the manner of the Greeks'; similarly it cannot be proved that the 'Hebrews' of Acts vi were simply Aramaic-speaking Christians. The question then is whether these 'Hellenists' were not really Jews who differed from the official Judaism, showing tendencies more or less of a hellenistic character and possibly a syncretistic origin[1] with their roots and background in the type of religious community which existed at Qumran.

[1] *JBL*, op. cit., 220ff.

Cullmann's thesis would have been more convincing if the link with Qumran had been through the party of the 'Hebrews' or 'the Hebraists' rather than with the 'Hellenists'. For the whole context of Acts vi (and of the later references) points unequivocally to a group of Greek-speaking Jews from the Diaspora (probably only temporarily in Jerusalem) who had accepted the Christian faith. Not only are the names of the seven all Greek names (Philip, Stephen, Prochorus, etc.), and one of them described as a proselyte of Antioch, but it is with Greek-speaking Jews of the Diaspora in Jerusalem that they engage in controversy, and who eventually denounce them to the Jerusalem authorities. No convincing reason has been given by Cullmann for departing from the traditional explanation of both names, Hellenists and Hebraists, or rejecting the verdict of H. J. Cadbury[1]:

The complaining party were Jews—Jews of the diaspora, who, though they were not few in Jerusalem and in the church of Jerusalem, were overshadowed by the Palestinian party to which the Twelve as Galilaeans naturally belonged. The committee of Seven chosen, as the sequel tells us, to remedy the difficulty all bear Greek names. One of them is called a proselyte of Antioch; another is at once involved in fatal controversy with Jews of the Synagogue of the Libertines. It is natural to suppose that all the Seven were 'Hellenists' and that Stephen's opponents were of the same class.

In view of the impressive *prima facie* case, however, for a connection between Qumran and the early Church, an alternative hypothesis is worth considering, namely, that the link with Qumran was *through the Hebraists*, the local Aramaic-speaking Jews.

The objection that the Jerusalem Church was not hostile to the Temple is met by the fact (as Cullmann himself recognizes) that Qumran itself, while preparing the way for the rejection of the Temple cultus by the substitution of the idea of a neo-Levitical community as the true Temple, did not in fact reject Temple worship outright. In his attack on the Temple Stephen was no doubt voicing more advanced views

[1] *Beginnings of Christianity*, London, 1933, Vol. V, p. 61.

than were countenanced by the 'Hebrews'. This alternative does not preclude the closest connection between Qumran and the Hellenists as well, for behind both Hebraists and Hellenists would then lie the community of Qumran. The affinities which Cullmann points out between the Acts and the Fourth Gospel and Qumran may still have to be explained as due to the greater initiative of the more radically minded Hellenists.

In his detailed discussion of Ἐβραῖοι-Ἰουδαῖοι[1], T. Zahn argued that the term Ἐβραῖοι stood for native Hebrew- (or Aramaic-) speaking Jews, in the Diaspora as well as in Palestine, in contrast to Ἐλληνισταί, Greek-speaking Jews. His conclusion was accepted by most scholars, but with several notable exceptions. The two famous inscriptions which refer to 'a synagogue of the Hebrews', the one in Rome, the second in Corinth, mean more, according to Deissmann, than synagogues of Aramaic-speaking Jews; the reference in the Corinthian synagogue is taken by him to be to the nationality and religion of the members of the synagogue: they were Hebrews, that is, Jews.[2]

Whatever the precise meaning of the term when applied to Jews, it came to be specially applied to Jewish Christians, as a description of their nationality and religion, as well as of their native language, and as a means of distinguishing them from Jews by religion as well as race.[3]    Indeed, Ἐβραῖοι appears to have been a very early description of the first Jewish Christians: the later Jewish Christian sects called the primitive Jerusalem Church under its Bishop James 'the Church of the Hebrews in Jerusalem'.[4]    The apocryphal 'Gospel to the Hebrews' and the title of the Epistle to the Hebrews are both late second-century echoes of this usage.

The designation, Ἐβραῖοι was an archaic form of speech; Josephus employs it usually when speaking of the 'Hebrews' of the patriarchal age.[5]    The way was prepared, however, for its special Christian use by the revival of the expression as a term for certain members of the Hebrew race in the last

---

[1] *Kommentar zum Neuen Testament, Die Apostelgeschichte des Lukas, Zweite Hälfte, Kap. 13-28*, Band V, 2, pp. 641-6.
[2] *Light from the Ancient East*, London, 1911, p. 13ff.
[3] Zahn, loc. cit.    [4] Clement, *Homilies*, XI.35.    [5] Zahn, op. cit. p. 641.

two centuries B.C. It came to be employed increasingly to describe loyal Jews, especially in the Maccabaean period, who displayed the traditional virtues of their patriarchal forefathers. It occurs in this sense at II Macc. vii.31,[1] xi.13, xv.37, and is especially frequent as a description of the 'Hebrew' martyrs in IV Maccabees (e.g., iv.11, viii.2, ix.6, 18, xvii.9). Too great importance cannot be placed on the usage of the word in the Sibyllines, for the poetic style of that work is deliberately archaizing: nevertheless, it is there the regular term (e.g. Sib. 1.344, 360-366, 5.161, 258) and used especially for the 'faithful elect'. Thus, Sib. 3.69:

ἐκ δὲ Σεβαστηνῶν[2] ἥξει Βελίαρ
.   .   .   .   πολλούς τε πλανήσει
πιστούς τ' ἐκλεκτούς θ' Ἑβραίους ἀνόμους τε καὶ ἄλλους
ἀνέρας . . .

In view of such a usage, it is possible that the description of synagogues of 'Hebrews' in the Diaspora means more than synagogues of Aramaic-speaking Jews, and that the reference is rather to Jews of the Hasidaean tradition, that is, of the Essene type. Some further support for this might be found in the use of the term in Plutarch[3] or in one hellenistic magical text to describe 'Hebrews' who practised some form of esoteric rites.[4]

We would then have an even closer link between the 'Hebrews' of Acts and the 'non-conformist' tradition of the scrolls.

In general, it seems likely that the term was used, not only to distinguish 'Jewish' Christians from Jews, but to include 'Hebrews' from Galilee as well as Judaea. In Palestine itself Ἰουδαῖοι would almost certainly tend to signify the 'inhabitants of Judaea' and (in a religious sense) the Pharisees and scribes of Jerusalem and their adherents.

The 'Hebrews' or 'Hebraists' of Acts would then provide

---

[1] Cf. F.-M. Abel, *Les Livres des Maccabées*, p. 370. 'L'emploi du terme *Hébreux* pour désigner le peuple fidèle se répandait de plus en plus depuis le IIᵉ siècle av. J.-C. Il est très fréquent dans iv Macc.'

[2] Samaria.

[3] *Quaest. conv. IV*, *probl.* 6; cf. Th. Reinach, *Textes relatifs aux Judaïsme* (*Fontes Rerum Judaicarum*), Paris, 1895, p. 142.

[4] R. Wünsch, *Antike Fluchtafeln*, Bonn, 1907, Kleine Texte, 20, p. 6ff.; Moulton-Milligan, *Vocabulary*, p. 178.

the general connection between the tradition of non-conformist Judaism and the Primitive Church.

In one further general aspect there is a close resemblance and affinity between Qumran and the Primitive Church.

Qumran Essenism was a *hierocracy*: it was a neo-Levitical community, and, in this respect, its sectarian character is derived from its ultimate priestly Hasidaean origins.

The Christian Church bears this same hieratic or sacerdotal character from its earliest beginnings; and this peculiar aspect of primitive Christianity has left its mark on most of the books of the New Testament. It was no coincidence that the cradle of the primitive community in the Book of Acts was not the Synagogue, but the Temple: though the movement of Jewish 'non-conformity' was a movement at times in conflict with the official Temple, it was itself a priestly movement. In his important study of the primitive Christian catechism, the late E. G. Selwyn wrote: 'The evidence we have been considering [the pattern of the primitive catechisms of the Church in the Epistles] points to a conception of the Church as a "neo-Levitical" or priestly community; . . . it is particularly noticeable in [I Peter] ii.1-10.'[1] (The pattern is traced by Selwyn in the Acts and in practically all the Pauline Epistles, but also in Hebrews and James.) Especially striking, as we have seen,[2] is the conception of the Church as a spiritual Temple, in which spiritual sacrifices are offered; we find an exact parallel to the New Testament passages in the Qumran texts—even the same Old Testament *testimonia* are employed.[3]

This conception of the Church as a sacerdotal community has left many traces in the language and thought of the New Testament writers; and it is of too frequent occurrence to be explained simply as a mere figure of speech. Christians are 'kings and priests' unto God (Rev. i.6), because they are the direct heirs of the ancient priestly tradition of Israel through Qumran. The Epistle to the Hebrews springs directly out of such a tradition. Even the Pharisaic Paul turns again

[1] *The First Epistle of St Peter*, p. 374.
[2] See supra, p. 42, and infra, p. 128.
[3] See infra, p. 129.

and again to the language of the Temple and the altar (cf. e.g., Rom. xv.16).

## II

### THE NORTH PALESTINIAN ORIGINS OF CHRISTIANITY

In his important monograph *Galiläa und Jerusalem*[1] the late Ernst Lohmeyer has conclusively shown that primitive Christianity had a double origin. The oldest roots of the primitive Church were in Galilee in the wide sense of 'Galilee of the Gentiles', extending beyond Galilee eastwards to include Peraea and the Decapolis (possibly reaching as far as Damascus) and to the North as far as Hermon. The development in Judaea and Jerusalem was an inevitable expansion as a result of the events which took place there.

Lohmeyer has drawn attention to the peculiar surrogate for the divine name which is used by Christ in his reply to the High Priest before the Sanhedrin:

ὄψεσθε τὸν υἱὸν τοῦ ἀνθρώπου ἐκ δεξίων καθημένον τῆς δυνάμεως καὶ ἐρχόμενον μετὰ τῶν νεφαλῶν τοῦ οὐρανοῦ (Mk. xiv.62).

The same substitute for the divine name (and the same type of 'Son of Man' Christology) is to be encountered in the famous reply of James, reported by Hegesippus (Eusebius, *Historia Ecclesiastica*, II.23.8-15): 'Why do ye ask me concerning the Son of Man? He sits in heaven at the right hand *of the great Power*, and will come in the clouds of heaven.'

As we have seen,[2] this was a northern form of speech, certainly Samaritan, and possibly no less Galilaean. There is no exact equivalent in rabbinical sources. What parallels do occur (as Lohmeyer noted) simply emphasize the rarity and unusual nature of the expression. We have to do with a North Palestinian idiom, attested especially in accounts of sectarian circles in this area. Here we have a very striking link between the 'Galilaean' Gospel tradition and North Palestinian forms of religion.

Lohmeyer was not satisfied with the traditional and accepted explanations of the oldest name for the Christian Church 'the sect of the Nazorenes' as the sect of the followers

---

of Jesus of Nazareth.[1] The debate about the name $Na\zeta\omega\rho a\hat{i}os$ has not yielded any conclusive result, and Lohmeyer avoids it.  He himself is not, however, convinced that the traditional explanation excludes an original reference to the Nazirite character of the earliest Christians.[2]  He draws attention to the evidence of Epiphanius for the attitude of the 'pre-Christian' $Na\sigma a\rho a\hat{i}oi$ to Temple sacrifice and their encratite asceticism, and to the later Nazorene rejection of the Temple cultus.  James, the Lord's brother, was a life-long Nazirite; one of the main elements in the Nazirite asceticism of James was his abstention from flesh.  As we have seen, this was one of the distinctive customs of the Jewish Nasaraeans of Epiphanius.[3]  Lohmeyer draws attention to the tradition that James wore the white linen garment of the priest and had daily access to the Temple: yet for James the Temple was a place of prayer only; any participation in the Temple cultus was avoided.  He prayed daily in the Temple, until his knees were swollen like those of a camel, for the forgiveness of the sins of his people, waiting for the deliverance of the coming Son of Man: but he did not take any part in the sacrifices and was eventually martyred on the instigation of the Sadducees.[4] It is perhaps significant that it is a Rechabite who seeks to intervene and prevent the martyrdom of James.[5]

The same Nazirite strain can be detected in the Baptist, a priest of the same character as James.

Especially instructive is the peculiar kind of Nazirite vow which St Paul undertakes in order to prove that he observed the Law (Acts xxi.18-27).  The length of the vow (seven days) does not correspond with the duration of the vow in the Mishnah (thirty days): more important is the fact that it was regarded by the early Church under James as mandatory, whereas the Nazirite vow of the Pharisaic tradition has more of the character of a work of supererogation.[6]

The association of the name $Na\zeta\omega\rho a\hat{i}os$ ($Na\zeta a\rho\eta\nu\acute{o}s$), in the Gospels and Acts, with Hebrew *Nazir*, is found more than once in the early Fathers: thus Tertullian on Mark iv.8 writes: *ipso nomine nos Judaei Nazarenos appellant per eum,*

---

[1] op. cit. p. 60ff.          [2] loc. cit.          [3] Supra, p. 66.
[4] Josephus, *Antiq.* XX.ix.1.    [5] *H.E.* II.23.17.    [6] Lohmeyer, loc. cit.

*Plate 6* A closer view of the excavated interior of the Qumran buildings, looking south towards 'Ain Feshka. The canal supplying the large cisterns or baptistries is seen in the immediate foreground. (*Sabine Weiss/Rapho, Paris*)

*Plate 7* The hoard of silver coins found in the ruins. They are for the most part Tyrian tetradrachms, the stater or shekel of Matthew xvii.24, 27, xxvi.15, the latest dated 9-8 B.C. *and* 1 B.C.-A.D. 1 (*Sabine Weiss/Rapho, Paris*)

*nam et sumus de quibus scriptum est: Nazaraei exalbati sunt super nivem (Lamentations* iv.7).[1] Similarly the anonymous *Book of Names,* edited by Lagarde,[2] explains Ναζωραῖος as καθαρός, Ναζαρέθ as καθαριότης: the Greek Ναζειραῖος is ἅγιος ἢ καθαρώτατος ἢ ἐκ κοιλίας μητρὸς ἀφωρισμένος θεῷ.

Such evidence by itself does not prove anything: all it means is that the similarity of the names Ναζωραῖος, Ναζιραῖος (Ναζηραῖος) may have suggested these associations to the patristic writers.

The case of Matthew ii.23, however, is somewhat different, for no sound exegesis can preclude an intentional allusion to the manner of the birth of Samson as analogous to that of Christ; and more particularly to Samson's vocation as a Nazir as prefiguring that of Christ (Judges xiii.5, 7, xvi.17, LXX Ναζιραῖος).[3] No doubt St Matthew also intended a reference to Isaiah xi.1: but in applying this traditional testimony text to Christ, he also has taken over the allusion to the Nazirate. This is confirmed by the Lucan parallel, i.35, which has ἅγιον, one of the LXX's translations of *Nazir.*[4]

All this would add up to the result that the oldest root of the Christian movement in 'Galilee' is to be sought in a group of dedicated Nazirites, sectarians who continued the ancient Israelite institution of the life-long Nazirate; and if there is any substance in the theory that Epiphanius's 'Nasaraeans' were a sectarian survival of this ancient order, then we may have in such a North Palestinian sect the actual historical link between the Primitive Church and Qumran Judaism.

### III

#### THE παρθένοι OF THE PRIMITIVE CHURCH

The celibacy of the Essenes is probably to be traced to a priestly origin: it may possibly be a legacy of the Hasidaean warrior's devotion of himself, or connected with the ancient life-long Nazirate.[5]

It is not surprising to find this ideal playing a significant

---

[1] Ed. Kroymann, 3, 437.

[2] *Onomastica Sacra* (1887), 175.24; 177.60; 196.90 (cf. 196.89).

[3] Cf. K. Stendahl, *The School of Matthew,* Uppsala, 1954, pp. 103, 198ff.; E. Lohmeyer, *Galiläa und Jerusalem,* p. 60, n. 1.

[4] Cf. 1 QSb iv.27, 28. See infra, p. 140.       [5] Supra, p. 76.

part among the early Jewish Christian heresies. Epiphanius
reveals that the ideal was once reverenced by the Ebionites,
on account of James, the Lord's brother, but that it latterly
changed into its opposite.[1] This violent antipathy to παρθενία
and ἐγκρατεῖα among these later Christian or Jewish groups
can only be explained as a reaction to the earlier monastic
ideal of celibacy of the classic period of Essene monasticism.
It is of particular interest to note that James is described by
Epiphanius as a παρθένος (so too, according to the anti-
Marcionite Prologue to his Gospel, was St Luke).

This is a feature of pre-Christian Judaism which was
completely alien to Pharisaic tradition, so that traces of such
an ideal in the New Testament may be set down with some
confidence to the influence of sectarian or Essene Judaism.

There are two New Testament passages of particular
interest, Rev. xiv.1-5 and I Cor. vii.

At Rev. xiv.1ff. the 144,000 followers of the Lamb are
given a position of special eminence. They belong to the
Temple choir of the heavenly Jerusalem, who are permitted
to sing, as it were, a new song before the heavenly Throne.
Their liturgy is known to them alone since no others can
learn it. They have been brought from among men to be
the first-fruits of mankind offered to God and the Lamb (2-5).
Verse 4 reveals an ascetic ideal of a distinctly Essene type:
οὗτοι εἰσιν οἳ μετὰ γυναικῶν οὐκ ἐμολύνθησαν· παρθένοι γὰρ εἰσιν.

The παρθένοι of I Cor. vii.25ff. have been variously identified and explained. The view appears to be gaining ground
that these Corinthian 'virgins' were not merely women who
did not happen to be married, but belonged to the same class
of people as are referred to at Rev. xiv.4, viz., celibate
Christians, either men or women.[2] Dr Chadwick, for instance, holds that 'the Corinthian situation being what it
was, the existence of such ascetics, both male and female, is
highly probable'.[3] It seems to the present writer that the

---

[1] Pan. 30.2.6.
[2] Cf. H. Chadwick, 'All Things to All Men', in NTS, 1, 266, n. 3. Chadwick
refers to the commentary of J. Weiss (p. 194), who is followed by Enslin (Ethics of
Paul, p. 176ff.); for alternative views cf. Jülicher, Protest. Monatshefte, 22, 1918,
110ff.
[3] loc. cit.

existence of such a class of Christian ascetics, in particular a
class of men dedicated to the celibate life, is demanded both
by the context and exegesis of I Cor. vii.25-28 and by the
early patristic evidence.

I Cor. vii.25-27 is best understood as referring primarily
to a class of *male* celibates. Paul had been asked for his
opinion about παρθένοι in the Corinthian letter of enquiry
(cf. vii.1). He does not, he replies, have any command of
the Lord, but he gives his own opinion ὡς ἠλεημένος ὑπὸ κυρίου
πιστὸς εἶναι. These last words seem to me to imply the
use of πιστός in the familiar sense of the Syriac *mehaimena*,
the rendering of the Syriac versions of εὐνοῦχος at Mt.
xix.12[1]; Paul was himself a παρθένος in this technical sense.[2]
The state of παρθενία, he declares, is a good thing, 'because
of the present tribulation', the reference being to the present
signs of the imminence of the End. 'Are you bound to a
wife? Do not seek to be loosed from your bonds. Are you
free from a woman? Do not seek one.' These words imply
that it is the position of the man, not the woman, of which St
Paul is speaking, first in general terms and then with particular reference to παρθένοι, so that his second question 'Are
you free from a woman?' includes a reference, in this context,
to the male παρθένος. To this individual St Paul declares:
'If a παρθένος[3] marries he does not sin.' Only such people
will have tribulation in their flesh, and St Paul is for sparing
them this. The time is short, and so it is better to remain
in the state we are in without seeking to change it.[4]

Chadwick notes that Theodore of Mopsuestia interprets

---

[1] This use of the word is well attested in Syriac: see Payne-Smith, *Thes. Syr.*,
col. 234. But it is not just a Christian (or a purely Syriac) usage. It is found in
Hebrew at Sir. xxx.20 where *ne'eman* is parallel to *saris* and rendered by LXX
εὐνοῦχος, Syr. *mehaimena*. See H. L. Strack, *Die Sprüche Jesus', des Sohnes Sirachs*
(*Schriften des Institutum Judaicum in Berlin*, Nr. 31, Leipzig, 1903), pp. 22, 58; cf.
also S. Schechter, *The Wisdom of Ben Sira*, Cambridge, 1899, pp. xxxvi, 54, Text
p. 11). Schechter suggests that the word should be read *'omen* (guardian). One of
the eunuchs of King Ahasuerus (Esther i.10) is called Mehuman.

[2] The masculine in this sense appears to be a Christian usage; the corresponding
Syriac term *bethul, bethula*, is regular for both male and female. Stephanus cites
Suicer (under παρθένος) for the definition: παρθένοι mares dicuntur Caelibes, qui nullam
feminarum notitiam unquam habuerunt.

[3] The best reading seems to me to be that which omits the article, with *B,G.*

[4] The words καὶ ἡ παρθένος at v.34 seem to me to be a gloss on ἡ γυνὴ ἡ ἄγαμος
(Nestlé's text) added by a pious scribe in order to exclude a possible misunderstanding
of ἡ γυνὴ ἡ ἄγαμος of a widow, about whom it would be impossible, from the strictly
ascetic viewpoint, to say that she could be ἁγία καὶ τῷ σώματι καὶ τῷ πνεύματι.

τῶν παρθένων at verse 25 of both men and women.[1]   Justin
Martyr both in his *Apology*, I.15.6ff. and in the fragment *De
Resurrectione*, 589, leaves us in no doubt that the παρθενία of
both men and women was an important feature of Christian
life in the second century.   *Ap.* I.15.6 follows on an exposition of Mt. xix.12: 'And there are many of both sexes in
their sixties and seventies, from their childhood disciples of
Christ, remain uncorrupted (ἄφθοροι).' The implication that
even lawful wedlock leads to corruption because of the
ἐπιθυμία involved in it is even more explicitly stated in the
second passage:

’Αλλὰ καὶ μὴ στεῖραι μὲν ἐξ ἀρχᾶς, παρθενεύουσαι δέ, κατήργησαν
καὶ τὴν συνουσίαν· ἕτεραι δὲ καὶ ἀπὸ χρόνου. καὶ τοὺς ἄρρενας δὲ τοὺς
μὲν ἀπ’ ἀρχῆς παρθενεύοντας ὁρῶμεν, τοὺς δὲ ἀπὸ χρόνου, ὥστε δι’
αὐτῶν καταλύεσθαι τὸν δι’ ἐπιθυμίας ἄνομον γάμον. [Ed. Otto, 589D][2]

The *Apology of Athenagoras* (fl. second century A.D.)
takes the same position: 'Nay, you would find many among
us, both men and women, growing old unmarried, in the
hope of living in closer communion with God.   But if the
remaining in virginity and in the state of an eunuch brings
nearer to God, while the indulgence of carnal thought and
desire leads away from him, in those cases in which we shun
the thoughts, much more do we reject the deeds.'[3]   In the
*Acts of Thekla*, § 6, St Paul is expounded: 'Blessed are the
souls and bodies of virgins, for they shall be pleasing to God
and shall not lose the reward of their chastity: for the working
of the Father's words shall be found in them, and they shall
inherit life in the day of the Son of God, and rest eternal
shall be theirs.'

Closely connected with this problem is the famous crux
of I Cor. vii.35-38.   The theory of Achelis that it referred to
unmarried female companions of the early Christians, in
particular early Christian leaders, the *virgines subintroductae*,
has been under constant attack since it was first published.[4]

---

[1] Migne, *P.G.* LXVI, col. 885.
[2] Cf. Conybeare, *About the Contemplative Life*, p. 241.
[3] Trans. Donaldson, Ante-Nicene Christian Library, *Justin Martyr and Athenagoras*, vol. II, p. 417.
[4] *Virgines subintroductae*, Leipzig, 1902; cf. also Hastings's *Encyclopaedia of
Religion and Ethics*, I, 1910, under *Agapetae*. Cf. Chadwick, op. cit. p. 267.

Chadwick (and before him Kümmel[1]) argued that the situation presupposed is rather that of a betrothed couple who are on the point of getting married, but decide to abstain because they have come under the influence of the ascetic teaching current at Corinth.[2] Even if this is the situation envisaged, Paul's statement that a man who keeps his παρθένος, yet remains unmarried, is in a position superior to one who marries, gives his sanction to a situation which is not so very different from that of the *virgines subintroductae*.[3] It seems much more likely that in the first flush of ascetic enthusiasm, when the End was imminently expected, such practices were found in the early Christian Church. It is in the Roman and North African Church we find the clearest evidence for this type of 'spiritual marriage',[4] just as it is also here that the celibate ideal flourished most vigorously.

Such practices recall, not only the Qumran celibates, but also, as Achelis noted, the Therapeutae: 'The Therapeutae in Egypt, who are there described, and who tabued marriage and sexual enjoyment, lived in union with female companions, just as the Christian monks did at a later date. It is the same combination of sexual asceticism and brotherly communion as in Syneisaktism, only that the personal intimacy between the individual pairs is wanting; the brotherly love is just the specifically Christian factor in the spiritual marriage.'[5]

One other passage in the New Testament, I Tim. iv.3 contains a warning against the teachings δαιμονίων, ἐν ὑποκρίσει ψευδολόγων, who are for stopping marriage and abstaining from meats (κωλυόντων γαμεῖν, ἀπέχεσθαι βρωμάτων). These were no doubt the forerunners of the Marcionite *Enkratites*. They were almost certainly Judaizing Christians. But we need not assume that these ascetic demands were innovations in the Church of the second century: they were

---

[1] 'Verlobung und Heirat bei Paulus', in *N.T. Studien für R. Bultmann*, pp. 275-95.

[2] Chadwick, op. cit. p. 267.

[3] Chadwick recognizes the logic of this argument, for he goes on to add (p. 268, n. 1): 'If the man followed Paul's stated ideal rather than his practical counsel, the ultimate result would have been a situation very like that of the *virgines subintroductae*.' 'Was the effect of Paul's opportunism', he asks, 'accidentally to create this practice?'

[4] Cf. Hermes, Vis. i.1.1; Sim. ix.11.3, 7, x.3. Cf. Tertullian, *De Exhort. Castit.*, 12; *De Monog.*, 16; Eusebius, *H.E.* vii.30.12ff.; Cyprian, *Epist.* 4.13.14.

[5] op. cit. p. 179.

more of the nature of surviving relics or throw-backs to the early sectarian origins and background of the Church. Indeed, it may be a wrong perspective altogether to view these heresies as innovations threatening to disturb the even tenor of the Church's way. The 'innovations' may have been the removal of the extravagancies and enthusiasms of the early period.

What emerges with ever-increasing clarity from the evidence is the strength of the link between the primitive Church in the New Testament period and its sectarian Jewish background: asceticism of a sexual type may have found encouragement from Hellenism, but it seems more likely to be an inheritance from Jewish sectarianism.

Undoubtedly, of course, the Christian ideal of voluntary celibacy—and the later institution of Christian monasticism —have been inspired by the dominical teaching of Mt. xix.12.[1] But the Jewish background of this ideal is to be found in sectarian, not Pharisaic, Judaism.

Three general conclusions seem to follow from this discussion: 1. The link between the primitive Church and the sectarian type of Judaism such as we find at Qumran, was through the 'Hebrews' or 'Hebraists' of Acts, Hebrew Christians, including 'Galilaeans' (in the wide sense used by Lohmeyer). Like Qumran, the Primitive Church was a neo-Levitical community. 2. The origins of Christianity are to be sought in Northern Palestine, and an even more specific connection with Qumran Judaism may have been through 'the sect of the Nasarenes', possibly a sectarian group descended from the Israelite institution of the life-long Nazirate. 3. The ascetic element in primitive Christianity, in particular its ideal of celibacy, is a strong link with sectarian Judaism, for this ideal is nowhere to be found among the Pharisees (or later rabbis).

[1] Cf. supra, p. 86.

# Part II: RELIGIOUS AND THEOLOGICAL

# CHAPTER V

# Qumran Baptismal Rites and Sacred Meal

## COVENANT, INITIATION, AND BAPTISMAL RITES

There seems little doubt that Qumran sectarianism, both in its beginnings and in its later forms in the 'Essenism' of New Testament times, was a genuine movement for internal reform within Judaism, on a strict principle of *apartheid*, or withdrawal from the world, but also on the basis of repentance and a vow to return to a new obedience to the Law of Moses.

The original Zadokites entered into a 'New Covenant' in 'Damascus' (which may be no more than a symbolic term for Trans-Jordan).

The idea of a Covenant-relationship between God and man is an inalienably Hebraic one: on the one hand is the divine initiative, on the other the response of Israel. The prophetic conception of a new Covenant, superseding the Old Covenant of Sinai, is classically presented at Jeremiah xxxi.31ff. It has its roots in Hosea and appears in variant forms in Ezekiel and in Second Isaiah. Fundamentally it represented a prophetic protest against the perils of an external legalism on which the old national covenants had foundered, calling for an inward and spiritual obedience in response to the divine initiative in mercy and forgiveness. Thus was to be created a new Israel out of the Remnant of the old Israel.

The name itself 'New Covenant' (*berith hadhasha*), occurs at least twice in the Qumran literature,[1] and points unmistakably in the direction of this prophetic ideal. Not much can be inferred from the description 'Covenant of God',[2] which the Qumran 'New Covenant' shares with Israel's

[1] *CD* viii.15, ix.8.       [2] *CD* xvi.7, 12: cf. iv.9, viii.21.

earlier Covenants; it does, however, place the Essene ideal in the same category as the great covenants of the past. More importance is to be attached to the description of it as '[the] Covenant of [divine] Mercy' (*berith hesedh*),[1] and 'the Covenant of Repentance' (*berith teshubha*),[2] for these names point unequivocally to the foundation of the whole Hasidaean-Essene movement in the prophetic ideal of Jeremiah-Ezekiel. It was a movement of repentance in response to the divine initiative in mercy; and 'repentance' appears to have been further construed as the condition of admission to the sect.

Again and again the writers dwell on the wonder of the divine forgiveness in God's 'Covenant of mercy', which brings the whole conception into line with the basis of Jeremiah's New Covenant, 'I will forgive their iniquity' (xxxi.34).

Entry into the New Covenant took place at a solemn assembly or convocation of the sect, and the *Manual of Discipline* has preserved two accounts of such a ceremony of 'entering into the New Covenant'. It is stated that this ceremony is to be repeated annually (ii.19), and it has been conjectured that the occasion was one not only of commemoration of the original 'New Covenant', but also a ceremony of admission of new members. It no doubt took place at one of the great Festivals, and Pentecost, with its associations with the giving of the Law, suggests itself at once.[3] Perhaps the main function of the Qumran 'monastery' was to provide a centre for the convocation of the sect, no doubt also at other feasts, but primarily at the Pentecost festival, when new members were admitted.

The central rite of the sect, the act of 'entering into the Covenant' (either for the first time or for a renewal of earlier vows) is described at 1 QS i, ii, and v, and alluded to elsewhere.

Before we study these passages, however, another aspect of the ritual and discipline of these sects calls for mention, their regulations about probation before admission.

According to Josephus[4]:

---

[1] 1 QS i.8.
[2] *CD* ix.15.
[3] Cf. Brownlee, *BASOR, Supp. Stud.* 10-12, 1951, 53.
[4] *B.J.* II.viii.7.

. . . Admission is not immediate for those who become enthusiastic for the sect. They lay down for him the same way of life for a year while he remains outside [the sect], providing him with a small axe and the loin-cloth mentioned above and white garment. When after this period he gives proof of self-control, he is brought into closer touch with their manner of life and shares in the purer waters for [ritual] cleansing, but is not yet allowed to join their common life. After this proof of fortitude, his character is tested for two further years, and when he is shown to be worthy, he is then enrolled in their company. But before he touches the common food he swears before them fearful oaths, first to hold God in reverence, then to maintain justice among men and neither to harm anyone deliberately nor under instructions, but always to hate the unjust and to strive on the side of the just; always to keep faith with all, especially with those in power, for office does not come to anyone apart from God; and should he himself bear rule that he will never abuse his authority, or, either in dress or by any superior decoration outshine those subordinate to him; always to love the truth and to expose liars; to keep his hands from theft and his soul from filthy lucre [lit. unholy gain]; not to conceal anything from his fellow-sectarians, nor to disclose anything of theirs to others, even if one should torture him to death. Besides these things, he swears to communicate their doctrine to no one otherwise than he himself has received it; to abstain from robbery, and, likewise carefully to preserve the books of their sect and the names of the angels. It is by such oaths they secure to themselves those who are being admitted.

The arrangements for admission to the Qumran sect are summarized by Millar Burrows from 1 QS vi.14-23 as follows[1]:

Candidates for admission are investigated by him [that is, the *mebaqqer* or Censor[2]]. If their wisdom and deeds are satisfactory, they are brought into the covenant and appear before the assembly. Lots are cast, and the candidate approaches or withdraws according to the result. If he is accepted, he still may not touch the 'purity' (that is, either the holy things or perhaps the rites of purification) until after a year's probation. Then he is investigated again, and the lot is cast a second time. If it is favorable, he enters the order, bringing his wealth and his work; but he still may not participate

---

[1] 'The Discipline Manual of the Judaean Covenanters', in *Oudtestamentische Studiën*, Vol. 8, p. 163.
[2] See infra, p. 116f.

in the common meal for another year, when the lot must be cast a third time.

The main difference appears to be that, according to Josephus, the probationary period is three years, in the *Manual* two; the difference, however, may be accounted for if we assume (as W. H. Brownlee suggested) that one year of probation is presupposed before the examination by the *mebaqqer*; Josephus's first year of testing takes place outside the sect.

Two different rites in Josephus are associated with admission, at these two stages; with the first stage, the 'rites of purification' (the ritual bath), and with the second, participation in a sacred meal.

The description of the ceremonies and prayers of admission and renewal of the covenant in 1 QS reveal a curious gap in the proceedings. We hear about the covenanters who are about to enter the New Covenant; mention is made of them entering the Covenant in the presence of God; we read about rites, blessings, and imprecations after they have entered, but once only do we learn of baptizing rites in the ceremony of entering into the New Covenant: 1 QS v.13 denies entrance *into the water* to the unrepentant, implying, not only that repentance alone qualifies for ritual cleansing, but the presence of such rites of purification (as Josephus reports) in the ceremony of admission. The act or ceremony was no doubt so well known that it was unnecessary even to mention it.

Both accounts begin with a list of obligations to be laid upon the members of the sect (the *adstipulationes* to which he will subscribe and bind himself by a solemn oath (cf. p. 120): the first account continues (i.16ff., in Brownlee's translation):

All who enter into the order of the Community shall enter into the covenant in God's presence, to do according to all that He commanded, and not to turn aside from following after Him, out of any terror or fright or ordeal. . . . And as they are entering into the covenant, the priests and Levites shall bless the God of deliverances and all His deeds of faithfulness. Then all who are entering into the covenant shall say after them 'Amen, Amen'.

After they have entered 'into the Covenant', there follows a public confession of sin by the assembled covenanting people:

Then all who enter into the Covenant shall confess after them [the Levites] saying: 'We have perverted ourselves, we have transgressed, we have sinned, we have done wickedly, both we and our fathers before us, because we have walked contrary to true ordinances. And God is righteous who has executed His justice upon us and upon our fathers; but the abundance of His grace He has bestowed upon us from everlasting to everlasting. [i.24ff.].

This is followed by a blessing by the priest in a new form of the Aaronic blessing:

> May He bless thee with every good,
> And keep thee from every evil,
> And illumine thy heart with life-giving wisdom,
> And favour thee with eternal knowledge,
> And lift up His face of mercy towards thee
>     for thy eternal peace.

The ceremony concludes with a double curse by the Levites, first on the 'men of Belial' (no doubt foreign oppressors and renegade Jews), then on backsliders from the 'New Covenant'. The section ends:

Thus shall they do year by year all the days of the dominion of Belial. The priests shall enter the covenant first in the order pertaining to their spirits, one after another; and after them the Levites shall enter; then thirdly, all the people shall enter in order one after another, by thousands and hundreds and fifties and tens ... each in the status of his office [ii.19ff.[1]].

Though it is difficult to form a clear picture of what actually took place, it is evident that the first account describes a general convention, the second refers to the admission of the neophyte as described by Josephus. The probability is, however, that the neophytes were admitted to the 'purer waters of baptism' in the sight of the assembled people. The size and formation of the baptistries at Qumran, exposed to full view in an area which forms a natural amphitheatre, the divided partitions on entering, point to their use in some

[1] Cf. M. Burrows, op. cit. p. 175.

public ceremony. It seems probable too that the renewal of covenant vows was also symbolized by the assembled people entering the baths in order of their rank and status.[1]

It does not seem unlikely that the 'entering' or 'renewing' of the Covenant was by descending into and ascending from the baptismal waters in the large Qumran baptisteries.

We would thus have a ritual corresponding to that of Exodus xx, the sprinkling and manipulation of dedicated blood. In a sect where Mosaic ideas are so prominent, the symbolism of the Covenant people crossing over the divided Red Sea at once comes to mind—or the symbolism in Genesis xv in the Covenant with Abraham (a light symbolizing the *numen praesens* of Yahweh passing between the pieces).

The occasion appears, therefore, to have been both a renewal of covenant vows by the whole sect and an admission of neophytes. The two-stage probation, according to Josephus, is marked by two rites or ceremonies; after the first year the neophyte is permitted to draw near to the 'purer waters of lustration', after the second two years to the 'sacred meal'. 1 QS vi.16 might seem to refer to the admission to the 'purer waters of lustration' ('he shall not touch the pure (*thrt*) things of the Many . . . until the completion of a full year . . . in the midst of the community'), but it seems more likely to refer to participation in the sacred meal.[2] The sequence of baptizing rites and sacred meal is clearly implied by 1 QS v.13: 'These (the unrepentant) shall not enter the water to draw near to the pure things of the holy men.' Again, 1 QS corresponds with the Josephan account. The statement in Josephus about drawing near to the '*purer* waters of lustration' after the completion of one year does not rule out the practice of such rites by the neophyte before acceptance, but appears to imply a special form of lustration marking the end of the first probationary year. As such lustrations were by total immersion we are here confronted with a ritual admitting a neophyte, on repentance,

---

[1] The numbers are, of course, fictitious and are obviously based on the accounts of the mustering of the Israelites at the time of the entry into the Promised Land.

[2] This seems the only possible sense of *thrt*, and is in agreement with rabbinical usage. (The expression may, of course, be a general one ('pure things'), and include the meal with other items. (Cf. Wernberg-Møller, op. cit. p. 96.))

by a bath by total immersion.[1]   All these ceremonies, including perhaps the renewal of the Covenant, may have taken
place in a general convention of the sect at Qumran.

We have thus a significant point of contact with the New
Testament in its general presentation of the baptism of John
as a baptism of repentance for the remission of sins.

The discovery that the Qumran sect practised such baptismal rites is nothing new; so too did most Jewish sects in
the New Testament period.  What is new is that these rites
were practised in relation to a movement of repentance, of
entry into a new Covenant (and a new Covenanted Israel,
the sect itself) in preparation for an impending divine judgment.[2]  The entry into the Covenant and the sect by a public
confession of sins recalls the scene in the Gospels where 'the
whole of Jerusalem' crowded to the banks of Jordan at the
call of the Baptist, 'confessing their sins'.  Like Johannite
'baptism for repentance unto the remission of sins', the
entire setting of Qumran repentance and enrolment into the
new Israel is eschatological.

This forms an impressive preparation for the New Testament, and it seems idle to deny that some connection exists
between the two movements; the same holds good of other
common features of the life of these two Jewish 'sectarian'
communities, Qumran and the Primitive Church.

Nevertheless, there are important differences, and they
are as significant as resemblances.  The new Covenant was
a renewal of the Old Covenant: it had probably little more in
common than its name with the New Covenant of Christianity; as we can see from the *Damascus Document*, the life of the
covenanter was subjected to all the restrictions of the Law,
even more rigidly interpreted than in Pharisaism; he was
enrolled into an exclusive sect; to become a covenanter a
Gentile had to become a Jew: Christianity (and the Baptist)
threw wide open the doors of repentance and the Kingdom of
God to all and sundry, Gentile and Jew, and in particular to
the despised masses, the *'am ha' areṣ*, contact with any of
whom would lead the Qumran covenanter, like the Samaritan,

---

[1] Cf. Rabin, *The Zadokite Documents*, XII (p. 50).
[2] See further infra, pp. 122, 133, 135.

to seek the nearest baptistry. Moreover, in view of the prevalence of the rite of baptism throughout Jewish non-conformity, it seems unlikely that the idea of preparation for an impending judgment was confined to one sect; it more probably represents a common belief of the apocalyptic Judaism of the period.

The main difference between the two movements lies quite simply in the persons of John and Jesus, both towering figures, transforming the practices of a sect into a universal religion by their proclamation: 'Repent, for the Kingdom of God is at hand', and by their prophetic and Messianic ministries.

The baptismal doctrine and rites of the scrolls offer too a striking contrast to Christian and even Johannite baptism in their New Testament forms. Though the Qumran Essenes practised a form of baptism by total immersion, it was a purely ritual act. At the most these rites may have been popularly construed as removing sins.[1] Such rites were multiplied for different purposes, though it does appear probable that they did form part of the ceremonies of initiation to the sect and the renewal of the covenant.

Christian baptism, on the other hand, was a single and unrepeatable act, and, in the New Testament, has no purificatory significance. The same is true of Johannite baptism as the New Testament represents it. The most that it appears possible to say of the Qumran rite is that it prepared the way, at some considerable remove, for the full Christian doctrine of Baptism. It may be a foreshadowing, but it is, in itself, a mere shadow of the full Christian rite.

The matter might be left there were it not for certain other facts. Josephus represents the baptism of John as an Essene lustration; it is for the purification of the body, the soul having already been purified by the practice of righteousness.[2] In this respect, it seems more probable, however, that Josephus has assimilated his account of John's baptism to Essene practice rather than that his account is to be preferred to the New Testament version.

[1] The claim that it was a baptism for sins is a capital error in K. G. Kuhn's account of these ceremonies; *The Scrolls and the New Testament*, p. 77.

[2] *Antiq.* XVIII.v.2.  Cf. 1 QS iii.6-12.

But the problem is not so simply disposed of, for there is other evidence for a form of baptism in Christian sources similar to the Qumran-Essene type.

A growing number of scholars are becoming impressed by the close resemblance—even if it is only outward and superficial and without any inner connection—between the religious rites and organization of the Qumran community and those of the early Church in Apostolic and sub-Apostolic times. It has now been proved beyond question that a close historical connection existed between this Essene sect and the later forms of heretical Palestinian Christianity among the Nazorenes, Ebionites, and the Jewish-Christian sect of the Pseudo-Clementine literature.[1] These resemblances have even been taken for identity.[2] But similar inner connections and not just chance external similarities have been claimed for the relationship of this Essene group and the early Apostolic and sub-Apostolic Church, in the main stream of tradition and especially in the emergence of Christian monasticism.[3]

The chief exponents of these views are Professor Oscar Cullmann and M. Jean Daniélou. Cullmann speaks of 'the absolutely astonishing agreement' between Qumran rites of initiation and the corresponding ceremonies among the heretical Palestinian sects, but mentions the possibility of a continuous tradition of such rites from the primitive Church only to reject it in favour of the view that these rites were introduced into Christian Palestinian heresies after A.D. 70, when the survivors of Essenism were swallowed up in such groups. M. Daniélou propounds a bolder hypothesis; he finds the same general Qumran pattern of initiation in the ordinals of the ancient Church, such as the second-century *Tradition of Hippolytus*, and concludes that this is a heritage from Essenism.

The main pattern of initiation which he traces is as follows. In our sect the neophyte is first examined by the

---

[1] See especially, Oscar Cullmann, 'Die neuentdeckten Qumrantexte und das Judenchristentum der Pseudoklementinen', in *Bultmann Festschrift*, p. 35ff.

[2] By J. L. Teicher, in *JJS*, 2 and 3, 1951, 1952.

[3] J. Daniélou, 'La communauté de Qumran et l'organisation de l'Eglise ancienne', in *RHPR*, 35e Année, 1955—No. 1, p. 104ff.

Censor (or Examiner), and if he is adjudged a fit person for instruction, he is admitted as a catechumen; part of this instruction (Daniélou suggests) was in the sect's doctrine of the two spirits, the spirit of light and the spirit of darkness, preserved in the *Manual of Discipline*.[1] Similarly the Christian catechumen is admitted to instruction which includes teaching on the two ways, the way of life and the way of death. In both Qumran and Church orders, the candidate is then presented to the congregation, and, if approved, enters on a secondary probationary period. In Essenism this is preceded by baptismal rites; and it is only after completion of the second grade and final approval by the congregation that the candidate is admitted to the sacred meal. In the Church, baptism and the eucharist follow the second probationary period. In both cases candidates are given a white robe, though again at different stages in the initiation (which also vary in their duration).

The main difference, according to Daniélou, between the two ceremonies lies in their central rite; this is a baptismal lustration in Essenism and could be repeated, whereas in the Church it is a single, unrepeatable act.

These are certainly impressive similarities, in particular the presentation of the candidate for election by the Examiner to the congregation, the two-stage probation in each case and the sequence, presentation, baptism, sacred meal. There may be a connection between the doctrine of the two spirits and the doctrine of the two ways, but we cannot be certain that the latter did form part of Christian baptismal instruction. At what period the white garment came into Christian baptismal ceremonies, it is difficult to say; it is not mentioned in the old Roman ordinal to which Daniélou appeals; Hippolytus mentions a 'white stone', which may be something concrete, but what it is no one seems to know.

Such evidence of resemblance and identity of practice cannot be set aside as coincidental. Even taken together, however, it may be felt to fall just short of a completely convincing case for derivation of the Christian rites from this side of Judaism. When there is then added the essential

[1] See further, infra p. 131ff.

difference which Daniélou claims for Christian baptism in the early Graeco-Roman Church, its single and unrepeatable character, the case for a close connection with or indebtedness to Essenism is weakened.

It is just in his reporting of the essential character of Christian baptism, however, that M. Daniélou has not given the full evidence, for example in the Hippolytean *Tradition. In fact, some forms of purificatory lustrations, as in Essenism, are found in the early Graeco-Roman Christian communities.* It is true, the rite of baptism as initiation into the Church remains the central act, and takes place, according to Hippolytus, on the Sunday: *but it is to be preceded on the previous Thursday by a ritual bath; and there are traces in the later part of the ordinal of surviving purificatory rites.*

As this evidence is of peculiar interest and importance, I give one passage from B. S. Easton's translation (p. 44):

Then those who are set apart for baptism shall be instructed to bathe and free themselves from impurity and wash themselves on Thursday. If a woman is menstruous she shall be set aside and baptized on some other day.

On other occasions in the ordinal where a ritual bath would have been prescribed in Judaism, the Church Father goes out of his way to point out that there is no need for such a measure. Thus: 'He who has used the marriage bed is not defiled; for they who are baptized have no need to wash again.'[1] Still he feels that something must be done and recommends: 'By signing thyself with thy moist breath, and so spreading spittle on the body with thy hand, thou art sanctified to thy feet; for the gift of the spirit and the sprinkling of water, when it is brought from a believing heart as it were from a fountain, sanctifies him who believes.'

What are we to make of this evidence as a whole, and in what way does it affect our answer to the main problem of Qumran and Christian origins? Before attempting some kind of a solution, I propose to turn to the second main rite of Qumran Judaism, the sacred meal.

[1] For such practices in Judaism, cf. Brandt, *Die jüdischen Baptismen*, p. 20.

## II

### THE QUMRAN CULT-MEAL

There are two passages in the Qumran texts where a sacred meal is fully described, 1 QS vi.2-8, and 1 QSa ii.11-22 (*Order of the Congregation, Discoveries in the Judaean Desert*, I, p. 110ff.).

(i)  1 QS vi.2-8:

They shall eat together, and worship [lit. bless] together, and take counsel together.  In every place where there are ten men of the Council of the Community, there shall not fail from among them a priest.  Each, according to his appointed rank, shall sit before him and in that order they shall be asked for their counsel with regard to every matter.  Whenever the Table is set out for eating or the wine for drinking, the Priest shall first stretch out his hand to bless the choice portion of the bread; or the wine for drinking, the Priest shall stretch out his hand first, to bless the choice portion of the bread and the wine.  Wherever the ten are, there shall not cease to be a man who expounds the Law, day and night continually, at length, one to the other.  Let the Many [the congregation] keep awake together a third of all the nights of the year to read in the Book, and to seek the right, and worship [bless] together. . . .

(ii)  1 QSa ii.11-22:

The following is the Session of the 'men of the Name', who are summoned in assembly to the Council of the Community in the event of God begetting the Messiah to be with them.  The High Priest of all the Congregation of Israel shall enter, and all the Fathers, the sons of Aaron, the Priests, who are called in assembly, the 'men of the Name'.  And they shall be seated before him [i.e. the High Priest], each man, according to his position [lit. honour], *and after [them] shall sit the Messiah of Israel [meshiah Israel]*; and there shall be seated before him the heads of the 'thousands' of Israel, each according to his position, according to his station in their camps and according to their campaigns.  And all the heads of the fathers of the congregation with the sages of the holy congregation shall be seated before them, each according to his position.  And if they are gathered together to the Table of the

Community or to drink the wine and there is an arranging of the
Table of the Community and a service of the wine, no one shall
stretch out his hand to the choice part of the bread or the wine
before the [High] Priest, for he it is that blesses the choice portion
of the bread and the wine; and he shall stretch out his hand to the
bread first, and thereafter the Messiah of Israel shall stretch out
his hand to the bread, and afterwards they shall bless all the
congregation of the Community, each man according to his
position; (and according to this regulation they shall do for every
arranging of the Table, when ten men are gathered together).

In both these accounts, the meal is described as part only
—clearly an integral part—of the communal activities of the
sect, its worship, deliberations in common, study of sacred
Scripture, and vigils.  The second description is primarily
concerned with the question of the order of precedence in
this hierocratic community at a full session or convocation
in the event of the 'divine begetting' of the Messiah, and his
presence in Israel.  The meal is part of a General Assembly
or Convocation and lays down the correct order of precedence,
the High Priest taking precedence of the 'Messiah of Israel'.
Since the second passage is obviously an account of an
'ideal' Messianic Session and an 'ideal' Messianic Meal it
is best studied separately, after the account of the regular
sacred meal.  The statement at the end of the second account,
'according to this regulation they shall do for every arranging
of the Table, if ten men are gathered together', may be an
indication that every sacramental meal of this kind had a
messianic significance (or the words may simply be the
remark of a glossator, who has noted the similarity of this
special meal with the ordinary celebration).
These passages have been the subject of study by Professor
K. G. Kuhn of Heidelberg.[1]  Dr  Kuhn starts from the
assumption of the identity of the Qumran sect with the ancient
Essenes, and his examination of the Qumran texts consists
mainly of a comparison with the account of the sacred meal
of the Essenes in Josephus.  Some interesting points of
similarity emerge: both are sacred meals, preceded by a

[1] K. G. Kuhn, 'The Lord's Supper and the Communal Meal at Qumran', in *The Scrolls and the New Testament*, p. 65ff.

priestly blessing. But there are also important differences; the Essenes of Josephus, for instance, are supplied with a cooked dish, and there is no mention of wine being served.

It seems best to approach the problem of these sectarian meals by examining first, in the light of their own first-hand evidence, the Qumran texts themselves; comparisons may help us later to understand the essential features and character of these sectarian cult-meals.

In the first place, this 'regular meal' is no ordinary meal of the community—one of the first errors into which a hasty comparison with Josephus leads us—but a meal confined to those full members of the sect who belonged to the Council of the Community. The opening words (1 QS vi.2) refer to all members of the sect for which communal worship and deliberation are prescribed. But the regulations for the sacred meal described in 1 QS apply to the members of the Council of the Community only: the ordinary members of the sect (the Many) keep vigil on certain prescribed nights of the year, but there is a clear distinction made between the members of the Council who participate in the meal, presided over by a Priest, and rabbim, the Many.[1] So too in the ideal 'messianic' meal, in addition to the priestly and military caste, the community is represented by 'the heads of the fathers of the congregation, with the sages (hakhamim) of the holy congregation'.

We do not, therefore, have any 'ordinary meal' described in 1 QS, but a special cult-meal in which only sectarians of the highest rank, the Council, are permitted to participate; these were, no doubt, the 'full members' of the sect.

It is a priestly celebration and consists solely of bread and wine or bread or wine (1 QS vi.4); a priest must preside and give his blessing, and to this presiding priest belong the choice portions of the bread and wine. There is no doubt that this regulation reflects the privileged position of the priesthood in the sect, corresponding to that of the Temple priesthood. It is to remain a hieratic institution even in messianic times; the Messiah of Israel is given precedence of everyone except the High Priest. Whether bread and

[1] Cf. infra, p. 177, n. 2.

wine were always served together, or whether such a sacred meal could consist of bread without wine is not clear from the text itself; and in view of this ambiguity we must, at least, allow for the possibility of a meal consisting of bread only.

The idealized account is of great importance for the sect's messianic beliefs and will be discussed in this connection later.[1] It clearly envisages a time when the Messiah of Israel will be divinely sent to the Community, and goes out of its way to lay down regulations which will preserve intact the priestly hierarchy and constitution of the sect—the High Priest (described in the old terminology[2]) takes precedence over the Messiah of Israel.

Is there any indication in these two accounts, taken together, of any particular religious significance attaching to this sacred meal? The second account resembles the Messianic Banquet of the Apocalypses (I Enoch xxiv, xxv, lxii.14; cf. Mt. viii.11, 12, Lk. xiv.15), and, in view of this, an eschatological significance has been ascribed to the sacred meal; it is interpreted as an anticipation of the Messianic Banquet, a meal eaten in expectation of this consummation. This may be a correct inference, but is obviously, so far, no more than an inference. If it is correct, however, then it is clearly important for an understanding of the origins of the Eucharist, which had from the beginning this forward-looking, eschatological meaning. The prescribed 'vigils' of the whole community (like the Easter vigil in the early Church) would also assume a 'messianic' character; the Qumran sectarians were awaiting the coming of the Messiah of Israel.

A parallel to this Qumran cult-meal has been found in the late (allegedly) Jewish writing 'Joseph and Aseneth',[3] a product of Alexandrian syncretism of the fourth or fifth century A.D.[4] The work is not only late, however, but obviously, in its only available form, a christianized document,

---

[1] See infra, p. 145ff.

[2] See my note on 'The Dating of the New Hebrew Scrolls on Internal Evidence', in *JJS*, 1, No. 4.

[3] By G. D. Kilpatrick, 'Living Issues in Biblical Scholarship, The Last Supper', *ET*, 64, No. 1, Oct. 1952. Cf. also K. G. Kuhn, op. cit.

[4] Edited by P. Battifol in *Studia Patristica*, i-ii (1889-90); an English translation by E. W. Brooks is published by S.P.C.K., *The Book of Joseph and Aseneth*.

and cannot be admitted as evidence.[1]   A close parallel might
be held to be the description in the *Testaments of the Twelve
Patriarchs*, Levi viii.2-5, of the installation of Levi as High
Priest.[2]   But here again Christian influences have been at
work.[3]   The unction and ablutions are parts of the ritual
investiture of High Priests in the Old Testament (cf. Exodus
xxviii.41 (37), xxix.7, Sir. xlv.15; Exodus xxix.4), but we
are probably to detect in the whole passage the influence of
the Christian baptismal ceremony.[4]

The only other description we possess of a sectarian meal
of the period is that of the Therapeutae, and, in this case,
there is no doubt that it is a Jewish sacred meal.

The Therapeutae, as we have seen,[5] are contrasted by
Philo with his Palestinian Essenes: the latter represent a
practical, the former a contemplative type.   The following
brief summary of the main points in Philo's account is taken
from F. H. Colson's introduction[6]:

Philo declares that the best of them [in Egypt?] resort from
every quarter to a particular spot near the Mareotic Lake.

Then follows a description of their manner of life concluding
with their 'Symposium':

First the date and occasion [Pentecost]; then the preliminaries
and prayers, the seating in order of seniority in the community,
with the sexes separate; then the nature of the couches used and
the qualifications of the attendants who are not slaves but young
freemen; the simplicity of the meal provided.   After they have
taken their places on the couches there follows a discourse by the
President on some scriptural point bringing out the spiritual lessons
that the literal text provides, which is received with all attention

---

[1] Cf. K. Kohler in *The Jewish Encyclopaedia*, ii, 1902, pp. 172-6, 'Aseneth, Life
and Confessions or Prayer of.'

[2] 'And I saw seven men in white raiment saying unto me: Arise, put on the robe
of the priesthood, and the crown of righteousness, and the breastplate of understanding, and the garment of truth, and the plate of faith, and the turban of the head,
and the ephod of prophecy.   And they severally carried [these things] and put [them]
on me, and said unto me: From henceforth become a priest of the Lord, thou and thy
seed for ever.   And the first anointed me with holy oil, and gave me the staff of
judgment.   The second washed me with pure water, and fed me with bread and wine
[even] the most holy things, and clad me with a holy and glorious robe.'

[3] Cf. M. de Jonge, *The Testaments of the Twelve Patriarchs*, p. 43ff.

[4] Cf. T. W. Manson, *JTS*, 98, 1947, 59-61.

[5] Cf. supra, p. 45ff.

[6] Loeb Classical Library, *Philo*, Vol. ix, p. 109ff.

followed by applause at the end. The discourse is followed by hymns, the first sung by the President, the others by the congregation each in turn, while all join in the refrain at the end. Then at last the meal itself is served. After this the vigil begins, the men and women each form a choir, the two choirs sing and dance in turn and then join together, thus resembling the songs of Moses and Miriam after the destruction of Pharaoh in the Red Sea, which is once more told in some detail. This is continued till dawn when they stand up and face the east and at sunrise after prayer return each to their prayer room. The concluding section sums up the virtues and blessedness of the Therapeutae.

Philo's statement that the Therapeutic mystics 'resort from every quarter' to Lake Mareotis may mean no more than that the settlement attracted devotees from all over the Graeco-Roman world. It may also, however, be interpreted to mean that (like Qumran) Lake Mareotis was *un centre de réunion*, especially on the occasion of their main festival, which was that of Pentecost, celebrating the giving of the Law (and possibly the deliverance from Egypt). There was, of course, no doubt also a permanent group resident at each centre.

The seating of the 'suppliants' (οἱ ἱκέται) in order of seniority at their sacred meal agrees with the account in 1 QSa. The meal, however, is one of leavened bread and water only; there is no flesh, 'The table . . . is kept pure from the flesh of animals' (ix.73), the meal consisting of loaves of bread, with salt as a seasoning, sometimes flavoured with hyssop. 'Abstinence from wine is enjoined . . . as for the priest when sacrificing, so to these for their life-time' (ix.74). ' . . . The young men bring in the tables on which is set the truly purified meal of leavened bread, seasoned with salt mixed with hyssop, out of reverence for the holy table enshrined in the sacred vestibule of the Temple on which lie loaves and salt without condiments, the loaves unleavened and the salt unmixed. For it was meet that the simplest and purest food should be assigned to the highest caste, namely the priests. . . .' (ix.82).

The asceticism of the Therapeutic mystics is similar to that of the ancient Israelite Rechabite ascetics, especially in their abstention from wine; in their abstention also from the flesh of animals they conform to the type of asceticism of some of the Palestinian sectarian groups.

The parallel which Philo draws between the 'tables' of the Therapeutae and the Table of the Shew-bread in the Temple is intended to remind us that, though the Thera-peutae were a lay order, their sacred meal *had the same cultic character as the offering of the Shew-bread by the priests in the Temple of Jerusalem*; the bread was consecrated bread, the Table was a 'holy table'; only, since the Therapeutae were laymen and belonged to an inferior rank, their bread was leavened bread.

In characterizing the meal in this way Philo reveals its origin and character.

It seems clear that the Qumran meal is to be derived from practices in the Temple itself.  To the priesthood were assigned the 'choice portions' of the daily offerings.  K. G. Kuhn made this point well:

. . . the Order originated with a group who severed their relations with the Jerusalem Temple and went out into the wilderness, and in the Jerusalem Temple the priests had to take a ritual bath before and after each cult action.  In the evening, their daily offices being concluded, the priests gathered—after a final bath— in a special room in the Temple set aside for them: here they partook of the priestly meal.  This consisted of 'holy things', i.e. those pieces of the offerings which were set aside for the priests. Once separated from the Temple, the Essenes discontinued the sacrificial cult, but continued to lead their lives in accordance with priestly purity.  They continued daily baths and sacral meals.[1]

The problem is to determine to which of the Temple meals the sacral meal of Qumran is to be traced.

Was it to the priests' participation in the Shew-bread, the 'bread of the Presence', and was the 'Table of the Com-munity (*shulḥan hayyaḥadh*)' the sect's substitute for this ancient piece of Temple (and Tabernacle) furniture?  The terminology employed (to arrange, '*arakh*, the Table) recalls the description of the Table of the Shew-bread at II Chron. xxix.18 (*shulḥan hamma'arekheth*).

[1] op. cit. p. 68.

In Ezekiel's Temple it was to be a table of plain, un-adorned wood; and it is there described as an altar (Ezek. xli.22).   Ezekiel provided the basis for the Qumran sect's priestly organization, and it is from Ezekiel it took its conception of the Messiah (see infra, p. 152).   It would not be surprising if its only altar, the Table of the Community, had a similar origin.   Moreover, we could then account for the character of this cult-meal as consisting of bread and/or wine. Since the sect did not fully participate in the sacrificial cultus of the Temple (and since bread and wine are universally available commodities), such a substitute would seem a natural and indeed inevitable one.   The Old Testament is silent, however, about the presence of wine as well as bread on the ancient Table of the Shew-bread.   It does mention 'flagons', however, as part of the appurtenances of the Table (Exodus xxv.29 R.V.); and the silence of the Biblical writers about the presence of wine has led rabbinical writers to give some novel and absurd explanations of the vessels of the Table. The LXX at Exodus xxxviii.12 tells us there were κύαθοι καὶ σπόνδια, 'bowls and flagons', ἐν οἷς σπείσει ἐν αὐταῖς 'with which libations are to be made'; these libations were quite certainly libations of wine, which we must suppose at some period also entered into the ritual of the Shew-bread.[1]

The association of bread and wine as cult offerings is very ancient; at Genesis xiv.18 the priest Melchizedek presents Abraham with consecrated gifts of bread and wine.

The source and inspiration of the sect's messianism is the form of the Davidic Messianic expectation in the Book of Ezekiel (the *Nasi'* or Prince).   At Ezekiel xliv.3ff, the Messianic Prince enters the ideal Temple of the future by a special gate, and then partakes of a festal meal: 'he shall . . . eat bread before the Lord'.[2]   The Messianic Banquet at Qumran may well be a description of the fulfilment of this prophecy. In that case, the regular cult-meal of participating in the Bread of the Presence may be a form of anticipation of the Messianic meal, when the Messiah of Israel would sit down at a Temple sacrificial meal with the true Israel.

---

[1] Cf. Hastings's *Dictionary of the Bible*, under Shew-bread.
[2] See infra, p. 148.

There is a further piece of evidence from Qumran itself
which supports this hypothesis of the origins of the Qumran
sacred meal.  Aramaic fragments from Qumran 2 contain a
description of a sacred meal.[1]  The text is fragmentary, but
the evidence is sufficient to show that the meal in question
consisted of the partaking of the Shew-bread.  The ritual
described occurs within a group of related fragments which
their editor suspects contained together a description of the
New Jerusalem.[2]  Fragment 1 contains the actual account of
the rite.  Fragments 2, 3, and 4 are concerned with the
dimensions of the Shew-bread Table, similar to those to be
found at Exodus xxv.23-30, Ezekiel xli.22, or in Josephus
(*Antiq.* III.vi.6) and the Mishnah (Men. xi.4-5).[3]  Fragment 1 gives regulations relating to the observance of the
rite, in particular the weekly renewal of the 'bread of the
presence' and its consumption by the priests.[4]  The first
concerns the need for the purification of 'their flesh' in
approaching the Table, and M. Baillet compares I Sam.
xxi.5-6: David and his companions are unable to partake of
the bread of the offering unless they have kept themselves
free from contact with women.[5]

The lines of special interest are 3 and 9:

3    *Then they shall enter the sanctuary . . .*
9    *. . . and they shall take the bread*[6]
     *and it shall be divided.*

The whole description appears to be in the same category as

[1] M. Baillet, 'Fragments araméens de Qumran 2.  Description de la Jérusalem
Nouvelle', in *RB*, 62 (2), April, 1955, 222ff.

[2] op. cit. pp. 244, 245: 'Quant à la présence d'un tel texte dans un lot provenant
sans doute d'une bibliothèque essénienne, elle nous montre que les cénobites de la
Mer Morte s'intéressaient aux choses du Temple et du culte, et rêvaient d'un Israël
messianique où le service du sanctuaire se déroulerait d'une manière sans doute en
partie nouvelle mais inspirée des bonnes traditions, et confirme qu'il ne faut voir en
eux que des gens séparés de Jérusalem pour un temps, en attendant la construction
de la Nouvelle Cité Sainte où tout sera parfait et le sacerdoce selon leur cœur.'

[3] M. Baillet, p. 238: ' . . . ce qui est plus intéressant que les dimensions elles-
mêmes, que d'ailleurs notre manuscrit ne donne pas, ce sont les parallèles littéraires
que l'on croit pouvoir relever avec le texte michnique, et qui se retrouvent partielle-
ment dans Ézéchiel.'  The Table found in the 'scriptorium' at Qumran (cf. Milik,
p. 22 and Plate 11) has been identified with a similar cult-object, cf. Del Medico, *The
Riddle of the Scrolls*, London, 1958, p. 89ff.

[4] Cf. Baillet, op. cit. p. 243.    [5] p. 228.

[6] The phrase is *nesabh laḥma*.  Cf. J. Jeremias, *Abendmahlsworte Jesu*[2], p. 88.
The oldest interpretation of the enigmatic ἄρτος ἐπιούσιος of the Lord's Prayer
identifies it with the Shew-bread.  Cf. D. E. Hadidian, in *NTS*, 5, 81.

that of the messianic meal: it is part of a vision of a future participation in the Shew-bread by the Zadokite priests in an ideal Temple in the future. But it may well reflect an actual custom of the sect.

The text, though fragmentary, appears to envisage a situation in a restored Temple where the priests would also participate in the Temple sacrifices: the consumption of the bread was probably envisaged as taking place in the course of a sacred meal which included the partaking by the priests of the portions of the animal sacrifices allotted to them.[1] This suggests that the sacred meal of bread and/or wine of the Qumran priestly sect was not only an anticipation of a messianic banquet, but also a foretaste of the full Temple rite when that had been fully restored in the New Jerusalem and in the new Temple of Ezekiel's vision, and when the Zadokite priesthood would once again have come into their ancient inheritance.

Other aspects of the sacral meal of the Therapeutae may contribute to further understanding of the Qumran texts. Especially characteristic of the Mareotis group is their hymn-singing, preceding and following the meal, the Vigil ($\pi\alpha\nu\nu\nu\chi\acute{\iota}s$) and the ritual dances:

After the supper they hold the sacred vigil which is conducted in the following way. They rise up all together and standing in the middle of the refectory form themselves first into two choirs, one of men and one of women, the leader and precentor chosen for each being the most honoured amongst them and also the most musical. Then they sing hymns to God composed of many measures and set to many melodies, sometimes chanting together, sometimes taking up the harmony antiphonally, hands and feet keeping time in accompaniment, and rapt with enthusiasm reproduce sometimes the lyrics of the procession, sometimes of the halt and of the wheeling and counterwheeling of a choric dance. Then when each choir has separately done its own part in the feast, having drunk as in the Bacchic rites of the strong wine of God's love they mix and both together become a single choir, a copy of the choir set up of old beside the Red Sea in honour of the wonders there wrought. For at the command of God the sea became a source of salvation to one party and of perdition to the other. As

[1] Cf. Baillet, p. 243.

it broke in twain and withdrew under the violence of the forces which swept it back there rose on either side, opposite to each other, the semblance of solid walls, while the space thus opened between them broadened into a highway smooth and dry throughout on which people marched under guidance right on until they reached the higher ground on the opposite mainland. But when the sea came rushing in with the returning tide, and from either side passed over the ground where dry land had appeared the pursuing enemy were submerged and perished. This wonderful sight and experience, an act transcending word and thought and hope, so filled with ecstasy both men and women that forming a single choir they sang hymns of thanksgiving to God their Saviour, the men led by the prophet Moses and the women by the prophetess Miriam.[1]

Hebrew hymns have now been discovered which were no doubt put to some similar use in the liturgy of Qumran. They have been called *Hymns of Thanksgiving* from the opening lines of some of the hymns, 'I thank Thee, O God.' They are all, for the most part hymns of deliverance, praising the divine mercy and goodness for his salvation of Israel. The mime or dance of the Therapeutae has the same theme, the celebration of the historic deliverance of Israel from Egyptian bondage. In these Qumran writings we encounter a spirit of almost evangelical piety, a sense of complete dependence upon God for life and salvation.[2]

Philo's description of the purpose of the mime and of the antiphonal singing of the Therapeutae (in honour of the wonders (there) wrought by God) brings us probably nearer to the fundamental religious meaning of the sacred meal of both Therapeutae and Qumran Essenes than any other source or document. It was a cultic action or drama, concerned with the celebration of the 'mighty acts' of deliverance of Israel by her God. But the sacred vigil suggests that this form of Jewish religion was forward, as well as backward looking.[3]

---

[1] xi.83-87 (Loeb translation).      [2] See further infra, p. 125ff.
[3] F. C. Conybeare wrote (op. cit. p. 314):
   'One would like to know whether the main aim of these Suppliants was not to make themselves ready by fasting and praying for the coming of the Messiah. Philo does not say so, and as he is silent, we must not give rein to our own mere conjectures. Yet we would not be imputing to them a motive quite foreign to Philo's own beliefs and aspirations. For that he contemplated the appearance of a divine personage who

Such a reconstruction of the character and significance of these sectarian cult-meals may be held to receive confirmation from the Qumran literature: the possible character of the meal as an anticipation of the Messianic Banquet, and the rules laid down in the event of the Messiah being 'born' suggest that these meals (like the Passover itself) had a messianic significance. They not only celebrated the past deliverance of Israel, but looked forward to her future deliverance by the 'Messiah of Aaron and Israel'. The character of the Qumran Messiah[1] and the *War* scroll, in particular, show that this future deliverance was conceived in terms of a triumphant military conquest of the Gentile world. At the same time, these ideas were combined with such deep religious longings and aspirations as we find in the Qumran hymns for a deliverance from all the powers of evil.

How are we to assess this evidence as a whole in relation to the study of Christian origins? Lieberman's comparison of Zadokite and Pharisaic initiation rites tends to rob the Essene parallels of some of their force.[2] Among the Pharisees too there was a two-stage probation, enquiry into the candidate's suitability, and the same concern for ritual purity; and initiation was accompanied by a ritual bath (the *tebilah*) and followed by participation in the ritually pure meals of the Haburah. The ritual bath, however, does not appear to have been repeated (hand-washings rather than immersion lustrations were the characteristic Pharisaic practice). The repetition of purificatory washings emerges as the most

should reunite the scattered faithful in a transfigured Jerusalem, is certain from a number of passages in his books. Thus in the *De Praemiis et Poenis*, 2.427, he expresses his conviction, "That God could easily, by a single call, bring together from the ends of the earth, into whatsoever place he will, men settled afar from their country in the recesses of the world." And in the closing chapters of the book on curses, he describes at length the salvation of Israel which he himself looked for, and which was to come whenever the backsliders from the law and the violaters of the sabbath should have turned from the evil of their ways and repented: "But when they shall have won this unlooked for freedom, those who were but scattered in Hellas and barbarous lands over islands and over continents, shall rise up with one impulse, and from the diverse regions flock together unto the one spot revealed to them, led on through strange lands by a certain apparition too divine to be esteemed merely human, unseen of others and only manifest to those who are saved" (ξεναγούμενοι πρὸς τινός θειοτέρας ἢ κατὰ φύσιν ἀνθρωπίνος(ην) ὄψεως, ἀδῆλον μὲν ἑτέροις, μόνοις δὲ τοῖς ἀνασωζομένοις ἐμφανοῦς).... And there shall be a change of all things on a sudden. For God will turn the curses upon the enemies of them that have repented, and on them that exulted in the calamities of our race, reviling and mocking at us,' etc.

[1] See further infra, p. 145ff.
[2] *JBL*, 71 1952, 199ff.

striking common feature between sectarian Judaism and certain branches of the early Church.

It has also recently been claimed that the *tebilah* alone had become the central rite of initiation among leading Hillelites of the first century,[1] so that Pharisaic practices may have contributed to the Christian doctrine and observance of baptism as a single unrepeatable act. In the New Testament the establishment of the 'one Baptism' is no doubt to be set down to the influence of the Pharisee Paul.

The persistence of ritual ablutions in the second-century Graeco-Roman Church need not oblige us to assume an inheritance from and continuity with the primitive Jerusalem church; these elements may be due to secondary not primary Jewish influences, and may be importations and accretions as the Church was reinforced, after the Fall of Jerusalem, by Essene groups insisting on continuing their ancestral rites. The presence of such features, however, in the main stream of the Church's life may, on the other hand, be held to support the alternative hypothesis that they formed part of the Church's ritual, in some form or another, from the earliest Johannite stages of development; and that Josephus may be historically accurate in his account of the baptism of John. Such rites may not have been finally shed till the Church's doctrinal position was fixed and accepted, when they survived, after the second century, in heretical Jewish-Christian circles only.

There is a third alternative. The *Tradition of Hippolytus* represents the situation in the non-Pauline Roman Church where we would expect earlier Jewish practices to survive. The Epistle to the Hebrews (perhaps intended especially for that Church and written not later than A.D. 90) counsels its readers to leave the 'elementary doctrines' of *baptismoi* and

---

[1] Cf. David Daube, *The New Testament and Rabbinic Judaism*, p. 109. Daube finds baptism the central rite in these rabbinic sources; it was in no sense a purificatory rite, but had a purely moral and spiritual significance. The central motif of pre-baptismal instruction is derived from the Exodus (a convert passes through the experience of Israel rescued from Egypt); such well-known Christian motifs as 'glorying in suffering', even the hope of heaven and charity, have their counterpart, according to Daube, in such pre-baptismal instruction.

Perhaps in this case more allowance should be made for the interplay of influence between the rival religions, and it might be better, in the matter of proselyte instruction, to reserve judgment until we know more about its oldest forms. Dr Daube's views do, however, provide a corrective to the Essene hypothesis.

*Plate 8* Inkwells from the ruins, the centre one of bronze, the others of terracotta.
*(Palestine Archaeological Museum)*

*Plate 9* Samples of the jars in which the scrolls were preserved See p. 22, n.1.
*(Palestine Archaeological Museum)*

*Plate 10 (left)* A close-up of the largest of the cisterns. The crack is due to earthquake disturbance (in 64 or 31 B.C.; see p. 138, n.1). Note the divided partitions for entering. (*Palestine Archaeological Museum*)

*Plate 11 (below)* A large open area lies to the south of this 'cistern', suitable for a gathering of the 'Many'. While the water system no doubt supplied fresh water to the community, this large cistern looks more like a public 'baptistry'. See p. 95. (*Palestine Archaeological Museum*)

go on to maturity (vi.2)—a clear enough indication that there were Jewish-Christian groups still practising purificatory washings when the Epistle was written.

The combined evidence of Hebrews and the *Tradition of Hippolytus* supports the view that where such washings did survive in the Graeco-Roman or Hellenistic Church it was in churches and circles with a predominantly Jewish element, perhaps even exclusively Jewish; the evidence of Hippolytus points to their survival in non-Pauline foundations only. But this clearly means that there were Jewish Christian groups outside Palestine practising the Essene type of ritual washing.

The main difficulty in trying to arrive at any firm conclusion about the sacred meal lies in our ignorance of other forms of such a meal in Judaism itself apart from the Passover meal. The Pharisees had also their religious meals in their Guilds or *Haburoth*; and, in any case, every meal in Judaism was, in some sense, a religious meal. It may well be, however, that this type of common sectarian meal rather than the Passover was the prototype of the Eucharist; the daily repetition of the breaking of the bread in the early Church can scarcely be traced to a paschal origin.

### ADDITIONAL NOTE

## The Organization of the Qumran Sect

Professor B. Reicke of Basel has drawn some interesting parallels between the constitution or organization of the Qumran sect and the Primitive Church.[1] The Qumran sect was a hierarchic, non-egalitarian body, the unity of which—and the texts make much of the 'unity' of the sect—depended on its 'aristocratic' or 'oligarchic' structure.

There are two features of special interest, the character and organization of a small body of 'saints' at the apex (or at the foundation) of the Qumran hierarchy, and the office of an individual known as the Examiner (*mebaqqer*). The first

[1] 'The Constitution of the Primitive Church in the Light of Jewish Documents', in *The Scrolls and the New Testament*, p. 143ff.

has been claimed as the prototype of the College of the Twelve Apostles in the early Jerusalem Church and the second as the forerunner of the Christian Bishop.[1]

1 QS viii.1ff. reads: 'In the Council of the Community [there are, or shall be] twelve men and three priests, perfect in all that is revealed from the whole Torah. . . .'

Dr Reicke is in error in describing this group as a 'council' in the community; it is a group or 'conclave' (so W. Brownlee) within the Council. Moreover, the most natural understanding of the words is that the number of this group is fifteen, twelve laymen *and* three priests. The inclusive reckoning is, however, both possible and defensible.[2]

It is not certain if there was an actual group or simply an ideal, and this second possibility would account for the fact that in *CD* there is an 'inner cabinet' in the Council totally different in character and structure (a special group of ten *shophetim* or 'judges', chosen by the community in assembly and consisting of four priests and Levites and six laymen *CD* xi.1-4). The ideal character of the 'twelve' (or 'fifteen') saints would also account for the soteriological functions assigned to them: they are given 'a theological significance as an instrument of salvation'.[3]

The function of the 'Censor of the Camps' presents an interesting analogy with the early Christian Bishop, but any suggestion of the direct derivation of the one from the other is ruled out, if only by the fact that ἐπίσκοπος is a Christian

---

[1] See B. Reicke, op. cit. p. 151.

[2] Cf. Reicke, p. 151: 'Perhaps the inclusion of the three priests is to be preferred, because it enables one to see in the expression "priest" an especial mark of honor and to avoid the rather improbable result that the other twelve were laymen. If the three priests can be included in the circle of the twelve, then we are reminded of the fact that Peter and the two sons of Zebedee, or later Peter, John and James the Lord's brother constituted a distinct group within the circle of the twelve. This is just a possibility; and it cannot be maintained with any certainty that those three priests constitute an analogy to the most intimate disciples of Jesus. On the other hand, the number twelve for the members of the Council of the Qumran Community is certainly significant. It is true that with Jesus, as probably with the Qumran Community, the number twelve is intended to correspond to the number of the tribes of Israel. In addition, the Jewish synagogue may have had colleges of twelve men. Thus we cannot say that Jesus is directly dependent on the Qumran sect in this matter. Still, it is valuable from a historical point of view to find here a partial analogy to the twelve apostles of the Church. In the primitive Christian community the Twelve constituted just such a council as our passage from the Qumran text indicates.'

It is perhaps worth adding that the number of the loaves of the Shew-bread was twelve, also corresponding to the twelve tribes of Israel.

[3] Cf. Reicke, op. cit. p. 152; cf. further infra, p. 128ff.

coinage for the office, with its origin almost certainly to be traced to the use of the word in trade guilds and societies of the Hellenistic world.[1] Nothing in the function of these lay ἐπίσκοποι, however, corresponds to the nature of the office of the Christian Bishop, and the Essene ἐπιμελητής and Qumran *mebaqqer* does provide a much closer analogy. He has the rôle both of judicial authority (the priests are obliged to consult him, *CD* xv.7) and he is also a teacher and a 'father in God' to the members of the sect (xvi.1-12). He has also the duties of examining novices (xvii.6-8).

[1] Cf. Kittel, *Th. W.* II, p. 608ff.

# CHAPTER VI

# Legalism, Prophetism, and Apocalyptic

## I

### LEGALISM

As in Pharisaism—and, indeed, in every form of contemporary and later Judaism—the Law of Moses provided the regulative norm of sectarian religion. The Qumran community differed from other forms of ancient Judaism in the almost equal place it accorded the Prophets, and to certain apocalyptic writings; and it is out of its 'prophetism' and related apocalyptic that some of its most characteristic doctrines developed. But it also had a distinctive type of priestly legalism; it was in fact known as a Torah Community (*yaḥadh Torah*), and it was its 'secession', in attempting to reform the Law, which led to its formation as a 'sect'; a new kind of legalistic heteropraxis came into being at Qumran.

In any attempt to isolate and define the main characteristics of this Qumran legalism, allowance must be made for its possible existence (in at least some of its elements) in other groups of the period, even within Pharisaism itself. The only known guide to ancient Pharisaism is in the forms of rabbinical Judaism which descended from it and in which the apocalyptic element has been eliminated altogether. Ancient Pharisaic legalism may also, like that of Qumran, have had an apocalyptic element. It is probably also misleading to take the Zadokite Fragments (where apocalyptic has at least suffered a partial eclipse) as representative, at all points, of the legalism of Qumran; they may owe something to rabbinical influence.

When such allowances are made, there remains a number of striking features of Qumran legalism which mark it off as a distinctive sectarian *genre*. While the evidence does not point directly to actual asceticism, or even, indisputably, to a monastic type of community, it points to a cult of what may be described as sacerdotal, legalistic 'puritanism', or 'perfectionism', only possible in a monastic or semi-monastic order with ascetic tendencies.

In an important article entitled 'Révélation des Mystères et Perfection à Qumran et dans le Nouveau Testament',[1] Père B. Rigaux of Brussels has drawn attention to the prominent place which the idea of Perfection has in the *Manual of Discipline*. 1 QS frequently employs such expressions as 'the perfect way', 'perfection of way' (viii.18, 21; ix.5, 6, 8, 9). The idea has its source in the Old Testament (cf. Ps. ci.6), but is developed at Qumran in several distinctive ways. Some of these distinctive aspects of this Perfection are noted by M. Rigaux: 'En résumé, nous avons rencontré dans les constituantes de la perfection qumrânienne un élément moral, l'obéissance et la marche dans la voie, un élément mystique, c'est-à-dire dépassant les catégories humaines du savoir, du vouloir et des actes, la purification et le don de l'esprit saint, enfin un élément gnostique, la connaissance du plan de Dieu et de la Loi de Dieu, aboutissant à une révélation de l'activité de Dieu et des destinées éternelles de l'homme.' (p. 240ff.)

The claim here made that Qumran Perfectionism included 'the purification and gift of the Holy Spirit' seems to me to be a misunderstanding of 1 QS; the Qumran saints were looking forward, at a future time of divine visitation, to such a 'purification' (nowhere, however, described as a 'gift'). The most that can be said is that the 'perfection of way' of these sectarians was related to the measure of their purification by the divinely created 'spirit of truth', which is, however, no more than a general expression to describe the fundamental basis of Qumran 'Perfection of Way', namely, its absolute and total obedience to the *divinely revealed tradition of the Law handed down and developed by the sect*. This comprises the moral element (though the revealed Law includes juridical, ceremonial, and other elements as well). It is this divinely imparted revelation of the Law (and, as we shall see, of the Prophets too) which constitutes the esoteric *gnosis* or 'mysteries' of Qumran.

An important passage for this basic conception is the interpretation attached to the oft-quoted *testimonium* from Is. xl.3: 'Prepare ye the way of the Lord,' etc. (1 QS viii.14ff.): the 'way of the Lord' which the sectarians are to prepare is defined as 'the study of the Torah by which God gave command through Moses for acting *according to everything that is revealed from time to time*, and according to what the Prophets revealed by His holy spirit'. The place of prophetic next to Mosaic revelation is characteristic for Qumran: their basic idea of revelation, with reference to both its main sources, Torah and Prophets, is one of a progressive disclosure to the sect of the revealed will of God from Holy Scripture. This is the function of the priestly teachers, the Bene Zadok, in the Community: 1 QS v.8ff. reads: 'He [the novice] shall bind himself by oath to return to the Law of Moses, after all that he commanded, with all his soul, *according . . . to everything revealed from it to the Bene Zadok, the priests*, the guardians of the Covenant who seek out His good pleasure, and according to the majority of the men of their covenant.' This last statement, 'according to the majority', implies that, in decisions of Torah to be made in any new circumstances, the whole community was consulted, and this is borne out by 1 QS i.7-9: 'All who dedicate themselves to carry out God's laws in the Covenant of Mercy shall be united in a Council of God to walk before Him perfectly *with regard to everything revealed to their* assemblies for the study of Torah.'[1] The idea that this was a progressive revelation in which Torah was interpreted and re-applied to the changing circumstances of the sect's life is well brought out by 1 QS ix.17ff., according to which the sectarians are exhorted 'to conceal the counsel of the Law among perverse men, but to edify with true knowledge and righteous law those who choose the way . . . *guiding them with knowledge, and instructing them in the mysteries of marvel and of truth . . . that they may walk perfectly each with his fellow in all that is*

---

[1] I have followed the interpretation of Sukenik, *Meg. Gen.* II, p. 28ff. Cf. W. H. Brownlee, *BASOR, Supplementary Studies,* 10-12, 1951, p. 8, n. 19.

*revealed for them . . . and to instruct them with regard to all
that is discovered to be carried out at this time . . .'*

What we have here is also a priestly *esoteric* legalism;
the study and interpretation of Torah constituted a kind of
secret gnosis to be closely guarded and revealed only to the
initiated. This aspect of the sect's attitude to Scripture
generally, and not only to the Law, becomes especially important in their interpretation of the Prophets; it was from
this source that the apocalypticism of the sect developed.[1]
(Whether this secret study of the Books involved what Philo
meant by the 'allegorical' interpretation of Scripture among
the Essenes is a moot point: but the emphasis of the ancient
Greek historians on the secrecy of the Essenes about their
doctrines is exactly paralleled in this side of Qumran
religion.)

This tradition of a progressive and esoteric revelation
goes back to the founder-fathers of the movement, in particular to the Teacher of Righteousness himself. The Zadokite
Fragments mention the 'hidden things' revealed to the
earliest Remnant and emphasize the validity of the legal
enactments of the founders of the sect.

*CD* v (Rabin's translation):

But with them that held fast to the commandments of God who
were left over of them, God established his covenant with Israel
even until eternity, by revealing to them hidden things concerning
which all Israel had gone astray. 'His holy sabbaths' and His
glorious appointed times, His righteous testimonies and His true
ways and the requirements of His desire, which man shall do and
live thereby, these he laid open before them; and they digged a well
for 'much water', and he that despises it (the water) shall not live.

The Well is the Law, as is explained later (*CD*, viii.3ff.),
where Numbers xxi.18 is so interpreted. In the Habakkuk
Commentary the Teacher of Righteousness is a new Ezekiel,
a prophet-priest who reveals all the words of His servants
the Prophets (i.5). The sect is also to be guided in disputes
about property 'according to the first decisions with which
the men of the community began to be disciplined' (1 QS
ix.10).

[1] See further infra, p. 125ff.

The element of 'perfectionism' in this secretly revealed legalism of Qumran is not only to be seen in the prominence of the description of the sectarians and their religion as 'the perfect way' or 'perfection of way', but also in the absolute and total demands which are made on their obedience to 'the whole Law' as thus secretly divulged by its priestly interpreters. It is difficult, indeed, to avoid the impression that 1 QS is not just the statement of an ideal, and not as it is usually taken to be, a 'Manual of Discipline'. The sectarians are to be obedient and perfect in *all* that is revealed to them (cf. 1 QS i.8-9; v.9; viii.1, 15; ix.13, 19), in 'everything which He has commanded' (i.17; v.1, 8; ix.24), to keep '*all* the words of God' (i.14; iii.11), to 'depart from *all* evil' (i.4, 7; ii.3; v.1), 'every perversity' (vi.15; viii.18; ix.21).[1]

This ideal of a 'legalistic perfection', secretly imparted, no doubt owes much to the unreal world of apocalyptic fantasy in which the sect lived. We may partly, no doubt, account for it as a reaction, in the direction of a priestly-ascetic type of life, from the corruption of the age, but it is only to be understood fully in the context of the other revealed 'mysteries' of the Sect—in its 'prophetism' and apocalypticism. The Age was an evil one moving to its end when it would fall under the catastrophic judgment of the Wrath of God. It was all the more necessary and urgent that this Remnant should keep the whole Law with perfect obedience.

The *Manual of Discipline* does not contain any actual 'legal' decisions, though we can infer that these were concerned with more than matters of conduct; the exact decisions about the times of the annual festivals almost certainly were among the '*revealed mysteries*'. So too must have been the details of the ceremonial Law. As we have seen, that some kind of community of possessions (not necessarily excluding all private property) was practised is clear from several passages, and this agrees with the reports of the Greek historians about the Essenes; apart, however, from the general condemnation of wealth to be found in Old Testament Scrip-

[1] Cf. H. Braun, *Spätjüdisch-häretischer und frühchristlicher Radikalismus, Beiträge zur historischen Theologie*, Tübingen, 1957, I, p. 28.

ture, we do not know the source of this *halakha* or legal
ruling, obviously a basic one, unless it is the old Targumic
version of the Shema (Deut. vi.4ff.), according to which
'Thou shalt love the Lord Thy God with all thy strength' is
interpreted 'with all thy possessions' (Targ. Pseudo-Jon.
*mammon*). 1 QS i.11 reads, 'All who dedicate themselves
to His Truth shall bring all their mind and their strength and
*their property* (*honam*) into the Community of God.'   The
Shema seems clearly in the background of this passage, and
the novice may have been obliged to recite it on this occasion
or hear it recited in his presence; these words certainly owe
something to the old Targumic interpretation of Deut. vi.

The Zadokite Fragments contain a considerable number
of *halakhoth*, some of which are non-Pharisaic, and can be
shown, on internal evidence, to be pre-Christian.   The prohibition of marriage with a niece links Qumran sectarianism
with the Samaritans, the Karaites, as well as with other
sectarian Jews.[1]   The view of Rabin that the Zadokites agreed
in this prohibition with the Pharisees (by whom it was
'either completely forbidden, or there were strong scruples'[2])
cannot be seriously maintained; apart from the absence of
evidence that the Pharisees forbade such marriages, one has
then the awkward problem that the rabbis favoured them.[3]
This legal controversy is of particular interest, since we
know from Josephus that it was a live issue in his day (*Antiq*.
XII.iv.6, *B.J.* I.xxii.4, *Antiq*. XVII.i.3; XVIII.v.1; XVIII.
v.4; XIX.v.1); and it was, of course, the burden of John the
Baptist's condemnation of Herod Antipas and the cause of
his death (cf. Mk. vi.17).

Two further examples of sectarian Law are noteworthy.
The Qumran sect condemned divorce and polygamy, and, as
at Mark x.6, cite Genesis i.27 as proof-text: 'the fundamental
principle of creation is "Male and female created he them"'
(*CD*, iv.21).   We do not know how they interpreted Deut.

---

[1] See Schechter, *Documents of Jewish Sectaries*, Vol. 1, pp. xviii, xxv.
[2] *Qumran Studies*, p. 92.
[3] 'The Rabbis . . . when faced with the alternative of disqualifying numbers of
priests or legalising past niece-marriages . . . allayed the uneasiness of their own
followers by making it a particularly meritorious type of union' (Rabin, loc. cit.).
It is much easier to account for the rabbinical attitude by seeing in them the faithful
pupils of the Pharisees.

xxiv.1, which permits divorce; their teaching almost obliges us to assume that they rejected altogether this part of the Law.

In the Zadokite Fragments there are twenty-eight Sabbath restrictions, twenty-three of which agree with rabbinical restrictions (and are probably all Pharisaic), but five of them are new, among them the total prohibition of freedom of movement on the Sabbath, in complete disagreement with the Mishnah.[1] One of the most interesting is the prohibition forbidding the removal of any animal which has stumbled into a pit on the Sabbath. The rabbis permitted this, and so too, we can infer from Luke xiv.5ff., did the Pharisees. The mention of this point of Sabbath legalism in the Gospels is clear proof that it was a debated issue at the time. The only people who could have maintained it are the Qumran sectarians or the Essenes.

Evidence of this kind, which we can be certain is ancient, underlines the rigorism of the sectarian legalism of Qumran. Among related sects it no doubt went to greater extremes, such as we find in the asceticism of the Therapeutae, the prohibition of marriage, and abstention from wine and flesh. In the form in which it confronts us in the actual documents from Qumran, it was a legalistic puritanism or perfectionism, with its secret code jealously guarded, and presented as a divine mystery or gnosis.

One further and important consequence of this extreme Torah radicalism of Qumran was its exclusiveness. The aloofness of the Pharisee and his distance from the 'am ha'areṣ is a relatively mild tolerance contrasted with the intolerant hatred of the sect for outsiders; the sectarians were 'sons of light', all others, especially foreigners, were the 'sons of darkness'. When ethical parallels with the Gospels are cited from the Manual of Discipline, such as sectarian teaching on anger and hatred, it should be remembered that such high standards did not apply outside the Qumran fraternity.

---

[1] See my article 'The Gospels and the Scrolls' in Studia Evangelica, T.U. 73 (1959), p. 571.

## II

### THE PROPHETIC TRADITION OF QUMRAN

In addition to the Law, the Qumran sectarians held the prophetic tradition of Israel in high esteem. This was pointed out by R. H. Charles in his edition of the *Damascus Document* and is confirmed by the new scrolls. It is not surprising to find Ezekiel occupying an important place in the writings of a priestly sect; Jeremiah and Daniel appear to have been no less influential, and the most surprising of all is the use made by this sect of II Isaiah.

The result is that a quite different note is struck again and again in these legalistic writings; and there emerges from time to time deeper spiritual insights which are in the spirit of the Gospels themselves. Perhaps we ought to allow more for different 'philosophies' within Qumran itself, that is, different schools of thought or *Richtungen*, as well as for the recognition of different stages in the sect's development.

Attention has been drawn more than once to the following verses from the hymns appended to the *Manual*:

*But as for me I belong to an evil humanity*
*And to the company of wicked flesh.*
*Mine iniquities, my transgressions, my sin . . .*
*Belong to . . . the things that move in darkness.*
*For a man's way is not his own*
*A man cannot direct his steps [Jer. x.23]:*
*But to God belongs justification*
*And from his hand is integrity of way, . . .*
*And if I stumble, God's mercy is my salvation for ever.*
*And if I stumble in carnal evil,*
*My justification through God's righteousness shall stand*
     *everlastingly. . . .*
*Even from the pit he will draw forth my soul,*
*And will direct in the way my steps.*
*In his compassion he has brought me near,*
*And in his mercy he will bring my justification;*
*In his steadfast righteousness he has justified me;*
*And in his great goodness he will atone for all mine iniquities,*

> *And in his righteousness he will cleanse me from man's impurity,*
> *And from the sin of the children of men.*
>
> XI.10ff.

On this last verse Dr Millar Burrows remarks: 'In this verse we seem to have not only justification but sanctification',[1] and adds: 'The point of prime importance here is that while man has no righteousness of his own, there is a righteousness which God, in his own righteousness, freely confers. The meaning of the righteousness of God in Rom. iii.21-26 is thus illustrated and shown to be rooted in pre-Christian Judaism.'[2]

This same note of almost 'evangelical' piety is struck again and again in the *Hodayoth* or *Hymns*; indeed one might almost refer to it as a recurring theme. It certainly gave the theological foundation for the religion of these sectarian saints. The condemnation of unaided human nature forms the foil or background to the doctrine of 'grace' or divine help by the spirit which God imparts to or has created for man. The two following hymns contain this fundamental sectarian theology, and give typical expression to it. It is not too much to say that, like the ancient psalmists and prophets (and following closely in their steps) the Qumran saints had discovered the secret of 'evangelical' religion, trust in the everlasting mercy of God alone, and in His spirit to guide and direct daily life and conduct.

1 QH iv.27-37:

> *By me Thou hast illumined the faces of the people* [lit. *the Many*]
> *And been magnified times without number,*
> *For Thou hast acquainted me with the mysteries of Thy wonders,*
> *And with the secret of Thy wonders Thou hast*
>     *made great my office,*
> *Dealing wondrously before the people for the sake of Thy glory*
> *To make known Thy might to all things living.*
>
> *What flesh is as this? And can a vessel of clay perform*
>     *wonders,*
> *That is sinful from the womb and unto old age guilty of*
>     *transgression;*

---

[1] Cited by Brownlee, op. cit. p. 45.
[2] *Dead Sea Scrolls*, p. 334. See further, infra, p. 160.

*I know that righteousness is not in man,*
*Nor perfection of way in the son of man.*
*To God Most High belong all righteous doings;*
*And the way of man cannot be made firm,*
*Except by the spirit which God has formed for him,*
*To make sound a way for the sons of men,*
*That they may know all his deeds by the power of his might,*
*And the multitude of his mercies*
*Unto all the sons of his good pleasure.*

*And as for me, trembling and quaking laid hold on me,*
*And all my bones shook,*
*My heart melted like wax before fire,*
*My knees became weak as water*
    *'poured down a steep place'* [Mic. i.4],
*When I remembered my guilt and the*
    *wickedness of my forbears,*
*When the wicked rose up against Thy Covenant*
*And the froward against Thy Word.*
*I declared by my transgressions I am lost to Thy Covenant.*

*But I remembered the strength of Thy hand,*
    *with the greatness of Thy mercies,*
*I was restored and stood upright,*
*And my spirit was strengthened to stand up to affliction;*
*For I lean upon Thy loving-kindness and abundant mercies*
*For Thou dost make expiation for sin. . . .*

1 QH vii.26-33:

*I give thanks unto Thee, [O Lord,]*
*For Thou hast given me understanding of Thy truth,*
*And with the secrets of Thy wonders Thou hast acquainted me.*
*In Thy mercies to man, in the multitude of Thy mercies*
    *to erring hearts,*
*Who is like unto Thee among gods, O Lord,*
*And what truth is like unto Thy Truth?*

*Who is there that is righteous before Thee,*
    *when Thou bringest him to judgment.*
*No spirit can reply to Thy charge,*
*None is able to withstand Thy wrath.*
*But all the children of Thy truth*
*Thou bringest, with forgiveness, before Thee,*
*Cleansing them of their transgressions by Thy great goodness,*

*And by the multitude of Thy mercies*
    *making them to stand before Thee forever.*
*For Thou art God everlasting,*
*And all Thy ways stand fast forever . . .*
*And there is none beside Thee*
*But what is man, a void and a vapour,*
*That he should understand Thy wondrous deeds.*

What we find in these verses certainly appears to approximate very closely to the Pauline doctrine of *justificatio sola fide*. It should be pointed out, however, that such religious sentiments do not only anticipate the Gospels as *praeparatio evangelica*; they are a continuation of *Psalmenfrömmigkeit*, the spirit of profound trust in God's mercy in the Psalms, and in the prophets, especially attributed to the Hasidim; it is significant that Jeremiah x.23 ('It is not in man to direct his steps') supplies the basic doctrine of these verses.

A specially noteworthy use is made of II Isaiah.

At fol. viii in the *Manual of Discipline* special mention is made of fifteen men, twelve laymen and three priests, who are said to be 'perfect in all that is revealed from the whole Torah'.[1]

'In the council of the community there shall be twelve men and three priests perfect in all that is revealed from the whole Torah, to act truly, rightly and justly and with a love of mercy; and to walk humbly each with his neighbour; to maintain loyalty in the land, with integrity of purpose and a broken spirit; to expiate wrongdoing as men who uphold the righteous cause [or who act justly] and who endure the afflictions of the refiner's furnace . . .

*For an eternal planting, a Temple for Israel,*
*A conclave which is an holy of holies for Aaron;*
*True witnesses to judgment, and the chosen of grace*
    *to atone for the land,*
*And to render to the wicked their desert.*
*This is the tested wall, the precious corner-stone;*
*Its foundations will not be shaken, nor be removed*
    *from their place.'*

'True witnesses to judgment': these Qumran saints are

[1] Cf. supra, pp. 42, 116.

to fulfil the mission of the Servant of the Lord (Is. xliii.10, 12: 'Ye are my witnesses, saith the Lord, and my servant whom I have chosen'), while the 'tested wall' and 'precious corner-stone' recalls Isaiah xxviii.16 and I Peter ii.4ff.

The most significant words, however, are the description of these Qumran saints as '*true witnesses to judgment, and the chosen of grace to atone for the land*'. Taken in conjunction with the earlier description of the fifteen saints as men who expiate wrongdoing by enduring the afflictions of the refiner's furnace (cf. Dan. xii.10), we have in these verses the devel-oped theological conception of a community or group within a community identifying itself with the Isaianic Remnant and attributing to its sufferings a redemptive function. (Else-where in the *Manual of Discipline* and the *Damascus Docu-ment* the individual makes atonement for his own sins by a renewed obedience to the Torah.) No less important is their work in judgment, for this corner-stone of the new Israel is not only to atone for the land but to render the wicked their deserts. As F. F. Bruce has remarked, the Servant who justifies many is also the Son of Man (in the Danielic sense) to whom has been given authority to execute judgment.[1]

This is one of the closest parallels to the Gospels in the scrolls. But in considering it we must again not overlook differences: the atonement is for Israel, and there does not seem to be any trace of the wider outlook of Second Isaiah which embraced the Gentiles in the redemptive purpose of the Servant.

These are important parallels, but there is nothing speci-fically sectarian about them; they spring from the prophetic tradition of Israel. That there were groups within Judaism, however, holding such views, is an important fact; and such groups may be viewed as forerunners, if they are not con-temporaries, of the Evangelists.

## Qumran Apocalyptic

It is known that the Qumran sect possessed some of our more familiar ancient apocalypses; fragments of Jubilees, of

[1] Cf. *NTS*, 2, 185.

an Aramaic version of the Testaments of the Twelve Patriarchs and of I Enoch have come from Cave 4.[1]  From *CD* we know that the Book of Jubilees was held in high esteem by the sect.

Qumran, however, had its own apocalypses; the *War* scroll or *Armageddon* is a type of apocalyptic writing.  However, what is most characteristic of Qumran is its esoteric interpretation of Scripture, which has developed into a distinctive type of Scriptural mysticism.  So far as the Torah is concerned this amounts to no more than a secret or esoteric legalism.  The same mystic terminology, however, is applied to the results of the study of the writings of the Prophets, 'mysteries' (*razim*), arcana (*nistaroth*).  The first term is of special interest since its Greek equivalent is μυστήρια.  It is an Aramaic (originally Persian) word, and Qumran usage derives ultimately from the Book of Daniel where the word means a 'secret' which is revealed by interpretation (*pesher*) of soothsayers, wise men, or of Daniel, the Prophet (cf. Dan. ii.18, iv.6).  The 'revealer of secrets' is God Himself (cf. ii.47; ii.28: 'there is a God in heaven that revealeth secrets, and maketh known to the king Nebuchadnezzar what shall be in the latter days').  In the closing chapters, the Book of Daniel is especially concerned with the revelation of the secrets of the 'latter days'; and its calculations about the seventy heptads come from a study of the prophet Jeremiah (Dan. ix.2); Daniel receives a special revelation of the future from the Angel Gabriel after he has confessed his people's iniquity (ix.20ff.).

These closing chapters of Daniel supplied the inspiration and pattern for the apocalyptic mysticism of Qumran; and research into the mysteries of the divine plan of salvation became an important preoccupation (if not a main occupation of the sect).[2]  It had its own *Book of Secrets*.[3]

These Mysteries of Qumran have been characterized by W. Grossouw[4]: 'Expressions like "the wonderful mys-

---

[1] See supra, p. 3, and Appendix B.
[2] I am indebted for much of the material in this paragraph to Père Rigaux's article, op. cit. p. 241ff.
[3] *Discoveries in the Judaean Desert*, I, pp. 102-7.
[4] In *Studia Catholica*, Jaargang cvii, Dec. 1951, p. 294.

teries" . . . "the truth of the secrets of knowledge", and such like occur continuously (cf. e.g., D.S.D. [ = 1 QS] 2, 23; 3, 15; 4, 6.18; 11, 3-6; D.S.H. 7.5; Hymn 4, 72ff.). What is primarily meant here is the decree or decrees of God regarding man's salvation, which were hidden and will remain hidden for the infidels but which God has revealed "through His servants, the prophets (D.S.D. 1, 3; D.S.H. 2, 9; 7, 5), and which are jealously guarded by the Sect".'

Fortunately, there has been included in the *Manual of Discipline* a long 'theological' section, intended for the guidance of the Instructor (*maskil*), no doubt in his 'preparation' of the novice for initiation. This important passage gives us a number of insights into the kind of 'mysteries' in which the sect believed. I give the passage first in translation and follow this with some comments upon it.

1 QS iii.13-iv.26:

For the sage [*lemaskil*], to instruct and to teach all the children 13 of light in the generation of all the sons of men about all the [different] kinds of spirits among them [lit. their spirits], with 14 their characteristics; about their actions in their classes and the afflictions which visit them, together with the periods of their well-being [*shelomam*]. From the God of knowledge comes all 15 that is and will be [or has been]. . . .

He created man to rule the world, and assigned him two spirits 18 in which to walk until the period of his visitation [*pequddah*, i.e. until God's final Visitation of man in judgment]; they are the spirits of truth and of wickedness [*ruḥoth ha'emeth weha'awel*]. In 19 a fountain of light [arise] the generations of truth, and from a spring of darkness the generations of wickedness. Under the hand 20 of the prince of light is the dominion of all the sons of righteousness; in the ways of light they walk. In the hand of the angel of 21 darkness is all the dominion of the sons of wickedness, and in the ways of darkness they walk. It is by the angel of darkness that all the sons of righteousness are led astray, and all their sins and 22 their iniquities and their guilt and the transgressions they commit are under his dominion, according to the divine mysteries, until the 23 time of his end [i.e. either Satan's or God's end-time]. And all their afflictions and the periods of their distress are under the dominion of his enmity. All the [evil] spirits belonging to him 24 are set to bring about the downfall of the children of light, but the

25 God of Israel and His angel of truth come to the aid of the children
of light.   He created the spirits of light and of darkness and on
26 them He founded all conduct . . . the one spirit God loved for all
the duration of the ages, and in all its deeds He takes pleasure
iv.1 forever.   But for the other, He has loathed its counsel, and all its
ways He has hated eternally.

2        These are the ways of these spirits [lit. their ways] in the
world.   [The spirit of light and truth] illumines the mind of a
man; makes straight before him all the ways of true righteousness;
inspires in his heart a fear of the divine judgments; [imparts]
3 humility, long-suffering [slowness to anger], great compassion,
eternal goodness [*tubh 'olemim*], understanding, discernment, strong
4 wisdom, believing in all God's works and relying in His great
mercy; and a spirit of knowledge in all plans for conduct, zeal for
5 righteous judgments and holy purposes, with integrity of mind and
great mercifulness towards all the children of truth; splendid
6 purity, and loathing for all the idols of impurity; humble conduct
with all prudence, and a faithful concealment of the mysteries of
knowledge.[1]

These are the counsels of [this] spirit for the children of truth
in the world, and the destiny [*pequddah*, visitation] of all who walk
7 in it [consists of] healing and great well-being [*shalom*] with length
of days, fruitfulness [of race], with all eternal blessings, everlasting
8 joy in eternal life and perfect glory with fullness of splendour in
eternal light [*wesimhath 'olamim behayye nesah ukhelil kabodh 'im
middath (middoth) hadhar be'or 'olamim*].

9        Now as to the spirit of wickedness—[to it belong] inordinate
desire, slackness in the service of righteousness, wrongdoing,
falsehood, arrogance and pride, dissimulation and deceit, cruelty
10 and gross profanity; quickness to anger, great foolishness, angry
insolence, deeds of abomination with an adulterous spirit, and ways
11 of impurity in the service of uncleanness; a blasphemous tongue,
blindness of eyes and dullness of ears, stubbornness and obtuseness,
so as to walk in all the ways of darkness and crafty purpose.

12        Now the destiny [visitation] of all who walk [in this spirit] is
a multitude of afflictions at the hands of all the afflicting angels,

---

[1] It would perhaps be a rewarding study to compare in detail the 'ways' of the
'spirits' with the 'fruits of the spirit' and the 'works of the flesh' in Gal. v.18ff.,
and with similar lists elsewhere.   Three of the 'ways' of the 'spirit of truth' are
closely parallel to the Pauline 'fruits of the spirit': 'humility' ('*anawah*) =πραΰτης;
'long suffering' ('*erekh 'appaim*) =μακροθυμία; 'goodness' (lit. eternal goodness) (*tubh
'olamim*) =ἀγαθοσύνη: 'compassion' (great compassion, *robh rahamim*) is not far
removed from χρηστότης; even πίστις may be held to be represented by the 'strong
wisdom believing in all the works of God and relying on His great mercy', 1 QS
iv.3ff.

everlasting ruin through the furious anger of a vengeful God; 13
everlasting terror, eternal ignominy, with the shame of destruction
in the fire of the dark regions.   And all their times in their
generations will be in mourning and grief, in bitter misfortunes
and dark calamities, until their destruction without remnant or 14
survivor for them.

Under these [two spirits] are the generations of all the sons 15
of men, and all their hosts in their classes have an inheritance in
one or the other [lit. in their divisions]; and in their ways do they 16
walk, and in either of them [lies] all their action and conduct,
according to the inheritance of each, whether great or little [in the
two spirits] in equal parts until the last period, and He has put 17
everlasting enmity between the one and the other [lit. between
their divisions]; an abomination to truth are the deeds of wickedness, and an abomination to wickedness are all the ways of truth.
Bitter contention lies between all their ways, for they cannot walk 18
together.

Now God, in the mysteries of His understanding and by His
glorious wisdom has appointed an end for the existence of wickedness; and at the season of Visitation [*pequddah*], He will destroy it 19
forever.   The truth of the world will emerge victorious [appear
forever], for it [the world] lies in the defiling ways of evil under
the dominion of wickedness until the season of the decreed judgment [*mishpaṭ neḥeresah*].   Then God will cleanse by His truth all 20
the deeds of a man [men], and will refine Him some of the children
of men in order to abolish every wicked spirit out of the midst of
their flesh; and to cleanse them by a holy spirit from all evil deeds; 21
and He will sprinkle upon him a spirit of truth like purifying water
[to cleanse him] from all lying abominations and from defilement
by the spirit of impurity.   Thus He will give the upright insight 22
into the knowledge of the Most High and the wisdom of the sons
of heaven; to give wisdom to the perfect way; for God has chosen
them for an eternal covenant; and to them belongs all the glory 23
of Adam.   And there shall be no more wickedness, and there will
be put to shame all deceitful works.

Until now the spirits of truth and wickedness strive within the
heart of man; men walk in wisdom and in folly.   According as a 24
man's inheritance is in truth and righteousness, he hates wickedness.   If, however, the lot of his inheritance is with wickedness
and wrongdoing, then he abhors the truth.   For God has set them 25
in equal parts until the decreed end and the New Creation ['*asoth*
*ḥadhasha*].   He knows their actions and deeds to all the ends of. . . . 26

## Dualistic World-View

This section contains the Qumran Essene doctrine of evil. The basic conception is that of an ethical dualism, similar to that of the New Testament and with special affinities with the Johannine writings. The world is divided sharply into a sphere of light under the dominion of the 'prince of lights' and the 'spirit of truth', and a realm of darkness ruled by the 'angel of darkness' and the 'spirit of perversity' (wickedness, *'awel*). The author does not hesitate to attribute evil as well as good to God ('He created the spirits of light . . . and darkness'), but is not further interested in the metaphysical problem, but in the realities of good and evil which his doctrine is intended to illumine. In this respect he stands in the Hebrew and Biblical, not the Greek tradition, though in comparison with the New Testament his speculative interest is slightly more pronounced: but it is in no way comparable to the later speculations and mythological systems of Gnosticism.

The sources and background of his doctrine of the two spirits are to be traced in the apocalyptic writings, for example in the Testament of Judah xx: 'Know therefore, my children, that two spirits wait upon man, the spirit of truth and the spirit of error' (τὸ τῆς πλάνης [πνεῦμα]), where the function of the 'spirit of truth' is 'to bear witness to all things and to indict [condemn] all things' (τὸ πνεῦμα τῆς ἀληθείας μαρτυρεῖ πάντα, καὶ κατηγορεῖ πάντων. Πλάνη may render *'awel*; later in the passage it is said that 'the angel of darkness' leads astray 'the sons of righteousness' (line 21).

The closest parallels are with the Johannine writings with their ethical dualism of 'light' and 'darkness' in which men 'walk' (cf. 1 QS iii.21, 'in the ways of darkness they walk'; cf. I Jn. ii.11); the doctrine of the 'spirits' (I Jn. iv.1ff.) is also similar; St John has the same distinction between 'the spirit of truth' and 'the spirit of error' (I Jn. iv.6). The Johannine Paraclete or Spirit of Truth shares the same two functions as the 'spirit of truth' in the Testament of Judah, but in St John the Paraclete bears witness to Christ and the things that are to come and condemns the world (Jn. xiv.17; xv.26; xvi.8, 13).

## Eschatology

The remaining section (iv.15-26) is, in some respects, of even greater interest, for it provides a fairly full picture of the sect's conception of the Last Judgment. It is not, however, intended primarily as a picture of the Last Judgment, but only of the Last Judgment in relation to the theology of the two spirits. It is precarious, therefore, to argue from its silence about the Messiah that the Qumran Messiah(s) had no rôle in the *eschata*.

The term used to describe this final drama, *piquddah*, is paralleled exactly in the New Testament by ἐπισκοπή, not just in its general sense of a divine 'visitation' (for good or evil), but in the specialized meaning it has in this passage of the Last Visitation of God; cf. I Peter ii.12 (v.6, *v.l.*), '... [that the Gentiles] may by your own good works, which they behold, glorify God in the day of visitation' (ἐν ἡμέρᾳ ἐπισκοπῆς). The expression at iv.19, 'the truth of the world will emerge victorious' is partly reminiscent of Isaiah xlii.3, describing the victorious mission of the Servant of the Lord, quoted by Jesus himself at Matthew xii.20. In its doctrine of a refining or purging of a portion of mankind, the language of the *Manual* directly recalls Malachi iii.3, and the idea is identical with the mission ascribed to the 'stronger one' by the Baptist (cf. Mt. iii.12, 'whose fan is in his hand, and he will thoroughly purge his threshing floor'). The description of the cleansing of the redeemed at line 21 ('and he will sprinkle upon him a spirit of truth like purifying water') may allude to Ezekiel xxxvi.25 ('Then will I sprinkle clean water upon you. . . . A new heart also will I give you and a new spirit will I put within you'), but the closest parallel is again with the Baptist's promise of one who will baptize with 'a holy spirit' (ἐν πνεύματι ἁγιῷ). The restoration of the state before the Fall ('to them belongs all the glory of Adam') is like the 'times of restoration of all things' of Acts iii.21 (ἀποκατάστασις πάντων), and is paralleled in St Paul, II Corinthians iii.17-iv.6. No one will have any difficulty in recognizing in the '*asoth hadhasha* the 'new heaven and the new earth' of Isaiah lxv. 17ff., I Enoch xci.16, the Ἀνακαίνωσις of the Apocalypses and the 'new world' of II Baruch and the Targums; and also the οὐρανὸς καινὸς καὶ ἡ γῆ καινή of Revelation xxi.1, and the παλιγγενεσία of Matthew xix.28.

When the evidence of this passage is taken in conjunction with the eschatology of the *Damascus Document*,[1] and, in particular, the prominence in the expectation of the sect of the idea of a New Temple in a restored Jerusalem,[2] the general type of eschatology would appear to be that of an expected Kingdom of God (or New Creation) of eternal duration on the present earth, with Jerusalem (and the Temple) as its centre. And this new creation, innocent of all evil, reproduces upon earth the state of Eden before the Fall.[3]

1 QH iii.19-36 (a Hymn of Deliverance) contains some important eschatological features.

19   *I give thanks unto Thee, O Lord,*
     *For Thou hast delivered my soul from the pit;*
20   *And from Sheol Abaddon Thou hast brought me up to the*
          *summit of the world* [to heaven?].
     *I walked on a plain without bounds;*
21   *and I knew that there is hope for him whom Thou hast*
     *fashioned from dust for the communion of eternity*
     [probably the company of the angels; cf. Ps. lxxxix.7].
     *The perverse spirit Thou hast cleansed from*
     *a great transgression,*
22   *To take its place with the host of the holy*
          *ones* [angels],
     *And to enter into fellowship with the company of the*
          *sons of heaven.*
     *For Thou hast appointed to man an eternal lot* [destiny]
23   *with the spirits that have intelligence,*
     *To praise Thy name together with them*
     *And to recount Thy wonders before all Thy works* [creatures].

24   *But I, creature of clay*
     *fashioned with water, what am I?*
     *Of what worth am I esteemed and what strength do I have?*

*For I was set in the circle of wickedness,*
25    *And with the froward was I assigned.*
*But Thou didst disturb my wretched soul with great alarms;*
*And fearful misfortune accompanied my steps,*
26    *As all the snares of the pit opened themselves.*
*All the nets of wickedness were spread out,*
*And the net of the froward upon the waters,*
27    *While all the arrows of the pit flew without being repelled,*
*And were shot forth relentlessly.*

27b    *As the measuring rod justly falls,*
28    *And the lot [of destruction] upon the forsaken;*
*And the outpouring of wrath on dissemblers,*
*And a period of fury for all Belial.*
*And bands of death encompass, without deliverance.*
29    *The rivers of Belial overflow all their lofty banks,*
*Like fire, devouring all that draw from them by their floods,*
30    *To consume every thing, green tree and dry, by their streams.*
*And it [the flood] roves about with tongues [as it were]*
      *of flame*
*Till there is no creature who drinks there.*

31    *The foundations of asphalt it [the fire] consumes*
    *and the firmament of the dry land.*
*The foundations of the mountains are*
    *given over to burning;*
*The roots of flint become torrents of pitch.*
32    *It consumes unto the great abyss.*
*The torrents of Belial burst into Abaddon.*
*The prisoners of the abyss make a roaring sound,*
    *throwing up mire,*
33    *And the earth cries out because of the disasters that*
    *are come upon the world.*
*And all its inhabitants cry aloud,*
*And all upon the earth rush madly to and fro:*
34    *They stagger in great disaster;*
*For God thunders with the noise of his strength,*
*And His holy abode resounds with his true glory;*
35    *The host of heaven utters its voice;*
*The foundations of the world tremble and reel;*
36    *The battle of the warriors of heaven sweeps across*
    *the world,*

*And returns not until it is finished and ended for ever
and ever.*[1]

Dupont-Sommer takes verses 19-23 to imply the immortality of the soul, comparing Josephus *B.J.* II.viii.11, where the belief is attributed to the Essenes that 'the soul, once detached from the ties of the flesh, . . . takes its joyful flight towards the heights . . .'.   The 'unsought level places' is translated by him as 'endless plain' and identified with the Elysian Fields of Pythagorean and Essene belief (cf. Josephus loc. cit.).   But the expression is an obscure one; nor is there any evidence in the passage which proves that the Qumran Essenes believed in the immortality of the soul as distinct from the body.   The suggestion has been made that their doctrine of immortality is similar to that of the New Testament conception of a 'spiritual body' and of I Enoch's 'garments of glory', but this also is doubtful.[2]

There seems to me to be no doubt, however, that as

---

[1] The hymn as it stands cannot be treated as a unity, and the breaks which are indicated in the translation seem to be the natural ones.   Lines 24-27a describe disasters that God is said to have sent upon the writer; these may include the 'period of fury for all Belial' of lines 27b-30, so that the division made at line 27a-b may not be a true one; lines 27b-30 can, however, be held to be a single and independent literary unit.

The division at line 31 of the last section is even more important.   It seems to mark a quite separate unit of composition united with the foregoing by the mere association of the terms for fire, conflagration, etc.   The reason is quite plain: in lines 29-30 fire is a mere metaphor for the overflowing floods of Belial, whereas in lines 31-36 it is no metaphor, but a grim eschatological reality.   The closing verses of the hymn (lines 35-36) oblige us further to divide it in this way: these verses underline the main theme, the End of all things and the vengeance of God by the armies of Heaven.   Here we have a brief description of the Armageddon of the *War* scroll.   What is of special interest is that Armageddon accompanies the fiery conflagration of the world.

The vivid description of the torrents of fire suggests that the author is describing an actual earthquake he has witnessed (note line 32, 'throwing up mire' (lava?)), perhaps one of those which caused the partial destruction of the monastery at Qumran in 64 or 31 B.C.   (Cf. Dupont-Sommer, *The Jewish Sect of Qumran and the Essenes*, p. 169.)   It may be from such experiences of actual earthquake that the expectation of world-destruction by fire arose.   The Biblical inspiration of this Essene doctrine may have been Ezek. xxxviii.22; cf. the allusions to this verse in the *War* scroll, infra, p. 153, n. 1.

[2] 1 QS iv.6ff. declares that those who walk according to the 'spirit of truth' will be rewarded by 'all everlasting blessings, and eternal rejoicing in the victorious life of eternity, and a crown of glory, together with raiment of majesty in eternal light' (Brownlee, op. cit.).   Brownlee compares with his translation I Peter v.4 (crown of glory) and I Enoch lxii.15 (garments of glory).   Cf., however, K. G. Kuhn, *Zeitschrift für Theologie und Kirche*, Jahrgang 49, 1952, Heft 3, *Die Sektenschrift und die iranische Religion*, p. 299, n. 1; he renders 'das Vollkommene der Herrlichkeit und das Vollmass des Glanzes in ewigen Licht'.   Over against 'joy in eternal life' (*ḥayye neṣaḥ* = ζωὴ αἰώνιος) is set the fire of the dark regions ('*esh maḥashakim*) (13).

contrasted with Sadducaean doctrine, the Zadokites did believe in a doctrine of immortal or eternal life. This is implied by the contrast between 'joy in eternal life', and the 'fire of the dark regions'[1]; the expression '(ever)lasting life' (ḥayye neṣaḥ) can only be the ζωὴ αἰώνιος of the New Testament. It is true the concept of 'eternity' is a quite different one in modern thought from the ancient Hebrew idea,[2] but in the case of the '(ever)lasting life' of the scrolls, we are almost certainly intended to take the term in the meaning of a life without any cessation by death.[3]   The clue to an understanding of the eschatology of the scrolls in this connection is to be found in its doctrine of the 'Ανακαίνωσις. The world is to be restored to its 'paradisiacal' state before the Fall; the glory which Adam lost at the Fall is to be restored to the renewed mankind,[4] sin and evil are to be banished from the earth,[5] and a renewed and obedient mankind are to live on for a thousand generations, an expression which in fact practically means 'eternal life'.[6]   Thus Adam is restored to his state before the Fall and lives for ever in his new Paradise.

The nature of this eternal life is given distinctive expression in the scrolls by the idea that the loyal covenanters will enjoy an angelic existence.   They are not only to live like angels and consort with angels, but to become as angels. The thought has no doubt developed out of the idea of God coming to dwell with men with His holy angels in a restored Temple in Jerusalem; we may compare Ezekiel xxxvii.27-28

[1] See previous note.

[2] 'olam means 'long-lastingness', and has a wide usage.  Cf. I Macc. xiv.41: 'Simon should be their governor and high priest *forever* (LXX εἰς τὸν αἰῶνα) until there should arise a faithful prophet.'  This does not mean, however, that 'olam *cannot have the sense of everlasting, eternal*.  Cf. F. Nötscher, Zur Theologischen Terminologie der Qumran-Texte, Bonn, 1956 (Bonner Biblische Beitrage, 10), p. 149ff.

[3] Cf. infra, p. 141.

[4] 1 QS iv.23, cf. CD v.5-6: 'God in His wonderful mysteries forgave their iniquity . . . and built them a sure house in Israel.  They that hold fast to it are destined for the life of eternity (ḥayye neṣaḥ) and all the glory of Adam is theirs.'

[5] 1 QS iv.18, 19, 23: God will destroy evil forever and there will be no more wrongdoing.

[6] CD vii(xix).5-6: ' . . . all those who walk in these things in the perfection of holiness . . . the Covenant of God standeth fast to preserve them to a thousand generations.'  Cf. H. W. Robinson, Inspiration and Revelation in the Old Testament, Clarendon Press, 1946, p. 119: 'The conception of eternity is reached by piling up limited time-periods, as with reference to a thousand generations in equivalence to 'olam.'

and especially Zechariah iii.7, xiv.5.   1 QS iv.22-23[1] speaks of
the cleansed spirit of man possessing the wisdom of the 'sons
of heaven' (angels).   The idea of likeness to the angels
occurs again in the *Benedictions* 1 QSb Cols. III, IV along
with a reference to God's Holy Dwelling-place in which the
covenanter is to find his place:

## Col. III.22-28:     [*Blessing on the Priests*]

22    *The words of blessing for the sage, for the blessing*
      *of the Bene Zadoq, the priests, whom God has*
      *chosen to confirm His Covenant. . . .*

25    *The Lord bless thee from His Holy Dwelling-*
      *place, and make thee a crown of*

26    *glory in the midst of the holy ones* [the
      saints or the angels, cf. infra], *and renew*
      *for thee the covenant of eternal priesthood*
      *and give thee thy place in* [His] *Holy*

27    *Dwelling-place; and by thy deeds he will*
      *judge all rulers* [*lit. noble ones*], *and by what proceeds*

28    *from thy mouth all the princes of the peoples.*
      *He will give you as an inheritance the*
      *first-fruits of all choice portions, and the*
      *counsel of all mankind will He bless by Thy hand.*

## Col. IV.24b-28:

25    *And thou shalt be as an angel of the Presence in*
      *the holy Dwelling-place, the glory of the*
      *God of hosts shall thou serve forever . . . serving in the*

26    *Temple of the Kingdom* [*of God*], *sharing*
      *in the lot of the Angels of the Presence and*
      *in the Council of the community of the people of*
      *the holy ones* [angels] *for ever and for ever.*

27    *For all His judgments are truth; and He will*
      *set* [*make*] *thee as holiness in His*
      *people, and as a great luminary to illumine*
      *the world with knowledge and the faces of*

28    *the many . . . as one consecrated* [*nezer*] *unto*
      [*for*] *the holy of holies, for thou shalt declare*
      *Him holy and glorify His name and His holiness.*

[1] See supra, p. 133.

It seems natural to interpret the Holy Dwelling-place as the Sanctuary in a (future) restored Jerusalem; and this may be the correct interpretation.   But it may also be understood to refer to the Holy Dwelling-place of God in heaven—the heavenly Paradise of God located by the Qumran Essenes in the north.[1]   In that case the sect's doctrine of immortality is identical with that of Luke xx.35ff. where in the Resurrection men and women become ἰσάγγελοι in heaven:

Οἱ δὲ καταξιωθέντες τοῦ αἰῶνος ἐκείνου τυχεῖν . . . οὔτε γαμοῦσιν οὔτε γαμίζονται· οὐδὲ γὰρ ἀποθανεῖν ἔτι δύνανται, ἰσάγγελοι γάρ εἰσιν, καὶ υἱοί εἰσιν Θεοῦ τῆς ἀναστάσεως υἱοὶ ὄντες.

Père Milik has (I believe) suggested that the north-south orientation of the graves at Qumran (with the head at the south end) was dictated by the wish that at the general Resurrection the pious Covenanter would rise to gaze on the Paradise of God in the north.

It is virtually certain that the sect had some form of belief in the Resurrection, though, so far, no unambiguously clear evidence for such has been produced.   Indeed, on the contrary, a number of passages appear to imply the old Biblical idea of Sheol, which seems to rule out, not only every form of belief in the Resurrection, but also, no less, any kind of hope of immortality.   For instance, 1 QS xi.20-22:

> For what, indeed, is the son of man among
>   Thy marvellous works . . .
> From dust is he formed and the food
>   of worms is his portion. . . .

No doubt the Psalmist is here thinking of old, unredeemed man, but it is also possible that the old Sheol concept survived, and was used in such contexts.   Side by side with it, however, is the Gehenna concept[2] so that we must also be prepared to find the ideas of immortality and resurrection.

The passage most frequently cited as evidence for a belief of some kind in a resurrection is 1 QH vi.29-34[3]:

[1] Cf. P. Grelot, 'La Géographie mythique d'Hénoch et ses sources orientales', J. T. Milik, 'Hénoch au pays des aromates', in *RB*, 65, 1958, pp. 33ff., 70ff.
[2] Cf. supra, p. 139.
[3] Cf., for example, Nötscher, op. cit. p. 151.

29    *Then will the sword of God come swiftly at the period*
          *of the judgment*
30    *And all the sons of His truth*
          *shall arise* [ya'uru]
          *. . . and all the sons of wickedness will*
          *cease to be . . .*
34    *And those that sleep in the dust*
          [shok hebhe 'aphar] *shall*
          *raise up a standard,*
       *And the worm among men* [among the
          dead] *lift up a sign. . . .*

A certain ambiguity, however, cannot be removed entirely
from the passage. The 'rising' of the sons of truth need not
refer to any resurrection, and, indeed, in the light of the
parallel ('and all the sons of wickedness will cease to be'),
the natural sense is that of the 'rising up' of the 'sons of
light' to do victorious battle with the sons of darkness. The
next line may refer, however, by way of contrast, to the
resurrection of the dead: it recalls Daniel xii.2, and verse 29
may refer to the Last Judgment.

The final section of 1 QH iii is concerned with a picture of
the doomsday of the world. The End will be a terrible
cataclysm where torrents of fire will destroy all life on the
earth and the material world will dissolve while the army
of heaven completes the work of destruction. The picture in
the author's mind appears to be that of a vast conflagration
accompanying the collapse of the Universe.

Here again is a point of contact with the New Testament
(cf. II Peter iii.7) as well as with a number of first-century
authors; the belief in the destruction of the world by fire is
attributed to the Essenes by Hippolytus.[1]

### 'Mysteries' of Redemption

There is one further association of the term 'wonders'
and 'mysteries' which is noteworthy, especially for the background it may supply to the special use of μυστήριον in the
New Testament as applied to the 'mystery' of redemption
in the suffering of Christ (cf. Col. i.24-26). The term

[1] See his *Refutatio Omnium Haeresium*, ix.27, and cf. infra, Appendix B, p. 190.

'wonders' or 'marvels' (*pela'oth*) is applied to the afflictions
of the Qumran 'saints' of the *Hymns of Thanksgiving*.
1 QH ix.6-8, 23-27:

> But as for me from ruin to desolation
> From pains to wounds, from pangs to torment
> Is my soul brought low in Thy marvels [*niphla'othekha*].
> But Thou didst not forsake me in Thy devotion;
> At the end will my soul delight in the multitude of Thy mercies.
> (6-8)
>
> Thou hast put supplication in the mouth of Thy servant,
> And hast not rebuked my life;
> My sacrifices Thou hast not rejected
> And hast not abandoned my hope . . . (10-12)
> For Thou art my God . . . Thou wilt plead my controversy,
> For in the mystery of Thy wisdom [*beraz hokhmathekha*]
>     Thou hast chastised me . . .
> And Thy chastisement was for me joy and gladness,
> And my wounds [*were*] for healing . . .
> And contempt of mine adversaries [*became*] a crown of glory,
> My misfortunes an eternal triumph . . .
> In Thy glory did my light shine forth,
> For a light out of darkness hast Thou caused to shine.   (23-27)

The text has another point of theological interest, for the
author of the hymn not only describes himself in these verses
as the Servant of the Lord ('Thy servant'), but employs the
language of Isaiah liii to describe his afflictions.   The last
couplet

> In Thy glory did my light shine forth
> For a light out of darkness hast Thou caused to shine.

echoes the thought and language of Isaiah liii.12, in the LXX
and the first Isaiah scroll: 'from the travail of his soul he
shall shed forth light and shall be satisfied'; we may compare
further 1 QH iv.27, 'And through me Thou hast illumined
the face of the Many, for Thou hast caused me to become
acquainted with the secrets of Thy wonders [*beraze pela'ekha*].'
No less significant are the words, 'my wounds were for
healing'; 'healing' is to be understood in the sense of the
divine pardon and forgiveness, for at 1 QH ii.8 we read

'... I became a snare for sinners, but healing for all that turned from transgression' (cf. Is. liii.4-5).

This language of redemptive suffering in such terms as 'Thy marvels', the 'mystery' of divine wisdom, raises acutely the question of the identity of the 'Servant' in these hymns, a problem to which I shall return in the next chapter.

# CHAPTER VII

# The Qumran Messiah and Related Beliefs

Until the actual discoveries in the caves, our only source of information on the subject of the Messiah of the Qumran or Zadokite sect was the so-called *Zadokite Fragments*, originally found in the Cairo Geniza and first edited by Solomon Schechter in 1910,[1] but now known to go back to an archetype from Qumran. The paucity and perplexing nature of this evidence posed more problems than were ever solved, and in the absence of other available sources, speculation tended to take the place of scientific hypotheses.

The situation has been changed by the new discoveries and their availability in recent editions. Ideas about the Messianic beliefs of the Qumran sect are now beginning to crystallize and take more definite shape; and the last text containing evidence on the subject has not yet been published.

Two main positions are held: 1. The first, based largely on the Zadokite Fragments, holds to the conception of a single Messiah, 'the Messiah of Aaron and Israel'. This was the view of Schechter, R. H. Charles, I. Lévi, M.-J. Lagrange, and others, and it has been maintained, in relation to the new evidence, by W. H. Brownlee, M. Lambert, and others. 2. According to the second view, the expectations of the sect were centred on a triumvirate of eschatological deliverers, of which the last two are claimed as Messiahs, the first being the prophet like Moses foretold at Deut. xviii.15, 18: the first Messiah is a High Priest, the second the Davidic Messiah of conventional Jewish belief, but with some new features. This view is maintained by scholars such as Millar Burrows,[2] L. Ginzberg, J. T. Milik, D. Barthélemy, K. G. Kuhn, L. H. Silbermann, among others.

For the two 'Messiahs' of Qumran, the primary documents for our consideration are, (a) the so-called *Serekh*

---

[1] *Documents of Jewish Sectaries*, Vol. I.
[2] 'The Messiahs of Aaron and Israel', *Anglican Theological Review*, 34, 1952, 203ff.

*ha'edhah* ( 1 QSa); ( *b* ) the collection of *Benedictions* published after the *Serekh ha'edhah* in the Barthélemy-Milik volume; ( *c* ) the *War* Scroll ( published by the University of Jerusalem ),[1] and finally ( *d* ) the *Zadokite Fragments* ( or *Damascus Document* ). The *Hodayoth* or *Hymns*, published in the Jerusalem University volume, raise a number of special problems, and I content myself here with one allegedly Messianic text.

The text of the 1 QSa passage is given in translation above (p. 102). The important words are those rendered 'in the event of God "begetting" [or sending] the Anointed One to be with them', and the description 'the Messiah of Israel' ( *meshiaḥ Israel* ).

The expression 'Messiah of Israel' is unique: it does not appear in the Old Testament, nor apparently in any form of later Judaism (in the Old Testament the king is always 'the Anointed of Yahweh ( *meshiaḥ Yahweh* )'). In the Zadokite Documents the expression is *mashiaḥ min Aaron we 'Israel*. In its context in the *Serekh* it obviously refers to the secular leader of Israel *par excellence*, the Messiah who is to be a mighty warrior for his people; just as the High Priest, who precedes him, is accompanied by the order of priests, so 'the Anointed One of Israel' takes his place with the 'heads of [the companies of] thousands', each being seated 'according to their station in the camps, and according to their campaigns', that is, according to military rank and experience. The 'Anointed of Israel' is thus clearly here the Warrior 'Messiah' in the familiar and traditional Jewish sense; and this must be one of the earliest uses of the expression in a non-Biblical document. The regulations about precedence (as we have seen[2]) are clearly designed to put this secular head, the Anointed of Israel, in his proper place in the hierocracy, a place subordinate to the High Priest.

As we have also seen above (p. 109), the scriptural basis for the ideal eschatological Banquet here described is to be found at Ezekiel xliv.3, which itself describes the sacred meal in the Temple to be celebrated at the entrance into the new Temple in the new Jerusalem of Ezekiel's Davidic Prince or

---

[1] Ed. E. L. Sukenik.
[2] Supra, p. 104ff.

Plate 12 (above) The Research Room, Musée de Jerusalem; in the foreground Père J. T. Milik, and, at the window, Père J. Starcky, engaged in deciphering the fragments. (Sabine Weiss/Rapho, Paris)

Plate 13 (right) The reconstructed 'bench' or 'table' thought to have come from the scriptorium of the monastery. See p. 110, n. 3. (Palestine Archaeological Museum)

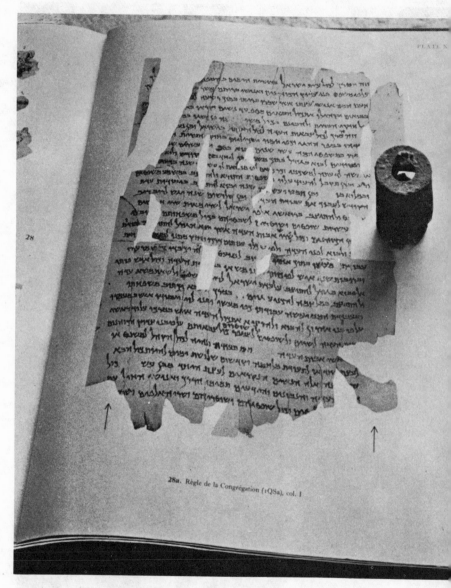

28

28a. Règle de la Congrégation (1QSa), col. I

*Plate 14* This scroll is the appendix to the *Manual of Discipline*, known as the
*Serekh ha'edhah* or *Rule of the Congregation*, and contains the passage describing
the sacred meal of the sect. See p. 102ff . (*Sabine Weiss/Rapho, Paris*)

*Nasi'*. The Ezekiel reference is to the Messianic Prince's participation in a Temple festal meal. The importance of Ezekiel generally for the sect, and the fact that their secular leader, the Messiah of Israel, is called (as we shall see) *Nasi'*, is further evidence for this connection. The Banquet is already an eschatological one in Ezekiel, that is, it is to take place at the fulfilment of Ezekiel's ideal for inauguration of his new Temple; the *Serekh* is no doubt giving the Zadokite version, based on Ezekiel, of the Messianic Banquet of the Apocalypses. In these circumstances it is not surprising to find the Anointed One of Israel subordinate to the High Priest; the Banquet is to be celebrated in a hierocratic Israel.

It is the evidence of this passage in 1 QSa which has provided the main basis for the theory of the two Messiahs of the sect, with parallels in the Old Testament, the Pseudepigrapha and later Jewish history. The theory has been most fully elaborated by K. G. Kuhn,[1] who draws attention further to the reading 'Messiahs of Aaron and Israel' at 1 QS ix.11 (in a passage where reference is also made to the coming of 'the prophet'), and to a parallel with the Testaments of the Twelve Patriarchs (Levi xviii and Judah xxiv), and the Moses-Aaron, Joshua-Zerubbabel, and, in later times, Eleazar-Bar-Cochba partnership. It is assumed that the *Serekh* is describing an eschatological banquet with *the two Messiahs* of the sect taking part in their appropriate rank.

That the Zadokite hierocracy envisaged a High Priest as its future 'ecclesiastical' Head need not be questioned. But the claim that he was also viewed as a 'Messiah' in the same sense (though with different functions) as 'the Messiah of Israel' must, I think, be viewed with reserve. The fact that the High Priest takes precedence of the Messiah of Israel may mean very little; presumably he would do so in any Temple rite or priestly function, but this does not mean that we are to regard the High Priest as in the strict sense a 'Messianic' figure. No doubt also in the ideal Temple of Ezekiel, the High Priest would take precedence of the Prince on 'ecclesiastical' occasions: but it is the Prince who is the

---

[1] 'Die beiden Messias Aarons und Israels', in *NTS*, 1, 168ff.; see also *The Scrolls and the New Testament*, p. 54ff.

deliverer of Israel and to the Prince alone belongs the honour of entering the Temple by the gate or 'porch' of the Lord (Ezek. xliv.1ff.).   The evidence of the parallels from the Testaments is to some extent invalidated by the fact that Christian influences have been strongly at work in the redaction of the Greek version.   The parallels from Zechariah and the Bar-Cochba situation support, if anything, *the superiority of the secular Head*.   The text of Zechariah vi.9ff. is notoriously corrupt, but the text of the LXX at V. 13 favours the substitution of the name of Zerubbabel for Joshua at V. 11; in the Bar-Cochba period, it was the secular leader who mattered. The textual tradition of Zechariah vi.9ff. reveals a conflict of claims to pre-eminence, priestly versus secular.

So far as the scrolls are concerned, the figure who emerges clearly in the *Serekh* and is called 'the Messiah of Israel' is the secular leader, the Warrior Messiah; and the fact that he takes second place to the High Priest on certain occasions is not sufficient in itself to warrant the inference that the High Priest too was a 'Messianic' figure in the same sense.

Before we speak about 'Messiah' or 'Messiahs' in these documents some further reflection seems desirable on the use of the expression (and title) 'Messiah'.   As a *terminus technicus* it undoubtedly was coined at a much later period. The eschatological leaders of this sect could all be called 'anointed ones', just as the prophets were.

What I am concerned to point out here is that *the Anointed One par excellence*, as in all subsequent Jewish tradition, was the secular leader; and this pre-eminence, if it has not become absolute, is beginning to emerge in such texts based on the 'Messianic' expectations of Ezekiel for a Prince of the lineage of David.   The High Priest plays no significant rôle in Ezekiel, and indeed is scarcely mentioned.

One further verse in the *Serekh* is in line with the conception of a single *Anointed One* as the central figure.   There are differences of reading and interpretation of the important words 'when God begets or sends the Messiah to be with them', though they do not affect the main position as I have reported it, namely, that these verses describe an eschatological Session of the Council *in the event of the Messiah being present.* The text seems to read: 'The following is a Session when God *begets* the Messiah [to be] with them.'[1] This may contain an allusion to Ezekiel xxxvi.12: its ultimate source I would suggest, however, is to be found in a Messianic interpretation of Psalm ii.7: 'Thou art my son; this day have I begotten thee [ילדתיך]'.

A parallel has been found in 1 QH iii.7-10, which reads as follows:

> *And I was in distress as a woman in travail,*
> *Bringing forth her first-born,*
> *For [her] birth-throes came suddenly,*
> *And agonizing pain to her pangs,*
> *To cause writhing in the womb of the pregnant one,*
> *For children have come to the pains of death;*
> *And she who conceived a male-child*
>    *was distressed by her pain;*
> *For with the 'waves of death' she shall be*
>    *delivered of a man-child,*
> *And with pains of Sheol there shall break*
>    *forth from the womb of the pregnant one*
> *A Wondrous Counsellor in his might.*
>    (cf. Is. ix.6)

W. H. Brownlee, who was among the first to call attention to this hymn,[2] identified the male-child with the Messiah; and the application to the man-child of the Hymn of the Messianic *testimonium* of Is. ix.6 'a Wonder of a Counsellor with his Might' is striking. Brownlee argues that the mother of the Messiah is the 'Essene Community'. The poet compares himself with a pregnant woman about to give birth: but like the 'I' of the Psalter he appears here to be speaking as representative of Israel or the faithful congregation of Israel; it is the true faithful Israel (and this sect is identified with it), which is the mother of the Messiah. J. Chamberlain[3] has noted the close parallel in Rev. xii.1ff.

---

[1] Milik proposed to read *yolikh* for *yolidh* and render: ' . . . in the event of God *sending* the Messiah [to be] with them', and this is how the text is translated: *yolidh* is, however, left in the text and Père Barthélemy states that after a very careful study of the text in ultra-violet light this reading seemed practically certain.

[2] *Interpretation*, 9, 1, Jan. 1955: 'John the Baptist in the New Light of Ancient Scrolls', p. 79. Cf. also *NTS*, 3, 24ff. A survey of recent literature on the hymns will be found in this article. See also O. Betz, 'Die Geburt der Gemeinde durch den Lehrer,' in *NTS*, 3, 314ff.    [3] *Interpretation*, loc. cit.

where the mother of the male-child, threatened by the Dragon, and who is to rule all nations with a rod of iron, is the true Israel. Though the hymn is employing the imagery of poetry, its apocalyptic language is also striking; through the birth of the man-child the world is to be overwhelmed as by a flood, and the enemies of Israel destroyed and engulfed in hell; the gates of Sheol are to open and close on them. The hymn following (to which attention has been drawn by Dupont-Sommer) further describes the last scenes of the world as a destruction[1] by fire—a well-known feature of Essene eschatological thought.

A closer study of this remarkable hymn, however, has yielded the quite certain result that it is not of the birth of any particular individual of which the author is speaking, but of the birth of a whole community of people.[2] The figure of birth belongs to a complex of confused and interwoven figures of speech, describing the throes of Israel—a storm at sea, earthquake, and upheaval on earth. The reference to the begetting of 'sons' (*banim*) makes it quite evident that it is of *a people* and not of an individual the author is thinking. But it is clearly a people with a 'messianic' mission ('Wonderful Counsellor'); and the eschatological setting of the hymn suggests that its subject is the 'birth-pangs of the Messiah' in the sense of the emergence through trial and suffering of the redeemed Israel.

The passage is not, therefore, exactly parallel, as has been claimed, to the passage in the *Serekh*.

It is, nevertheless, a remarkable parallel to Rev. xii.1-6, and there may be some connection. The Qumran hymn, at any rate, prepares the way for the later idea of the birth of the Messiah.

The evidence next in importance for the Qumran conception of the Messiah occurs in the collection of *Benedictions* (Barthélemy-Milik, p. 110ff.). These have the same general character as the *Manual of Discipline*; they are no doubt modelled on actual benedictions employed by the sect (themselves expanded versions of the Aaronic blessing; cf. 1 QS ii.2ff.), but in this present form, at any rate, in at least one

certain case, ideal forms for a still unrealized future. They
are divided by their editors into, *a*. benediction of the faithful;
*b*. benediction of the High Priest; *c*. benediction of the
Priests[1]; *d*. benediction of the Prince, the latter clearly a
Messianic figure.

The reconstruction of the text and fragments has been a
work of considerable difficulty. The conjecturally reconstructed benediction of the High Priest is the least certain:
the editors have recognized these verses correctly as a benediction, but a certain doubt attaches to the identity of the
individual who is blessed. There is no doubt about the
identity of the *Nasi'* or *Prince of the Congregation*.

( 1 QSb v.20-28)

20  [*For the Blessing of the Prince of the Congregation, . . .*]
23  *May the Lord exalt thee to an everlasting height, and as a tower*
24  *of strength on a lofty rampart.*
     *Thou shalt smite the peoples with the power of Thy word* [*lit.
       mouth*];
     *With thy rod thou shalt lay waste . . . the earth,*
25  *And with the breath of thy lips thou shalt slay the wicked,*
     *With a spirit of counsel and eternal might;*
     *A spirit of knowledge and of the fear of God;*
26  *Righteousness shall be the girdle of Thy loins,*
     *And faithfulness the girdle of Thy reins;*
     *And He will set thy horn with iron and thy hoofs with brass . . .*
27  *. . . Thou shalt tread down the nations as mud in the streets,*
     *For God has raised thee up as the sceptre of rulers.*
28  *They shall come before thee and worship thee,*
     *And all the nations will serve thee,*
     *And by His holy name He will make thee great*
     *And thou shalt be as a lion*
     *. . . tearing and there is none to restore. . . .*

A number of traditional Messianic features reappear in
these verses, such as the slaying of the wicked with the breath
of his lips. The most important, however, are the reference
to the Lion of Judah and the Messianic prophecy of Gen.
xlix.9; the allusion to the Messiah as the Sceptre of rulers,
recalling the same prophecy, but particularly, Numbers

[1] Supra, p. 140.

xxiv.17[1]; and in lines 25-26 the application to the *nasi'* of Isaiah xi.1-2, 5: '(And there shall come forth a rod out of the stem of Jesse, and a Branch shall grow out of his roots:) and the spirit of the Lord shall rest upon him, the spirit of wisdom and understanding, the spirit of counsel and might, the spirit of knowledge and of fear of the Lord . . . (5) and righteousness shall be the girdle of his loins and faithfulness the girdle of his reins.'[2]    Here is the Davidic Warrior Messiah in his most familiar Old Testament form.    Highly significant, however, is the avoidance of the title 'king' and its substitute *nasi'*; the form of the Messianic hope is clearly that of the closing chapters of Ezekiel (cf. especially Ezek. xlv, xlvi, xlviii), and I want to suggest again that it is in these chapters we are to look for the key to the Zadokite ideal of a new Israelite hierocracy.

The text of the scroll entitled 'The War of the Sons of Light against the Sons of Darkness' presents many difficulties, and these are increased by its frequent *lacunae* (part of the end of every folio is lost).    It is still uncertain with whom we are to identify the 'Sons of Darkness', whether with the Seleucids and Ptolemies or the Romans; the 'Sons of Light' are the true Israel, no doubt as represented by the Qumran sect.

The greater portion of the text is occupied with a description of a battle-scene, and with detailed regulations for its conduct, the deployment of forces, their description, with accounts of the banners, trumpets, etc. which go into considerable detail.[3]    The central interest of the writer is a priestly one.    The regulations are designed to ensure that this holy warfare should be conducted according to the rules of the priestly code: thus, though the High Priest and Levites play an important part in the battle, the former in passing in front of the ranks and addressing the army, and the latter in sounding the trumpets for attack and retreat etc.,

---

[1] The *Damascus Document* (at ix.8-10) equates the Sceptre with the 'Prince of the Congregation', and the same individual is apparently meant as 'the Messiah of Aaron and Israel'.

[2] In 1 QH iii.13, we may have another 'Messianic' reference from Isaiah: 'Thou didst make me a standard to the chosen of righteousness'; cf. Is. xi.10.

[3] On the basis of the measurements and descriptions of the various weapons, Mr Yadin of the Hebrew University has assigned the scroll to the Roman period; the weapons are alleged to correspond with Roman weapons.

the priests are forbidden any part in the actual battle which involves contact with blood or with the slain (Pl. 24, line 8ff.).

The whole account is a *tour de force* of priestly imagination, out-romancing the Chronicler himself in some of his military operations. The Battle is an ideal one still to be fought out in the visionary future; and like so much else in the Qumran texts is again a kind of blue-print, in this case for an Apocalyptic or Messianic War which will finally bring to an end the oppressions and sufferings of Israel at the hands of one of the great Empires and place the true Israel, as represented and led by this priestly sect, in the dominant world-rôle now occupied by her enemies, the Kittiim.

The first two folios describe wars, extending over a lengthy period of years, against Israel's traditional enemies, and the list, compiled from the Old Testament, appears to be an entirely artificial and imaginary one. The clue to an understanding of the main battle seems to be given by several references to Ezek. xxxviii (the destruction of the armies of Gog investing Jerusalem,[1] and by the statements in the first folio that the final conflict with the Kittiim is 'an appointed Day', 'the Day of Destruction',[2] lines 10, 11. When this is taken together with an earlier statement in the same folio (line 3) that the warfare is to take place 'at the return of the Captivity of the sons of light from the desert of the nations to encamp in the desert of Jerusalem', we are perhaps justified in concluding that the final battle-scene is an account of Armageddon, based mainly on the Gog prophecy of Ezekiel. This is confirmed by the fact that the battle-scene takes place with Jerusalem as its base, the priests and the divisions of the army emerging for the battle from the gates of the city.

---

[1] Pl. 26, lines 15-18, cf. Ezek. xxxviii.23, xxxix.1; Pl. 31, line 1, Ezek. xxxviii.21. Gog is connected with 'the mighty men of the peoples' (Pl. 26, line 13; cf. line 16), and apparently symbolizes the Kittiim, the last enemies of Israel. The Ezekiel passages to which allusion is made read: 'And I will call for a sword against him throughout all my mountains, saith the Lord God: ... and I will plead against him. ... Thus will I magnify myself; and I will be known in the eyes of many nations, and they shall know that I am the Lord.' Cf. also Pl. 27, line 8, and Pl. 34, line 2 with Ezek. xxxviii.9. The cloud to cover the land, which in Ezekiel refers to the enemies of God, is here the hosts of angels which intervene in the battle together with a figure known as 'the man of war', identified by Barthélemy-Milik with the Messiah. See infra, p. 155. Cf. J. Carmignac, *La Règle de la guerre*, Paris, 1958, p. 168.

[2] *yom howa*. Is this a cryptic allusion to the *yom Yahweh*?

The *War* scroll, if I have understood it rightly, is thus a midrashic development, in relation to the writer's own times and experience, and with, as we shall see, some striking apocalyptic features, of the description of the Day of the Lord in Ezek. xxxviii, when the exiles return to Jerusalem and are attacked by Gog and his allies. If we set the scroll (with Yadin) in the Roman period, the author may have had the investment and destruction of Jerusalem by Roman armies vividly in mind.

The most characteristic feature of the scroll is its apocalyptic element. The earthly stage where the final conflict is fought out is the mountains or desert of Jerusalem, but the whole conflict is lifted on to the plane of the supernatural by the part played by the angelic hosts and Israel's protecting angels, among them Michael himself. This is stated in so many words in the lines describing the final conflict in Pl. 16, folio 1, line 10ff.: 'A congregation of gods and an assembly of men, the sons of light, and the lot of darkness will fight together . . . with great noise and confusion and the blasts of the trumpets of gods and men on the Day of Destruction.' It reappears again in the scroll (Pl. 28, lines 10-11), where mention is made of the 'Prince of Light', appointed for the help of Israel, where God is declared to have brought the angel Mastema to the pit. Later (Pl. 32, line 5ff.), after a reference to the subduing of the Prince of the dominion of darkness, God sends the glorious angel, Michael, with eternal light, to give light to Israel.

The motif of angelic help at the climax of a battle is familiar from II Maccabees x.29ff.,[1] and the *War* scroll is a development of this kind of primitive Jewish apocalyptic. The final angelic visitation or intervention, however, is described (Pl. 27, lines 6-14) in terms which may imply the presence with the angels of the Warrior Messiah, and perhaps also the High Priest, who plays so prominent a rôle in the earlier battle-scenes.

---

[1] 'But when the battle waxed strong, there appeared out of heaven unto their adversaries five men on horses with bridles of gold, in splendid array; and two of them, leading on the Jews, and taking Maccabaeus in the midst of them, and covering him with their armour, guarded him from wounds, while on the adversaries they shot forth arrows and thunderbolts; by reason whereof they were blinded and thrown into confusion, and were cut to pieces, filled with bewilderment.'

*And Thou, O God . . .*[1] *with the glory of Thy Kingdom, and the congregation of Thine angels is in our midst as an everlasting help. We shall turn kings to mockery and mighty men to scorn, for the holy one of Adonai and the King of glory* [קדוש יהוה ומלך הכבוד] *is with us, with the holy angels . . . the mighty ones, the host of the angels are with our commanders, and the mighty man of war is in our congregation, and the host of his spirits with our army. And they will cover the land as clouds and as a thick mist, and as a stream of copious showers, to cause judgment to flow for all her descendants.*

> *Arise, O Mighty One,*
> *Take Thy captivity captive, O man of glory,*
> *And take Thy spoils, O valiant one;*
> *Set Thy hand on the neck of Thine enemies,*
> *And Thy foot on the heap of the slain;*
> *Strike the nations that are Thine adversaries,*
> *And let Thy sword devour the guilty flesh,*
> *Fill Thy land with glory and Thy heritage with blessing,*
> *A multitude of cattle in Thy allotted lands,*
> *Silver and gold, and precious stones in Thy palaces;*
> *O Zion rejoice greatly,*
> *Shine forth with cries of exultation, O Jerusalem.*
> *Exult, all ye towns of Judah*
> *Open Thy gates continually to bring unto Thee the*
>     *wealth of the nations;*
> *And their kings will serve Thee*
> *And all thine oppressors will prostrate themselves*
>     *before Thee.*

A number of scholars (among them Sukenik, Dupont-Sommer, Barthélemy) have recognized the Warrior Messiah in the 'man of glory', to whom this hymn of triumph is addressed. But with whom are we to identify 'the holy one of Adonai'[2] and 'the King of glory'? If two persons are intended, the first is possibly the High Priest, who plays so prominent a rôle in the Battle; cf. the use of the expression 'holy one of Yahweh' (קדוש יהוה) at Psalm cvi.16 to designate Aaron. If this is the right explanation, then the 'King of glory' who accompanies the High Priest must be the same

---

[1] [*dost reveal Thyself?*]

[2] The hymn 'Arise, O mighty one' is repeated with introduction at Pl. 34, with an occasional variant, the most significant of which is the substitution of 'the holy one, our glorious one' for 'the holy one of Adonai'.

individual as 'the man of glory' in the following hymn, that is, the Messiah of Israel.  It is also possible, however, to regard the two expressions, 'holy one of Adonai' and 'King of glory' as in apposition, referring to one person, the Messiah.[1]

The feature of special interest for the apocalyptic of the scroll is the close association of these figures or this figure with the angelic hosts.  If the one figure is intended, this angelic intervention suggests the appearance of the Messiah as 'the man from the plains of heaven' of the Fifth Book of the Sibyllines (l. 414ff.), that is as a supernatural figure, coming to the rescue and deliverance of Israel with his legions of angels at the climax of Armageddon.  But this is almost certainly to read too much into the passage; and we have no right to assume that the eschatology of the *War* scroll is necessarily the same as that of the *Manual of Discipline*, which thinks definitely in terms of an otherworldly Divine Intervention, though it contains no reference in its account of this divine judgment to a Messiah.  We may have little more in the *War* scroll than an apocalyptic developed out of the conceptions to be found in the Second Book of Maccabees. At the same time it is clearly in the direction of the Messianism of the Ezra and Enoch apocalypses.

The *Damascus Document* contains some six references, where the description occurs, in most cases in the form 'the Messiah of [from] Aaron and Israel' (ii.10; viii.2; ix.10 (B); xv.4; xviii.8).    Attention has already been drawn to one reference where the 'Messiah of Aaron and Israel' is identified with the *nasi'* or Sceptre of Numbers xxiv.17.[2]  Not all of these references to *mashiah* necessarily refer to this figure (in one case, viii.2, the allusion to 'the anointed one' may be to Aaron[3]): most of them, however, clearly do, and the functions attributed to the 'Messiah of Aaron and Israel' agree with the statements from the sources already discussed: he is the Warrior figure, who is to come at the period of divine visita-

---

[1] The passage is translated by van der Ploeg: 'car le Seigneur saint et le roi de gloire est avec nous. . . .'   The words could be rendered 'for holy is Adonai and the King of Glory is with us', and my former pupil Dr R. Laurin suggests that the 'man of glory' in the later verses is Yahweh Himself.  Cf. also J. Carmignac, *La Règle de la Guerre*, p. 180ff.

[2] Cf. supra, p. 152.

[3] Cf. I. Lévi, *REJ*, 61, 182.  It is also possible to interpret the words as a reference to Messiahs (plur.).

tion (*pequddah*), when the 'poor of the flock' are to escape, the rest to be delivered up to the sword. So far as I can discover, nothing in the *Damascus Document* itself can be taken as pointing conclusively to the supernatural character of the Messiah (all that is said is that he will 'arise' at the end of the days).[1]

Several problems remain. 1. There is a change in title from 'Messiah of Israel' in the *Serekh ha'edhah* to 'the Messiah of Aaron and Israel'. Perhaps the second title was intended to underline the fact that, while the Messiah is the Davidic Prince, he is to rule within the hierocratic Israel of Ezekiel's prophecies. 2. More difficult is the change from the plural in 1 QS ix.11, 'the Messiahs or Anointed Ones of Aaron and Israel', to the singular in the *Damascus Document*. Kuhn explains the singular as a deliberate scribal alteration once the expectation of 'two Anointed Ones', a priestly Messiah and a secular leader, had ceased to be understood.[2] This may be the correct explanation; or the alteration may reflect a change in doctrine when a High Priestly 'Messiah' ceased to hold any interest for the sect. Perhaps too much importance has been attached in this discussion to the plural reading in 1 QS ix.11; it may in fact be a scribal error, or simply a general reference to Israel's future leaders, High Priests and secular rulers (its use in referring to the prophets has already been noted).

## THE PROPHET

The expectation of a Moses-like Prophet is found at 1 QS ix.11, and in a collection of *testimonia* or proof texts from Cave 4 (reported on by Milik, *Discoveries in the Judaean Desert*, Vol. I, p. 121ff.), where Deut. xviii.18 is followed by Numbers xxiv.15-17 (the Star and the Sceptre prophecy), and Deut. xxxiii.8-11 (the blessing of Levi by Jacob). The last two passages have been taken to refer to the

---

[1] The much discussed passage viii.10 (vi.11) which refers to the 'rising' of 'the Teacher of Righteousness' at the end of the days can be explained (with Lagrange) as referring to the Messiah and the words 'Teacher of Righteousness' regarded as a Messianic title. Cf. my article 'Theological Conceptions in the Dead Sea Scrolls', *Svensk Exegetisk Arsbok*, 18-19, 1953-4, 86. Dupont-Sommer holds that the text means that the martyred Teacher will return 'at the end of the days'. See also infra, p. . 160

[2] op. cit., *NTS*, 1, 173ff.

Messiah of the sect and the eschatological High Priest (the priestly Messiah).[1]

There is reason to believe that the expectation of a Moses-like Prophet was one of the liveliest popular beliefs in pre-Christian Judaism. Critical opinion has been divided on the question whether this figure was a Messianic one in Judaism; Bultmann maintains against Jeremias that the recognition of Deut. xviii.15 as a Messianic proof-text was a purely Christian, never a Jewish insight.[2] There is general agreement, however, that it was an extraordinarily influential form of belief, among Samaritans as well as among Jews and Christians; we learn this from patristic writers and from Josephus as well as from the New Testament.[3] In the New Testament itself, the Moses-Messiah typology lies behind far more in St Matthew's Gospel than the Sermon on the Mount. The 'Prophet' reappears as a Jewish figure in St John; at i.31 the Baptist is asked if he is the Prophet, and after the miracle of the Feeding, the people cry: 'This is of a truth the prophet that cometh into the world' (vi.14; cf. vii.40). In this last case (vi.14) John may have preserved the most primitive tradition of the story, for in representing Jesus as a 'second Moses' repeating the miracle of the manna, he is making Him fulfil a Jewish expectation that a miraculous feeding, like the manna, would be performed by the second Moses-like Deliverer.[4]

This form of expectation is one of the most striking points of contact between Samaritanism and the Scrolls, for it is well known that the so-called 'Samaritan Messiah' the Taeb (the title 'Messiah' is never applied to him) was conceived either as a returning Moses (the name Taeb means either the Restorer or the Returning One), or as a *Moses secundarius*. The prophetic function and character of the Samaritan Taeb are described in one of our oldest Samaritan sources, an Aramaic liturgical hymn for the Day of Atonement.[5]

---

[1] Cf. Milik, loc. cit., and J. M. Allegro, *JBL*, 75, 1956, 182ff.
[2] *Das Evangelium des Johannes*, p. 61.
[3] Cf. F. W. Young, 'Jesus the Prophet', in *JBL*, 68, 285ff.
[4] Cf. Keim, *Jesus of Nazara*, Vol. 4, p. 197ff.
[5] See A. Hilgenfeld, *Zeitschrift für wissenschaftliche Theologie*, 37, 1894, p. 234, and A. E. Cowley, *Expositor*, 5th series, 1, 1895, p. 163. The poem is attributed to

*When he is born in peace*
*His majesty shall shine forth in the heavens*
*    and the earth,*
*And his star in the midst of its heavens.*
*When the Taheb groweth up, his righteousness*
*    shall be revealed.*
*The Lord shall call him and teach him*
*    his laws.*
*He shall give him a new scripture and clothe*
*    him with prophecy.*

(Cowley's translation)

The hymn goes on to describe the restoration of the 'true worship' of the Tabernacle on Mount Gerizim at the coming of the Taeb: 'Then the Tabernacle shall be discovered . . . the Table and the Candlestick, the Ark of the Covenant and its Tables . . . (cf. *Antiq.* XVIII.iv.1). The Priest [that is, the High Priest] shall offer his incense, and go into the Tabernacle and make atonement . . . for all the Congregation of Israel.' A time of prosperity follows:

*Water shall flow from his [the Taeb's]*
*    vessels [cf. Jn. iv.13, 14],*
*And his king [malko] will be greater than Gog,*
*And his kingdom shall be exalted.*

The Taeb's king corresponds to the Zadokite 'Messiah of Israel', and the eschatological High Priest to the Zadokite high-priestly Deliverer.[1]

This Samaritan type of messianism provides a clue to a hitherto obscure problem in *CD*. According to *CD* ix.39, the 'Messiah of Aaron and Israel' was apparently expected to appear within forty years of the death of the Teacher of Righteousness. The description of the latter in these Fragments strongly suggests that the sect regarded him as the second Moses[2]; in that case the Messianic king was expected to accompany him, and the (unrealized) belief that he would

Abisha ben Pinhas (fourteenth century A.D.) but incorporates traditional Samaritan material.

[1] Neither Hilgenfeld nor Cowley recognized the clear distinction which is here made between the Taeb or second Moses himself and 'the Priest' and 'the king' who accompanies his appearance. The reading of the text, however, is quite clear.

[2] Cf. J. Jeremias, Article Μωϋσῆς, *Th. W.* Band IV, p. 865, line 27ff.

appear shortly after the death of the Teacher reflects this early stage in the messianism of the sect.

### THE TEACHER OF RIGHTEOUSNESS

What place was held by the Teacher of Righteousness in the religious beliefs of Qumran?  It is clear that he was not the Messiah,[1] in any later technical sense,[2] but, like the Samaritan Taeb (or Moses himself) he appears to have occupied a position of great authority and importance in the life of the sect, even after his death.[3]   In commenting on the Qumran sectarians' doctrine of 'justificatio fide',[4] Dr Millar Burrows writes:

not only is salvation dependent upon God's righteousness; it is also connected in the Habakkuk Commentary with faith in the teacher of righteousness.  The passage where this appears is a part of the commentary on Habakkuk ii.4, one of Paul's favorite proof texts for his doctrine of justification by faith in Christ. What the commentator means by faith in the teacher of righteousness, however, is not the same as what faith in Christ meant to Paul. Three elements are more or less involved: fidelity to the teacher of righteousness, confidence in him, and a belief about him.  Some

---

[1] The view that they were one and the same individual was first put forward by S. Schechter (op. cit., p. xiiff.), and since Schechter distinguishes between a *first appearance* of the Teacher-Messiah as the founder of the New Covenant *on earth* (his death or 'gathering in' is stated at ix.29) and a *second advent* as a supernatural being at 'the end of the days' (vi.11), we would then already have in the Messianic doctrine of the sect the conception of the Incarnation and Second Advent of the Messiah.  (This remarkable theory has been accepted and developed by Dupont-Sommer, according to whom the Messiah, a divine being, became incarnate in the Teacher of Righteousness, suffered under Pompey at the hands of a High Priest (after a life like Christ's on earth) and will return for judgment at the end of the days.  (See his *Dead Sea Scrolls*, especially pp. 34 and 99).

The crucial passage for Schechter's theory is *CD* viii.10 (vi.11) which apparently refers in unmistakable terms to the 'rising' ('arising') of the Teacher of Righteousness at the 'end of the days' ('*adh 'omedh yoreh haṣṣedheq be'aḥarith hayyamim*'); the 'rising' of the Messiah of Aaron and Israel is described in practically the same language (cf. *CD* ix.29 B).

As Lagrange pointed out, however, (*RB*, N.S. 9 (1912), p. 223 n. (4)) *yoreh haṣṣedheq* in this passage need have no more significance than that of a general title applied to the Messiah; similarly, as applied to the Founder of the sect it is to be regarded essentially as a title and certainly not as a proper name.   At viii.10 it is quite unnecessary (and extremely misleading) to explain the words as referring to the historical Teacher of Righteousness and founder of the sect.   Moreover, as Charles showed (op. cit., p. 800, n. 7), *CD* ix.29, which bans from the sect all who fall away from the New Covenant 'from the day when there was gathered in the Unique Teacher until there arise the Messiah of Aaron and Israel', clearly distinguished between the Founder of the sect and the expected Messiah.   Two different individuals are meant.

[2] See further supra, p. 148.

[3] Cf. supra, p. 20.          [4] See supra, p. 126.

scholars see here only the first of these three ideas, but it seems clear to me that more than this is meant. Confident acceptance of his teaching and leadership is presupposed, and this implies also the belief that he knows by revelation the true meaning of prophecy. The same three elements are included also in what Paul means by faith in Christ, but the belief about Christ which he considers necessary for salvation goes much farther than anything that was believed about the teacher of righteousness. There is no implication in the Dead Sea Scrolls that the teacher of righteousness had himself accomplished a redemptive work in any way comparable to the saving work of Christ.

(*The Dead Sea Scrolls*, p. 334ff.)

One of the central theological issues of the scrolls is raised in this last sentence. Claims are now being made for some kind of redemptive function for the Founder of the sect.

The question revolves round the identity of the writer of the hymns referred to above. The view that the 'Servant' figure in these hymns is the Teacher of Righteousness himself and the Founder of the Qumran sect has now been argued by many writers.[1] If this identification is correct then we may be obliged to regard the 'Teacher' as a cult-figure in the life of the sect to whose vicarious suffering some kind of redemptive significance was attached. Have we to do, in these psalms or hymns, with an early pre-Christian Jewish martyr-cult? It is certainly in this area of religious devotion rather than in pre-Christian Jewish messianism that these hymns would most naturally be located. Eduard Lohse's recent book on *Martyrer und Gottesknecht* has reminded us of the antecedents of the veneration of the martyrs in early Christianity in post-Maccabaean Judaism[2]; such martyr-cults (to which Bousset drew attention in his *Religion des Judenthums*[3]) sprang up in post-Maccabaean times around the reputed site of the martyrdom or the tomb of the martyr; one of Julius Wellhausen's brilliant insights was to infer the existence of such cults from the words of Jesus in his

---

[1] For a discussion of this hotly debated issue, see the article of Père Rigaux, 'Révélation des mystères et Perfection à Qumran et dans le Nouveau Testament', in *NTS*, 4, p. 244ff. Cf. also Dupont-Sommer, 'Le Livre des Hymnes' in *Semitica*, 7, 1957, 13ff.

[2] Göttingen, 1955, p. 72.

[3] Berlin, 1903, p. 181ff.

denunciation of the Pharisees at Mt. xxiii.29: 'Woe to you, scribes and Pharisees, hypocrites! for you build the tombs of the prophets and adorn the monuments of the righteous, saying, "If we had lived in the days of our fathers, we would not have taken part with them in the shedding of the blood of the prophets."' The rabbinical idea of the propitiatory power of the shed blood of the heroes and saints of Israel has also roots that lie deeply buried in pre-Christian antiquity; already in I Maccabees an atoning efficacy is attributed to the deaths of the martyrs.

Some conclusions to which this discussion has been leading may be tentatively stated:

1. The influence of Ezekiel has been evident in more than one text, in the Messianic Banquet, the Benediction of the *Nasi'*, the *War* scroll. This is not surprising in a priestly sect calling itself the Bene Zadok, which, in the *Damascus Document*, derives its charter of a hierocratic Israel from Ezekiel. The closing chapters of Ezekiel, describing the new Temple in a New Jerusalem, in which the *Nasi'* or Prince Saviour of Israel, of Davidic line, will rule in his appropriate sphere, supply the key to the Zadokite conception of the Messiah in the New Israel.[1]

2. The *Nasi'* is the Davidic Warrior Messiah of traditional Jewish belief, whose office will be to bring Israel to final triumph over her enemies, in particular the Kittiim. This is stated in the Benediction of the Prince, and the same figure is recognizable in the *Serekh ha'edhah's* account of the Messianic Banquet, in the *War* scroll, and in the *Damascus Document*: Ps. ii.7 may have been messianically interpreted in relation to the *Nasi'*. In Ezekiel, a sacred meal for the *nasi'* is described, as we have noted, at Ezek. xliv.3[2]; this takes place in the ideal Temple envisaged in the new Jerusalem after the defeat of Gog and the enemies of Israel. We may perhaps conclude that the *Serekh* scroll contains a version

---

[1] Further confirmation of this conclusion may be found in Aramaic fragments which have been claimed as descriptions of the new Jerusalem and its ideal Temple service, the latter demonstrably related to Ezekiel. M. Baillet, 'Fragments araméens de Qumran 2. Descriptions de la Jérusalem Nouvelle', in *RB*, 62, 1955, 222ff. Cf. Barthélemy-Milik, op. cit. p. 134, and Appendix C, p. 192.

[2] Supra, p. 109.

of the Messianic Banquet based on Ezekiel xliv, which will follow the destruction of Israel's enemies, as described in the *War* scroll, and the establishment of the ideal Temple in the new Jerusalem.

3. In a hierocratic Israel, such as Ezekiel describes, the *Nasi'* would be subordinate to the High Priest. This is, however, assumed rather than explicitly stated in Ezekiel; no mention is made of the office of the High Priest in the contemplated hierocracy of Ezekiel.[1] In the *Serekh ha'edhah*, and perhaps in the *Benedictions* and *War* scroll, the *Nasi'* is subordinated to the High Priest. The latter plays an important rôle in the *War* scroll, along with the Warrior figure. Whether we have any right to regard him as a 'Messianic' figure in the same category as 'the Messiah of Israel' must still be a debatable point.

4. The *War* scroll connects the Messiah with the angelic hosts to appear on Israel's side. This appears to be a development of a motif found in II Maccabees. It is possible to interpret the evidence as supporting a belief in a supernatural Warrior Messiah, such as we find in the Sibylline Oracles. If our interpretation of 1 QH iii.19-36 is sound, this Armageddon was to be followed by the universal conflagration and the Judgment.[2]

5. The Prophet like Moses, was evidently an important figure for the Qumran sect; this belief represents one of the most striking points of contact between Qumran and Samaritanism.

6. The Teacher of Righteousness, perhaps identified at one time with the Prophet, may have been invested with 'redemptive' functions, if the identification of the speaker in the Hymns with this figure is correct. The language employed suggests a pre-Christian martyr-cult.

[1] Supra, p. 148.　　　　　　　　　　[2] Supra, p. 138, n. 1.

# CHAPTER VIII

# Summary and Conclusions

The purpose of this concluding chapter is to summarize briefly the conclusions which have emerged from this study, so that the reader, in particular the non-expert, may acquaint himself at once with the main results of the argument.

It goes without saying that we are dealing, in most cases, with fresh working hypotheses only; and these will stand or fall as fresh evidence comes to hand.

## PART ONE: HISTORICAL

1. In the first place, it seemed prudent to emphasize that firm and final conclusions have not yet been reached about the date of the Qumran documents, though a date between Daniel (second century B.C.) and Bar-Cochba (second century A.D.) give the outer limits of possibility.

It is the period of maximum interest to the student of Christian origins.

2. The identification of the sect of the scrolls with the ancient Essenes is accepted as the best working hypothesis hitherto advanced.

The evidence of the scrolls confirms the older explanation of the name Essene as a Greek equivalent of the Hebrew Hasidim, the pious ones or saints.

The origins of Essenism can now be traced into the Hasmonaean period: the ancestors of the Essenes were the Hasidim.

As a religious order of ascetics, Essenism crystallized out of the older Hasidaean movement some time in the reign of Jonathan (160-142 B.C.).

According to rabbinical tradition, the earliest Hasidim were all Nazirites: it seems likely that the asceticism of the later Essene order was a development of this side of the Hasidaean movement, coming in particular from their priestly character and their consecration as warrior-saints to the Law;

it probably also had earlier roots in the ancient tribal asceticism of Israel.

In view of the close connection between the requirements of the Nazirate—the most ancient form of Hebrew asceticism —and the priesthood, it seems likely that, when the Zadokite priests seceded from Jerusalem and the service of the altar, they became virtually and in practice Nazirites.

3. There seems little doubt about the identity of the Qumran sect with the ancient Essenes of Josephus, Philo, and Pliny the Elder. But, while the study of the Qumran writings confirms this identity, it at the same time corrects and fills out the picture, by supplying a great deal of detail, hitherto unknown. It is unlikely, for instance, that celibacy was the universal rule; it may, in fact, have been the exception. It seems likely too that the complete community of property which the Greek historians report was, in fact, confined only to the priests. The picture of the Essenes as engaging only in a spiritual form of worship is also probably an idealized one; they did, in fact, participate in the sacrificial worship of the Temple, though on their own conditions.

Together, the reports of the ancient historians and the scrolls supply us with invaluable information about one of the most remarkable phenomena in ancient Judaism—the life of a priestly (or monastic) sect of Torah Judaism, descendants and guardians of the tradition of the Hasidim of Maccabaean times, and also, beyond them, of the ancient asceticism of Israelite Yahwism; like their ancestors they were themselves ascetics and dwellers in the desert of Judaea.

The movement may have been as great and as influential as that of the Pharisees themselves. It was a peripheral sect only in the sense that it was pursuing an unworldly life, but not in the extent of its influence on the religion of the period.

Their main centre appears to have been at Qumran, but a related group had established itself at Lake Mareotis in Egypt—the Therapeutae of Philo.

4. A study of patristic sources for early Jewish sectarianism in the light of the scrolls yields some interesting results. There is credible patristic evidence for the existence in pre-70

Palestine of a widespread movement of Jewish or para-Jewish 'non-conformity', characterized by its ascetic or puritanical tendencies and manner of life, and by its baptizing cult, holding a different canon of Scripture and different customs from the orthodoxy (or orthopraxis) of the Pharisees. The Qumran Essenes were one branch only of this movement.

As we view these different sects through the eyes of the Greek historians and patristic authors, what we tend to see is their differences: but the really impressive fact about the entire movement, in spite of its fissiparous nature, is its surprising unity; at the main points of its heteropraxis (asceticism, monasticism, rejection of sacrifice, of the Jerusalem Torah, baptismal rites, etc.), it presents a solid and unbroken front of opposition to the established religion of the day, while at the same time sharing much in common with it.

A parallel is to be found in the splinter-groups of Scottish Presbyterianism in the eighteenth and nineteenth centuries—Burghers and anti-Burghers, Auld Lichts, New Lichts, Wee Frees, United Presbyterians, Established Kirk. To the outsider it presents a somewhat bewildering variety: yet in fact and history, these groups often hived off for unimportant and even trivial causes. What they held in common was far more important, the heritage of the Reformation, an agreed Protestant faith, solidly united against the sacrificial cultus of the Mass and the practices of Rome. Translate Rome into Jerusalem in the first century and Protestant Presbyterianism or non-conformity into Jewish sectarian non-conformity, and one obtains a fairly accurate picture of the sectarian situation in first-century Palestine.

Presbyterianism in Great Britain has two main branches, a northern, represented by the Church of Scotland, and a southern, the Presbyterian Church in England. The same geographical pattern can be traced in first-century Palestine, corresponding broadly to the ancient division of the Kingdom. The northern group was headed by the Samaritan schism. The most influential sects in the south, if not the entire southern movement, are in some ways connected with the Qumran 'Essenes'.

It seems probable that this vast movement of 'Jewish' or 'Hebrew' sectarianism represents the survival into New Testament times of the old pre-Ezra type of Hebrew religion; and its puritanism would then stem from the ancient asceticism of the religion of Israel.

5. Where, if any, is the link between this side of Judaism and the New Testament? It has been argued by Professor Oscar Cullmann that the contact between the primitive Church and Qumran was through the 'Hellenists' of the Acts. It is now suggested that the historical link was through the Hebraists of Acts. It is contended that the latter name had been revived in Maccabaean times to describe the Hasidim, and came later to be employed to distinguish Pharisaic (rabbinical) 'Jews' from their co-religionists of Hebrew nationality, but with anti-Pharisaic beliefs, mainly the group known as 'Essenes'.

The 'Hebraists' or 'Hebrews' of Acts would then provide the general connection between the movement and tradition of non-conformist baptizing Judaism and the Primitive Church.

A closer connection still would be through the so-called 'sect of the Nazarenes' of Acts xxiv.5, if there is historical foundation for Epiphanius's Jewish Nasarenes of Trans-Jordan. On the whole, the cumulative evidence seemed to support Epiphanius. The oldest roots of the Christian movement were certainly in Galilee and the North; and one of these may have sprung from a group of dedicated Nazirites, sectarians who continued the ancient Israelite institution of the life-long Nazirate. There would then be the closest of connections between John the Baptist and his baptizing movement and the Galilaean movement; and a similar close tie would exist with the priestly 'Nazirites' of Qumran.

There is certainly a Nazirite element in Christian origins, as is witnessed, for instance, by Matthew ii.23.

The celibacy of Qumran (and the wider movement out of which it sprang) is perhaps its one absolutely unique feature. Where traces of this ideal are found in the New Testament, as, for example, in Revelation xiv and I Corinthians vii, they almost certainly derive from this non-conformist, anti-Pharisaic type of Judaism.

PART TWO:   RELIGIOUS AND THEOLOGICAL

It must be the theological evidence which the scrolls supply by which the general thesis of the emergence of the Primitive Church from this side of Judaism stands or falls.

Study of several of the main aspects of Qumran religion and theology, while evincing notable differences, shows clearly a close affinity and resemblance which seems conclusive for some historical connection.

1. The discovery that the Qumran Essenes practised baptismal rites is no new thing in Judaism: so too did most Jewish sects in the New Testament period.  What is unique about Qumran is that such rites were practised in relation to a movement of repentance, of entry into a New Covenant (that of Jeremiah and Ezekiel) and of a New Covenanted Israel—the sect itself—in preparation for an impending divine Judgment.

This forms an impressive preparation for New Testament religion; and it seems idle to deny that some connection exists between the two movements.

At the same time important differences ought not to be overlooked.  The Qumran New Covenant was largely a renewal of the Old Covenant; and the life of the new covenanter was subjected to an even more rigorous and burdensome legalism than that of the strictest Pharisee.  He became a member of an exclusive sect, of a saved Remnant (at least in its own eyes), but not of a saving Remnant.

The main differences between the primitive Christian movement and Qumran are to be sought in the persons of John and Jesus, both towering figures, transforming the practices of a sect into a universal religion by their proclamation: 'Repent, for the Kingdom of God is at hand', and by their prophetic and Messianic ministries.

Nevertheless, the background of Christianity in a Qumran-type Judaism seems indisputable; and the institutions of Qumran, such as their repeated baptismal practices and rites of initiation, appear to have cast a very long shadow indeed, for they are still to be found in the non-Pauline Roman Church of the late second century A.D.

The sacred meal of Qumran consisted solely of bread and/or wine; the presence of wine does not seem to have been an indispensable feature of the meal. These sacred or ceremonial meals are to be distinguished from the regular daily meals reported for the Essenes by Josephus, though, in so far as all meals in Judaism are sacred meals, too great emphasis ought not perhaps to be placed on this distinction.

The meal was that of the Shew-bread, and was regularly celebrated wherever there was a quorum of ten members—and only full members of the sect could participate.

When the Zadokite priests went into exile, the main Temple rite they appear to have continued was that of the Table of Shew-bread, in which they regularly and solemnly participated in their community gathering.

The close parallel with the sacred meal of the Therapeutae, consisting of bread and water only, and Philo's comparison of the latter with the priests' participation in the Bread of the Presence or Shew-bread supports such an explanation of the origins of the sacred meal.

It is highly significant that of the three passages which have survived and which describe such a meal, one portrays it as a Messianic Banquet, another as participation in the meal of the Shew-bread. It may be that such a meal was eaten in anticipation of the coming of the Prince of David's line (or *Nasi'*), and of his participation in the sacred meal of Ezekiel xliv.3 (supra, p. 109). The meals of the Therapeutae may have had a similar messianic significance.

It seems more probable that a sacred meal of this type lies behind the daily 'breaking of bread' in the Primitive Christian community in Acts than a meal such as that of the Passover. But our ignorance of other forms of sacred meals in ancient Judaism must not be forgotten. Nevertheless, the Qumran material has immensely enriched our knowledge of first-century Judaism, and added a fresh possibility to the solution of the age-old problem of the origins of the Eucharist.

2. Qumran developed a peculiar type of *legalistic tradition*. It was, from the beginning, a Zadokite, that is, priestly, legalism and in its later forms it shows some remarkable

features which mark it off as a peculiar and distinctive sectarian *genre*. It was a perfectionist 'mystery' cult, a priestly 'esoteric' legalism, its primary aim and ideal being the fulfilment of all the righteousness of the Law, as interpreted from time to time (and from situation to situation) by the Qumran Zadokite priestly hierarchy.

It is interesting to note that one of its *halakhoth*, its teaching about divorce, agrees with the teaching of Christ at Mk. x.6, even utilizing the same proof-text (Gen. i.27). It also agrees, in its condemnation of marriage with a niece, with the position attributed to John the Baptist in the Gospels (Mk. vi.17), and with the position of the Samaritans and other sectarian groups. Rejection of such marriages was held strongly by such groups against the position of the Pharisees, who appear not only to have condoned or permitted, but even to have encouraged such practices.

But if there are these parallels to the Gospels, on the whole the 'legalism' of Qumran represents one of the chief points of difference from the Gospels and the New Testament; thus the Qumran sectarians appear to have been even stricter in their Sabbath observance than the Pharisees themselves (supra, p. 124).

In addition to the Law the prophetic tradition was held in high esteem by the Qumran sect; and it is in their 'prophetism' and its closely related Apocalyptic that we enter a universe of discourse shared with the New Testament writers, in particular by St Paul and St John.

There is a note of almost evangelical piety struck, again and again, in the Hymns or *Hodayoth*. What we in fact find is a doctrine very closely approximating to the Pauline *justificatio sola fide*. It was pointed out, however, that here we do not only have a *praeparatio evangelica*, but also a continuation of the *Psalmenfrömmigkeit* of the Hasidim.

Qumran appears also to have developed a doctrine of redemption by vicarious suffering and to have viewed this as among its chief *arcana* or 'mysteries'. These 'mysteries of redemption', however, were exclusively for the redemption of Israel, and the vicarious suffering through which they were to be wrought was not that of a single individual (cf., however, p. 160), but of a small group of consecrated saints.

The famous Servant Prophecies of II Isaiah are applied to this group of saints and potential martyrs.

That there were groups within Judaism holding such views is again an important *praeparatio evangelica*; these are the forerunners of the disciples and evangelists.

Qumran Apocalyptic assumes a dualistic universe, of light and darkness, the spirit of truth and the spirit of error (or perversity), similar to that of the Johannine writings. It looked forward to a final Visitation (*peqqudah*) or Judgment (*mishpaṭ*) in which there would be a divine purification of mankind. The state ensuing appears to be conceived as that of the New Creation or the 'Ανακαίνωσις or renewal of Creation; it is the return to the state of innocence before the Fall when Adam's lost 'glory' is restored again and he enjoys an everlasting life, undisturbed by sin or death. The actual destruction of the present world at the Judgment appears to have been envisaged as a universal conflagration. This New Creation of eternal duration appears to have its location on this earth, for the restoration of the Temple in a New Jerusalem seems to have been an integral part of their expectations for the new age.

This was accompanied by a belief in an eternal life, a life to be shared with the angels in heaven, a form of belief which is similar to that expressed at Luke xx.36. There was also probably some form of resurrection hope, though unequivocal evidence for belief in resurrection is not yet forthcoming.

3. According to most authorities the sect expected two Messiahs, a Messiah of Aaron and Israel and a high-priestly Messiah, the two constituting a partnership similar to the Moses-Aaron, Joshua-Zerubbabel partnership. The sect also cherished the expectation of the coming of the Moses-like Prophet of Deut. xviii.18. There is certainly a triumvirate of deliverers, though this does not mean that they were all expected at the same time. It may be that, in the strict sense, the title Messiah should be confined to the secular leader, the Messiah of Aaron and Israel, now clearly to be identified with the Davidic Messiah of popular expectation.

Apart from the addition of the High Priest and the Prophet as eschatological figures, the only distinctive feature of the Qumran Messianic hope would seem to be that it took its ideal of the Davidic Prince from the Book of Ezekiel.

All three motifs, prophet, priest and king, are, of course, found applied to Jesus in the gospels.

# THE ACCOUNTS OF THE ESSENES IN
# JOSEPHUS AND PHILO

I

## JOSEPHUS

### *Vita 2*

At about sixteen years of age, I made up my mind to
acquire some experience of the 'sects' [αἱρέσεων][1] among us.
There are three such, as we have frequently said, the first
that of the Pharisees and the second of the Sadducees, and
the third of the Essenes. For in this way I thought to choose
the best, if I had knowledge of all. I therefore disciplined
myself severely, and with much toil passed through the three
of them [τὰς τρεῖς διῆλθον].[2] Since I did not consider even
the experience thus gained sufficient for myself, and had
learned that a certain Banus by name was living in the
wilderness, wearing clothes from trees, using as food what
grew of itself, and frequently bathing himself with cold
water by day and night for purification, I became his devoted
disciple. I lived with him for three years and when I had
done what I wanted to do, returned to the city. Being now
nineteen years old, I began to regulate my conduct following

---

[1] On Josephus's use of this word, see supra, p. 5.

[2] These words can only mean that Josephus became a pupil of the Pharisees,
Sadducees, and Essenes between his sixteenth and nineteenth years, before, finally,
after his sojourn with Banus, settling down as a Pharisee. Since he lived with the
eremite baptist Banus for three years he can hardly have spent much time with any
of the other three 'sects', and can certainly not have served as a novice in any one of
them. No doubt he attended occasionally the lectures of a well-known teacher, but
the statement about the 'discipline and toil' he underwent *in passing through the three
sects* is clearly an exaggeration and distortion of the facts. He may have submitted
himself to the most rigorous discipline according to the rules which he had learned as
Pharisaic or Essene rules, but he can never have been a member of either sect; as a
member of a priestly Sadducaean family, his closest acquaintances must have been
with the Sadducees.

Josephus's knowledge of the Jewish sects, and, in particular, of the Essenes, must
be regarded, therefore, as for the most part information acquired at second hand; he
was an outsider to these sects and had probably no inside information about them (see
supra, p. 26).

the 'sect' of the Pharisees, which resembles the Stoic school among the Greeks.

*Bellum Judaicum*, II.viii.2-13

(2) There are three schools of thought among the Jews, the followers of the first being Pharisees, of the second Sadducees; the third, which is indeed reputed to lead a noble kind of life, are called Essenes, being Jews by race, and also loving one another more than the other sects. These shun the pleasures as evil, and regard self-control and not yielding to the passions virtue. Marriage they hold in little esteem, but they adopt the children of others while they are still pliable and docile, regarding them as their own kinsfolk and imprinting on their minds their ways and customs. It is not that they are for doing away with marriage, and thereby the continuance of the race, but they seek to protect themselves against the wanton ways of women, and are convinced that no woman keeps faith with one man.

(3) They are despisers of wealth, and a thing to wonder at among them is their community of goods; it is not possible to find anyone among them possessing more than another. They have a law that those who enter the sect should turn over their property for the public use of the order, the consequence being that among them all there does not appear either the degradation of poverty or excess of wealth, the possessions of each individual being put all together to be the common property of all as brethren.

They regard oil as a defilement, and if anyone is smeared with it against his will, he wipes his body clean. For they consider it a good thing to keep a dry skin and always to be clad in white garments.

The overseers of their common property are elected and chosen by the whole body, each with regard to his special functions.

(4) They do not have one city, but many settle in each city.

Sectarians arriving from elsewhere have all the resources of the community placed at their disposal, just as if they were their own; and they enter the houses of those they have

KANSAS CENTER
for
PUBLIC EDUCATION RELIGION STUDIES
APPENDIX A
1300 Oread
Lawrence, Kansas 66045
175

never seen before as if they were their closest friends. Consequently, when they make their journeys they do not carry anything at all with them, but they are armed on account of robbers. An officer to look after strangers is chosen and appointed in each city where the Order is found, furnishing them with clothing and necessities. Their manner of dress and deportment is like that of youths being brought up in fear. They do not change their clothes or shoes till they are first completely in rags and tatters or worn-out with age. Among themselves they do not either buy or sell, but each gives what he has to one in need, and receives something useful from him in exchange. There is nothing to prevent them sharing or using whatever they want without any return for it.

(5) With regard to their religion, they have their own distinctive piety. For before the sun rises they utter no word on common matters, but offer to him certain ancestral prayers, as if entreating him to rise. Thereafter, they are dismissed by their overseers to the occupations in which they are severally skilled, and work without a break until the fifth hour when they again assemble together in one place. They gird themselves with linen loin-cloths, and thus bathe their bodies in cold water.

After this rite of purification they come together in a special room, where no one of another sect is permitted to enter, and being themselves purified they arrive in their refectory as if they were entering a sacred shrine. When they have seated themselves silently their baker serves them with bread in order, and their cook sets before each one dish consisting of a single course.

The [Chief] Priest says a prayer before meat and no one may partake before the prayer. When the meat is over, he prays again—at the beginning and the end they do honour to God as the provider of life. Thereafter, laying aside their garments as sacred vestments, they return to work till evening. On their return they dine in the same way, though guests sit along with them, if any happen to be present with them. No shouting or uproar ever disturbs their dwelling, and in their discussions they give way among themselves to those senior to them in rank. To persons outside, the silence of those within appears as some dreadful mystery; the reason for it is their constant sobriety and the limiting of their food and drink to what satisfies nature.[1]

(6) In everything else they do nothing without instructions from their overseers, but these two matters are left to their own free will, giving help and [deeds of] mercy; for to assist the deserving, whenever they ask, and to supply food to those in need, these things are left to themselves to decide.

Gifts to relatives may not be made without the permission of the stewards. They know how to use a righteous indignation, but anger they control; they are champions of loyalty, ministers of peace.

Everything that is said by them is more binding than an oath and they avoid swearing, regarding it as worse than perjury, for they declare that anyone who is not believed without having to appeal to God is already condemned.

They show an extraordinary interest in the writings of the ancients, selecting especially those that refer to the welfare of soul and body; hence their research for the healing of diseases into medicinal roots and the properties of stones.

(7) Admission is not immediate for those who become enthusiastic for the sect. They lay down for him the same way of life for a year while he remains outside [the sect], providing him with a small axe and the loin-cloth mentioned above and white garment [λευκὴν ἐσθῆτα[2]]. When after this period he gives proof of self-control, he is brought into closer touch with their manner of life and shares in the purer waters for [ritual] cleansing [καθαρωτέρων τῶν πρὸς ἀγνείαν ὑδάτων μεταλαμβάνει], but is not yet allowed to join their common life. After this proof of fortitude, his character is tested for two further years, and when he is shown to be worthy, he is then enrolled in their company. But before he

---

[1] The ideal is that of Dan. i: they almost certainly abstained from flesh and wine, except on special (ceremonial) occasions.

[2] This is the first mention of 'a white garment', though earlier we are told that they dressed in white and wore their garments till they were old. The 'loin-cloth' was for use in bathing. The statement above that they set aside these garments after dining as if they were sacred vestments suggests that the white garment was not worn when they were engaged in their crafts or toil. Was it worn on all other occasions or was it reserved for ceremonial use only?

Its origin probably goes back to the vestments of the Temple priesthood.

touches the common food he swears before them fearful oaths,
first to hold God in reverence, then to maintain justice among
men and neither to harm anyone deliberately nor under
instructions, but always to hate the unjust and to strive on
the side of the just; always to keep faith with all, especially
with those in power, for office does not come to anyone apart
from God[1]; and should he himself bear rule that he will never
abuse his authority, or, either in dress or by any superior
decoration, outshine those subordinate to him; always to love
the truth and to expose liars; to keep his hands from theft
and his soul clean from filthy lucre [lit. unholy gain]; not to
conceal anything from his fellow-sectarians, nor to disclose
anything of theirs to others, even if one should torture him to
death. Besides these things, he swears to communicate their
doctrine to no one otherwise than he himself has received it;
to abstain from robbery, and likewise carefully to preserve
the books of their sect and the names of the angels. It is by
such oaths they secure to themselves those who are admitted.

(8) They expel from the order those convicted of grave
offences. The condemned outcast often meets his end in a
most lamentable fate. For since he is bound by their oaths
and customs, and unable to partake of other men's food, he
eats grass, and so, wasted in body by starvation, he perishes.
That is why many have been taken back through pity at their
last gasp, since it is thought that torment to the point of
death is a sufficient punishment for their offences.

(9) In their administration of justice, they are most
scrupulous and just, and they do not pass sentence with less
than 100 present: what is decided by them is irrevocable.
Their great object of reverence next to God is the name of
their Law-giver, and if any is guilty of blasphemy against
this, he is punished by death. They hold in esteem obedience
to elders and the majority [$\tau o \hat{\imath} s \ \pi \lambda \epsilon i o \sigma \iota \nu$, that is, the Many].[2]
When ten are seated together no one would speak against

---

[1] Cf. Rom. xiii.1, and O. Cullmann, *The State in the New Testament*, New York,
1956, p. 55ff.

[2] Cf. C. Rabin, *The Zadokite Documents*, p. 65 (note on CD xiii.8). Josephus's
($o i$) $\pi \lambda \epsilon i o \nu \epsilon s$ is the Greek equivalent of *rabbim* '(the) Many', i.e. 'the main body
of the people' as opposed to the Hellenizers (Charles), or the elders (Josephus, *B.J.*
ii.8, 9). Cf. II Cor. ii.16. See also D. Daube, *HTR*, 40, 1947, 119. Mark uses
$\delta \chi \lambda o s$ in the same sense. The source of the expression appears to be Daniel, for
example xii.3 (quoting Is. liii.11); ix.27; xi.33, 39; Esth. iv.3(?).

the will of the other nine. They forbid spitting into the midst of a company or to the right, and, even more strictly than all other Jews, engaging in work on the sabbath. For they not only prepare their food a day ahead, in order not to kindle a fire for that day, but they do not even venture to remove any vessel, or even to go to the stool. On other days they dig a foot-deep pit with their mattock—for of such a nature is the hatchet[1] given by them to their neophytes, and covering themselves up with their cloak, that they may not give offence to the rays of the god [that is, the sun], they sit above it. They then draw the earth they have dug out back into the pit; and they choose the most deserted place to do this, although this discharge of excrement is a natural function; they are accustomed to wash themselves afterwards, as if defiled.

(10) They are divided, according to the duration of their life under discipline, into four grades; and so great is the inferiority of juniors to seniors that, if a junior should touch a senior, the latter takes a bath, just as if he had been in contact with a foreigner. They are long-lived, many of them attaining to more than a hundred years, on account of the simplicity, I suppose, and orderliness of their manner of life. They despise dangers, overcoming pain by their powers of mind, and deeming death, if it come with honour, as better than immortality. The war against the Romans tested their souls to the utmost [διήλεγξεν—v.l. διήλεξεν—δὲ αὐτῶν ἐν ἅπασιν τὰς ψυχὰς ὁ πρὸς 'Ρωμαίους πόλεμος],[2] in which, tortured and racked, burned and broken, and having to pass through all manners of instruments of torture, that they might blaspheme the name of their Law-giver, or eat one of the forbidden foods, they submitted to neither, nor stooped even to flattery of their tormentors or to tears. But smiling in their pains and engaging in light banter with their executioners, they gave up their souls cheerfully as those about to receive them back again.

---

[1] ἀξινίδιον. Cf. Deut. xxiii.13 and supra, p. 30.

[2] The verb διελέγχω, 'to refute utterly' does not give a suitable meaning. Whiston renders 'and indeed our war with the Romans gave abundant evidence what great souls they had in their trials'. Thackeray (Loeb) translates: 'The war with the Romans tried their souls through and through by every variety of test.' The varia lectio διήλεξεν gives no satisfactory sense either.

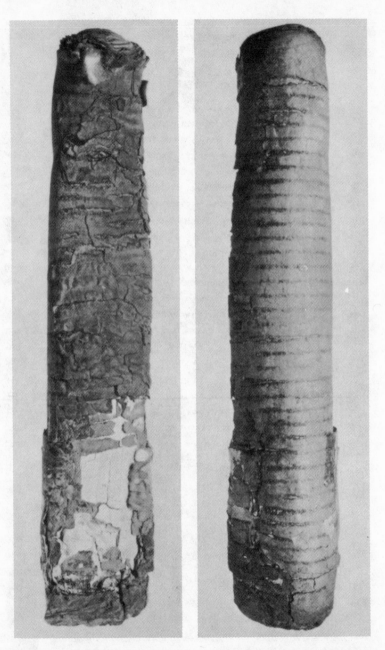

*Plate 15* The unopened scroll of the *Genesis Apocryphon. Left,* the badly pre-served side; *right,* the better preserved side. *(Hebrew University of Jerusalem)*

*Plate 16* This is part of a folio from the *Hymns of Thanksgiving*. These are in many respects the most important of all the Qumran texts from a theological point of view. (*Hebrew University of Jerusalem*)

(11) For the following doctrine is firmly held among them that, while bodies are corruptible and their material substance has no permanency, souls are immortal and continue forever; and that, emanating from the finest atmosphere, they are bound up in their bodies as in prisons, into which they are drawn as by a natural spell: but when they are released from the bonds of the flesh, they rejoice and are borne upwards, as it were, freed from a long slavery. In agreement with the Greeks, they maintain that a life is reserved for the good beyond the Ocean, a place oppressed neither by rain, snow or heat, but which an even gentle zephyr, blowing in from the Ocean, keeps refreshed. But for the wicked souls they set apart a murky and wintry cave, filled with unending punishments. The Greeks, it seems to me, entertained the same idea when they set apart for their brave men, those they call heroes and demi-gods, the Islands of the Blest, and for the souls of evil-doers a place of the impious down in Hades where their myths held that certain persons are actually undergoing punishment, such as Sisyphus, Tantalus, Ixion, and Tityus: they were first seeking to establish that souls were imperishable, and then to promote virtue and deter from evil. For the good become better in their lifetime by the hope of reward even after death, and the passions of the wicked are restrained by the fear that even though they should escape detection while alive, they must expect to undergo everlasting punishment after their decease. Such are the theological views of the Essenes on the soul, setting an irresistible bait for those who have once tasted their philosophy.

(12) There are among them some who profess to foreknow even things to come, being well versed in sacred books and various forms of purification, and utterances of prophets; and it is seldom that they ever go astray in their predictions.

(13) There is still another Order of Essenes, agreeing with the rest in manner of life, customs, and regulations, but differing in its opinion with regard to marriage. They think that those who do not marry cut off the greatest part of life, the succession: and, what is more, if all were to hold this view, the race would very soon disappear. All the same,

they put their brides to the test over a three-year period; and when they have had three purifications to prove that they can produce children, they then marry them. They do not have intercourse with them when they are pregnant, proving that they marry not for pleasure but to produce children. The women are covered with a garment when a ritual washing takes place, just as men have a loin-cloth. Such then are the ways of this Order.

## II

### PHILO AND THE ESSENES

Philo, *Quod omnis probus liber*, XII

75    Palestine Syria too, which a by no means small portion of the very populous nation of the Jews inhabits, is not unproductive of high moral excellence. There are said to be some among them, in number more than four thousand, certain people called Essenes, a name derived in my opinion from ὁσιότης, though not as an exact equivalent of the Greek: the reason for their name is that they are primarily religious devotees [θεραπευταί θεοῦ], not by any cult of animal sacrifices but in their resolve to maintain the sanctity of their minds.

76    First of all, they live in villages, avoiding cities because of the lawlessness which has become inveterate among city dwellers, knowing that from association with such there comes a deadly influence on their souls, like that of a disease arising from a pestilential atmosphere. Some of them work on the land. Others follow crafts that make for peace, so helping both themselves and their neighbours. They do not amass silver or gold, nor do they acquire large tracts of land out of

77    greed for revenue, but provide just as much as the necessities of life require. For alone of practically all men they become moneyless and propertyless, by deliberate policy rather than by lack of good fortune:

yet they are deemed the wealthiest of all, since they judge frugality and contentment to be, as indeed they

78   are, riches. Nor would you find any artificer of arrows, javelins, daggers, helmets, breast-plates, or shields among them, nor, in a word, any armourer or manufacturer of weapons, or anyone concerned with anything connected with war, nor for that matter any occupation connected with peace which tends towards corruption; for they have not the vaguest idea about buying or selling or of seafaring, since they reject with abhorrence such inducements to covetousness.

79        There is not among them a single slave, but all are free, exchanging mutual services with one another. They condemn owners of slaves, not only on the grounds of their injustice, which is destructive of equality, but also as irreligious people who abolish the laws of Nature, which, like a mother, has borne and reared all men alike and made them genuine brothers, not in name only, but in very truth—a kinship which malevolent covetousness, like a rank growth, has disrupted, working estrangement in place of affinity and enmity instead of friendliness.

80        As for philosophy, logical subtleties they leave to verbalists as unnecessary for the acquisition of virtue, metaphysics to speculative talkers, as something beyond the reach of human nature, except for that part which deals with the existence of God and the creation of the Universe. They make a very special study of Ethics, taking as their sources their ancestral Laws which the human soul could not possibly have conceived without

81   divine instruction. In these Laws they receive instruction not only at other times, but especially on the seventh day. For the seventh day is held as holy; on it they abstain from all their other works, betaking themselves to sacred places, which are called synagogues. There they are seated according to their ages, the younger below their elders, with a fitting orderli-

82   ness and listening attentively. Then, while one takes the Books and reads, another of those who are most

proficient comes forward and expounds all that is not understood. For most of their study consists of allegorical interpretations of Scripture [pursued] with an
83    ardour like that in olden times. They are trained in piety, holiness, justice, domestic administration, citizenship and the understanding of things truly good, evil or indifferent, the choice of what is right and the avoidance of the opposite, taking three things as their definitive standards, love of God, love of goodness, love
84    of man. They offer many proofs of their love to God, a purity which is constant and uninterrupted through their whole life, by abstaining from oaths, by veracity, by their belief that the deity is the cause of all good and of nothing evil. [As to proof of] their love of goodness, there is their freedom from the love of money, or of praise, or of pleasure, their self-control, endurance, or again their frugality, simplicity, contentment, humility; they are law-abiding, possess stability and many other similar qualities. In their love of men [they show] goodwill, a sense of equality, and a fellowship which is beyond all words, though to say something about it briefly may not be out of place.

85    First of all, there is no house belonging to anyone which is not in effect shared by all. For in addition to their living together in fraternities their door is open also to those of their fellow-enthusiasts arriving from
86    elsewhere. Then there is a single treasury for all, common disbursements, a common wardrobe, and common food when they hold their communal meals. Among no other people will you find such things as having a common roof, a common life, and a common board more firmly established in practice. That is only to be expected, for all that they receive in wages in their daily work they do not keep as their own private property, but contributing it to the common purse they thus provide a means of benefiting those who wish to
87    avail themselves of such help. The sick are not neglected because of any inability to provide for themselves, since they have the cost of their treatment available

from the common purse, so that expenses can be met
out of these ample funds, giving them a complete sense
of security. To elders there is accorded respect and
consideration such as is given by real children to their
parents: and their old age is cared for by all manner of
generosity by countless hands and minds.

# XIII

88       Such are the athletes of virtue produced by a philosophy free from excessive pedantry about Greek words
but which sets before itself praiseworthy actions as the
exercises by which freedom, that can never be enslaved,
89   is consolidated. Whereof here is proof. There are
many potentates who have ruled at different times over
the country. [Digression describing the characters of
these kings and rulers in Palestine under whom the
91   Essenes have lived.] None of these, neither the extremely cruel nor the altogether treacherous and
hypocritical, has been able to lay any charge against
the congregation of the Essenes or 'holy ones' I have
here described. Unable to resist the high excellence
of these men, they all treated them as independent and
free-men by nature, praising their communal meals and
their ineffable fellowship, which is the clearest proof of
a perfect and completely blessed life.

*Hypothetica*, 11.1-18

1   Great numbers of his own people has our Law-giver
trained for [the life of] fellowship. They are called
Essenes, having been deemed worthy of the appellation
—I think—on account of their holiness. They dwell in
many towns in Judaea, in many villages, and in large
and populous communities.

2   Their vocation is not connected with birth—for birth
is not a thing to reckon among objects we can choose—
but with their zeal for virtue and desire to love their
fellowmen.

3   No Essene is a mere child or even a stripling or a youth,
since the characters of such are unstable, changing in

keeping with the immaturity of their age. [Essenes are] full-grown men, already declining towards age, no longer led away by their passions, but men who are enjoying the pure and really only [true] freedom.

4  Their [manner of] life bears testimony to their freedom. No one suffers himself to possess any private property at all, neither house nor slave nor land, nor cattle, nor any of the other provisions and resources of wealth. They bring everything together into a common stock and enjoy the benefit of everything in common.

5  They live together in the same place forming themselves into fraternities and clubs with communal meals. They conduct all their affairs continually for the common weal.

6  They have each different occupations, in which they work with untiring labour, excusing themselves neither on the grounds of heat or cold or any other changes in weather. Before the sun rises they betake themselves to their customary tasks, and reluctantly return when it sets, for they delight [in their work] no less than those who are in training for gymnastic exercises.

7  For they hold that whatever exercises they engage in are more valuable for life, more agreeable for soul and body and more enduring, than those of athletes, since they do not cease when the body passes its prime.

8  Some of them are agricultural workers, skilled in sowing and planting; others are herdsmen, in charge of all kinds of animals; some look after swarms of bees.

9  Others are craftsmen that they may not suffer on account of things which our unavoidable needs force upon us; thus they do not neglect any means of obtaining an innocent provision for such needs.

10  Each group, when it has received the wages of those who are thus differently employed, gives them to one who has been appointed treasurer. On receiving it, he immediately buys what is required, and provides food in abundance, and everything else which human life requires.

11  Thus, sharing each day a common life and a common table, they are content with the same conditions, being

lovers of happy frugality, shunning luxury as a disease of soul and body.

12    They do not have only a common table, but share a common wardrobe: for winter they have laid up stout clothes, and for summer cheap tunics, so that it is easily possible for anyone who wishes to take whatever he wants, since the property of each belongs to all, and of all again to each.

13    More than this, should any one of them fall ill, he is treated at the common expense and nursed with the care and consideration of all.  The old, even if they are children, are accustomed to spend their last days in an extremely happy and comfortable old age, as if they belonged not just to a large family but to a family of dutiful children: they are deemed worthy of precedence and honour by so many who do so with a willing mind, rather than thinking of tending them through a necessity of nature.

14    Furthermore, since they very clearly see that marriage is the sole or main disruptive influence on their common life, they eschew it, as well as for the reason that they practise self-control to an unusual degree.  For no Essene takes a wife, because a wife is selfish, jealous to an immoderate extent, an adept at corrupting her husband's morals and leading him astray by her constant enticements.

15    For by the flattering words she releases and her other pretences, as if she were on the stage, she first entices sight and hearing, and when these have been duped into subjection she bewitches the sovereign mind.

16    And if children are born, filled with effrontery and boldness she utters with audacity and hardihood things which she had before only by dissembling and hypocrisy hinted at.  Casting away all shame, she compels each

17    to do what is hostile to the life of fellowship.  For he who is bound by the love-potions of his wife or caring, by the necessity of nature, for his children, is no longer the same person to others, but has unconsciously become a different person, a slave instead of a free man.

18    Such then is the life of the Essenes, a life highly sought after, so that not only private persons but also great kings regard such men with wonder and admiration, and even further contribute to the veneration of them by the approbation and honours they bestow upon them.

# THE ESSENES IN HIPPOLYTUS AND JOSEPHUS

The possibility that the new Zadokite documents from the region of the Dead Sea have some connection with the ancient Essenes[1] has sent a number of students of the Jewish background of the New Testament back again to the primary sources for our knowledge of that influential pre-Christian 'sect'. Our chief information about it comes from Josephus' *Bellum Judaicum* II.viii-xiii. From these chapters in Josephus descriptive passages have been apparently excerpted by patristic writers such as Hippolytus, Porphyry and Origen, of which by far the most interesting is the long 'version' of Josephus embedded in Hippolytus' *Refutatio Omnium Haeresium* (ix.18-28).

That the Hippolytean description of the Essenes is substantially the same in contents (and in arrangement of topics) as that in Josephus is apparent from a comparison of the first few paragraphs of each account. But differences are as striking as agreements; Hippolytus gives us a number of fresh facts about the Essenes of which there is no trace in our Josephus text, and, together with a marked difference throughout in style and language, his whole account creates the strong impression of being a closely related but independent version. It would be quite impossible, for instance, to collate the 'variants' in Hippolytus and include them in a critical apparatus to Josephus: Duncker, in his edition of Hippolytus,[2] prints the entire Josephus text underneath his text of the *Refutatio*. Moreover, the introduction of fresh information by Hippolytus is difficult to reconcile with a theory of free adaptation and paraphrase, though such a view is tenable. It seems more likely, either that Hippolytus had a different edition of Josephus from ours, or that he is reproducing one of Josephus' own sources.[3]

---

[1] Cf. Millar Burrows, 'The Discipline Manual of the Judaean Covenanters', in *Oudtestamentische Studiën*, Vol. 8, Leiden, 1950, p. 165ff.

[2] Göttingen, 1859.

[3] Cf. Duncker, p. 471, l. 90 n.: *quae sequuntur* (ix.18-28) *Hippolytus e Flavio*

In view of this second possibility, the points of greatest interest in Hippolytus' account are: 1. those where it supplements Josephus and gives fresh facts, especially on topics directly bearing on subjects of interest to the New Testament student; and 2. when his version contradicts the traditional account of Josephus.

One feature of Hippolytus' description, however, must first be noted, as it constitutes a strong argument for its independent origin. It is at once a much simpler, and, from the literary point of view, a less elegant version, and, at the same time (and in keeping with its literary plainness) a much more factual account. The Josephan version, in comparison, reveals a characteristic tendency to hyperbole and extravagance. An example of Hippolytus' literary style is the unadorned statement at § 20, οὐδὲν δὲ ὅλως οὔτε ἀγοράζουσιν οὔτε πωλοῦσιν, ὃ δ' ἂν ἔχῃ τις τῷ μὴ ἔχοντι δούς, ὃ οὐκ ἔχει λαμβάνει. Josephus confronts us with the following (somewhat prolix) period: οὐδὲν δὲ ἐν ἀλλήλοις οὔτε ἀγοράζουσιν οὔτε πωλοῦσιν ἀλλὰ τῷ χρήζοντι διδοὺς ἕκαστος τὰ παρ' αὐτοῦ, τὸ παρ' ἐκείνου χρήσιμον ἀντικομίζεται. καὶ χωρὶς δὲ τῆς ἀντιδόσεως ἀκώλυτος ἡ μετάληψις αὐτοῖς, παρ' ὧν ἂν ἐθελήσωσι. It is arguable that here (and perhaps in other passages) Hippolytus is simplifying Josephus and at the same time adding a 'Christian touch'.[1] But why a Christian Father should thus deliberately assimilate his account of a 'heresy' to a Synoptic saying of Christ is difficult to explain—or why he should depart at all from the text of Josephus, if it lay before him in its present form.

Examples of Josephan hyperbole (and perhaps even of distortion of his source) occur more than once: thus the statement at § 18 in Hippolytus that the Essenes are φιλάλληλοι is in Josephus that they are φιλάλληλοι δὲ καὶ τῶν ἄλλων πλέον; where Hippolytus informs us about the Essenes' attitude to women, he tells us simply that even though women should want to become adherents of the sect, they are not admitted, since the Essenes in no way trust women (κατὰ μηδένα τρόπον

---

*Iosepho . . . hausisse videtur, nisi uterque unum eundemque auctorem secutus.* The first to draw the consequences of Duncker's second alternative for the study of the Essenes was Dr K. Kohler in his article on the Essenes in the *Jewish Encyclopedia.*

[1] Cf. Conybeare on the Essenes in Hastings's *Dictionary of the Bible*, p. 770.

γυναιξὶ πιστεύοντες); in Josephus we are told that they take special precautions against the wantonnesses of the sex, καὶ μηδεμίαν τηρεῖν πεπεισμένοι τὴν πρὸς ἕνα πίστιν.

If Josephus has introduced something of himself into this last passage, it is probably not the only occasion. Thus the statement that the Essenes were sun-worshippers is based on *B.J.* viii.5, πρὶν γὰρ ἀνασχεῖν τὸν ἥλιον οὐδὲν φθέγγονται τῶν βεβήλων, πατρίους δέ τινας εἰς αὐτὸν εὐχὰς ὥσπερ ἱκετεύοντες ἀνατεῖλαι: over against this Hippolytus has simply παραμένουσι δὲ εὐτάκτως καὶ ἐπιμόνως εὐχόμενοι ἕωθεν, μηδὲν πρότερον φθεγξάμενοι εἰ μὴ τὸν θεὸν ὑμνήσωσι.

Hippolytus' version in general is a much fuller and more circumstantial account, occasionally adding a fresh detail which has a ring of authenticity, such as the statement that some of the stricter members of the sect refused even to leave their beds on the Sabbath ( § 25, τινὲς δὲ οὐδὲ κλινιδίου χωρίζονται). The longest 'interpolation' occurs at § 26 where Hippolytus goes on to describe some further traits of the stricter *renuntiantes*. Some of these will not even carry a coin about with them, declaring that it is wrong even to look on an image, and for the same reason refusing to enter a city gate over which a statue stands. Others still, if they heard any Gentile discussing God or his laws would lie in wait for him and threaten him with death if he refused to be circumcised, an excess of zeal which earned for them the name of Zealots or Sicarii.

None of this information is contained in Josephus, whose brief account of the Zealots (*Antiq.* XVIII.i.6) is confined to a statement, the gist of which is given in a single sentence in Hippolytus, that their love of liberty is such that the fear of death itself would not induce them to call any man lord, since God is their only Lord (Hippolytus § 26, ἕτεροι δὲ αὐτῶν οὐδένα κύριον ὀνομάζουσι πλὴν τὸν θεόν, εἰ καὶ αἰκίζοιτό τις ἢ καὶ ἀναιροῖτο.[1]

An instance where Hippolytus introduces another unexpected and perhaps a 'Christian touch' is in his account of the Essenes' attitude to those who wrong them. Josephus

---

[1] For the identity of Josephus's 'fourth philosophy' with the Zealots, cf. *B.J.*, VII.viii.1.

(viii.7) tells us that among their 'fearful oaths' is a promise μήτε κατὰ γνώμην βλάψειν τινὰ μήτε ἐξ ἐπιτάγματος, μισήσειν δὲ ἀεὶ τοὺς ἀδίκους καὶ συναγωνιεῖσθαι τοῖς δικαίοις. Hippolytus has (they swear) κατὰ μηδένα τρόπον ἀδικήσειν τινα, μηδένα δὲ μήτε ἀδικοῦντα μήτε ἐχθρὸν μισήσειν, προσεύχεσθαι δὲ ὑπὲρ αὐτῶν, συναγωνίζεσθαι ἀεὶ τοῖς δικαίοις.

The passage which stands in direct contradiction to Josephus' account and which is of greatest interest to the New Testament student is Hippolytus' version of the Essene doctrine of immortality.

Josephus, *B.J.* viii.11: Now the following opinion is firmly held among them (καὶ γὰρ ἔρρωται παρ' αὐτοῖς ἥδε ἡ δόξα) that while bodies are corruptible and their material substance has no permanency, souls are immortal and continue for ever; and that, emanating from the finest atmosphere, they are bound up in their bodies as in prisons, into which they are drawn by a certain natural attraction: but when they are released from the bonds of the flesh, they rejoice and are borne upwards, freed from a long slavery.

Hippolytus, 27: Now the dogma (word) of the resurrection also is firmly held among them (ἔρρωται δὲ παρ' αὐτοῖς καὶ ὁ τῆς ἀναστάσεως λόγος). For they confess that the flesh also will rise and be immortal as the soul is already immortal, which they now say, when separated from the body, enters a place of fragrant air and light, to rest until the judgment ... for they say that there will be a judgment and a conflagration of everything, and that the wicked will be eternally punished.

There are two possible interpretations of this last evidence: 1. that Josephus is adapting and conforming his account to Greek conceptions, whereas Hippolytus is remaining faithful to his source; or 2. that it is Hippolytus who is conforming his report of Josephus to Christian ideas and attributing such beliefs wrongly to the Essenes. In the first case the motive is plain enough; in the second it is more difficult to discern; moreover, it is the Jewish doctrine, not the Greek, that we would expect in a Jewish sect. At one point at least the new scrolls agree with Hippolytus' account; there is little doubt that the Zadokites believed in a final 'conflagration of everything'.[1] But whether the Essenes

---

[1] Cf. G. Vermès, *La Communauté de la Nouvelle Alliance* (*Analecta Lovaniensia Biblica et Orientalia*, ser. II, fasc. 22), and supra, p. 142.

taught a resurrection of the body (or prayer for enemies) must still remain in doubt.   Hippolytus may equally well, however, be faithful to his source, and the ancient Essenes may have taught both.

## Appendix C

# ARAMAIC TEXTS FROM QUMRAN

In comparison with the extensive Hebrew discoveries made at Qumran, only a small number of Aramaic texts have so far come to light. They consist, for the most part, of small fragments, miscellaneous 'bits and pieces', sometimes containing no more than one word or even just a single letter,[1] and only occasionally extending to several lines or more substantial portions of text, as, for instance, in the fragments from 'apocryphal works' (from the Book of Enoch, or the Testaments of the Twelve Patriarchs).[2] Where, in one case, a longer text has existed, it has been preserved in so dilapidated a condition as to be at times barely legible.[3] In view of this situation, the discovery at Qumran of an entire scroll of twenty-two columns, with approximately thirty-five lines to each column, makes a welcome and significant addition to the Qumran library, and, in particular, to its sadly decimated Aramaic contents.[4]

How are we to classify and describe this new Aramaic document? Since only five of the scroll's twenty-two columns have so far been published, it might be deemed advisable to await the publication of the complete scroll before venturing

[1] See D. Barthélemy and J. T. Milik, *Discoveries in the Judaean Desert I, Qumran Cave I*, Oxford, 1955, pp. 97, 147.

[2] op. cit., pp. 84, 87. The following communication was made by Père Milik in *RB*, 63, 1956, 60: 'Le livre d'Hénoch, qui, comme on sait, se divise en cinq parties, possède dans 4Q huit mss. Ils sont tous en araméen. La relation aux versions grecques et éthiopienne se révèle plutôt complexe. Dans quatre mss. on relève des correspondances assez exactes aux parties I, IV, et V (ch. CVI s.) de l'ouvrage. Mais il s'y trouve des sections qui ont été omises par les versions, ainsi une lettre d'Hénoch à Shamazya et ses compagnons, qui commence par les mots: *ydy' lhw' lkwn* [ . . . ]. La partie II, livre des Paraboles, manque entièrement et cela ne semble pas être dû au hasard. Trois mss. ne contiennent que la partie III, astronomique, mais dans une rédaction plus longue, plus détaillée et plus intelligible que celle de l'Hénoch éthiopien. Pourtant, vers la fin de cette section (Ch. LXXVI-LXXIX), les deux textes redeviennent à peu près identiques. Un petit rouleau ne contenait sans doute que la partie V, donc probablement l'original de l'*Épître d'Hénoch* du pap. Chester Beatty-Michigan.'

[3] Cf. M. Baillet, 'Fragments araméens de Qumran 2. Description de la Jérusalem Nouvelle', in *RB*, 62, 1955, 222ff.

[4] *A Genesis Apocryphon, A Scroll from the Wilderness of Judaea*, Description and Contents of the Scroll, Facsimiles, Transcription and Translation of Columns II, xix-xxii, by Nahman Avigad and Yigael Yadin, Jerusalem, 1956.

on any characterization of it. The substantial portions of the
scroll already published, however, ought to be sufficient to
enable us to describe, in general terms at least, the character
of the document.

This is, in fact, what the two editors of the five columns
so far published have sought to do. The new Aramaic
document has been described and named by them an 'Apocryphon', not only because it was 'hidden away', but mainly
since its first editors, Mr Nahman Avigad and General Yigael
Yadin, regard the scroll as 'a sort of apocryphal version of
stories from Genesis' (op. cit. p. 38), and 'the earliest
example of pseudepigraphic literature that has come down
to us. It not only helps us to reconstruct and understand
obscure passages in that literature, but fills a distinct gap in
the history of Aramaic during one of the most decisive
periods of its history' (*The Nature of the Scroll and its Date*,
p. 39). The editors emphasize 'the close connection between
the scroll and many parts of the Book of Enoch and the Book
of Jubilees, leading at times to the conclusion that *the scroll
may have served as a source for a number of stories told more
concisely in those two books*' (p. 38).

The question I wish to raise is whether, in fact, this is
an adequate or even correct description of the character of
this old Aramaic text. It is, of course, a general description:
nevertheless, too much stress on the apocryphal character of
the scroll may have the effect of obscuring or even mis-
representing its essential nature—even granted a close
affinity with the apocrypha and pseudepigrapha of the Old
Testament.

Almost as soon as the text was available, I had the
opportunity of discussing it with Dr Paul Kahle, of Oxford.
It was he who first suggested—or rather raised the question
—whether we may not actually possess, in this ancient
Aramaic document, an early specimen of a written Aramaic
Pentateuch Targum from Palestine, perhaps a prototype and
forerunner of the old Palestinian Pentateuch Targum Dr
Kahle himself published in his *Masoreten des Westens*, Band II,
and of the so-called Fragment Targum.

At this stage, with the bulk of the scroll unpublished, one

can do no more than raise the question whether the so-called Genesis 'Apocryphon' is, in fact, an old Aramaic Targum, and give some reasons for thinking that it may be.    Confirmation or rejection of what can only be a provisional and tentative working hypothesis must await the publication of the rest of the scroll and the observations and views of other scholars.

As in all Targums, the order of the Aramaic text in the scroll follows chapter and verse of the Hebrew original.

The editors of the five columns note this correspondence with the chapter order in the Hebrew text of Genesis, but do not give any detailed comparison of chapter with chapter or verse with verse: they simply observe that 'some of the chapters begin and end precisely as the comparable chapters of Genesis do' (p. 38), or that 'lines 28-30 [of col. xxii] correspond to verses 5-7 in Genesis xiv of which they are an almost literal translation' (p. 35).    On col. xxii.1-26, they note: 'These lines correspond to verses 13-24 of Genesis xiv. The narrative, on the whole, is very similar to Genesis xiv and is at times almost a literal translation, particularly beginning with the passage that deals with the King of Sodom, Abram and Melchizedek, etc.' (p. 36).    At one point, comparison is made with the Targums:

In both structure and style, this chapter [cols. xxi-xxii] is closer to the Biblical source than any other part of the scroll.    It should in fact be pointed out that, despite a number of additions which serve as a sort of commentary on the Scriptural passages *in the manner of the Targumim* [italics mine], the version of the scroll is almost identical with that of Genesis xiv, and in a number of passages is actually a literal translation.    This is of great importance in helping us to determine the relationship of the scroll to the various Targumim.    (p. 33)

This last important point, however, is not further developed.

Detailed comparison shows that, in fact, the Aramaic paraphrase follows the order of chapter and verse in the Hebrew.    Thus col. xxii is a rendering of Genesis xiv.13-20, verse by verse:

(col. xxii)

| lines | 1- 4 | Gen. xiv. 13 |
|-------|------|--------------|
| ,, | 5- 7 | ,, 14 |
| ,, | 8- 9 | ,, 15 |
| ,, | 10-11 | ,, 16 |
| ,, | 12-13 | ,, 17 |
| ,, | 14-15 | ,, 18 |
| ,, | 15-16 | ,, 19 |
| line | 17 | ,, 20 |

Even where the paraphrase is freer than in this column and embellished with haggadic additions, legend, poetry, or parable, the underlying pattern of Hebrew text and verse order can still be traced.

(col. xix)

| lines | 9-10 | Gen. xii. 9 |
|-------|------|-------------|
| ,, | 10-12 | ,, 10 |
| ,, | 13-19 | ,, 11 |
| ,, | 19-23 | ,, 12 |
| ,, | 24-27 | ,, 14 |

In the light of these facts the division of the text into a series of 'Books', a 'Book of Lamech', a 'Book of Enoch', a 'Book of Noah', a 'Book of Abraham', seems unnecessary; like any other Targum text, the Aramaic translation is simply following the sections of Scripture in their canonical order, Lamech (Gen. iv), Enoch (Gen. v), Noah (Gen. vi), etc., etc.

Further support for this hypothesis may be found in the contacts between the new text and the Targum tradition, in particular with the pre-Onkelos Palestinian Pentateuch Targum. There is, of course, no identity of text or translation: the new scroll is a hitherto unknown Aramaic paraphrase, as different from Targum Onkelos or the Geniza or Fragment Targum as these are from the Samaritan Targum or from one another: but there are *factual* agreements which betray the same origin in a Palestinian Aramaic tradition of paraphrasing Scripture.

A striking example of such an agreement with the

Palestinian Targum tradition occurs at Gen. xiv.6, where Mount Seir is identified with the mountain of Gebal (col. xxi, line 11), in agreement with the Pseudo-Jonathan Targum (P-J) *contra* Onkelos (O) [ = Seir]. This agrees also with the Samaritan Targum and is clearly an old Palestinian identification.[1]

At Gen. xiv.18 (col. xxii.13-14) Salem is identified with Jerusalem in agreement with all the Targums. Melchizedek, however, is described as a *priest unto God* (*kohen le'el*) in agreement with the Hebrew followed by the Fragment and Samaritan Targums, but *contra* O and P-J. The avoidance of the designation *kohen* in the Onkelos Targum is significant: it was no doubt motivated by the same reason as led to the gloss on Salem, equating it with Jerusalem. The identification of the Salem of Genesis xiv.18 with the Samaritan town of that name and the designation of Melchizedek as 'priest' would form the basis for Samaritan priestly claims. The new scroll preserves an ancient Palestinian tradition.

In another passage, the 'Targumic' character of the version (and, incidentally, its antiquity) can be determined by an agreement with the New Testament.[2]

At col. xxii, line 27, Gen. xv.1 is rendered:

> *After these things God appeared to Abram in a vision and said to him—*

It is not surprising to find such 'anthropomorphic' language avoided in all our Targums, especially as it does not correspond to the Hebrew.[3]

Acts vii.2 alludes to the parallel passage Genesis xii.1, where the Lord spoke to Abram, in the form ὁ θεὸς τῆς δόξης ὤφθη τῷ πατρὶ ἡμῶν Ἀβραάμ . . . καὶ εἶπεν πρὸς αὐτόν . . .

Though the two passages are different, the use of an

---

[1] Avigad and Yadin write (p. 29): 'During the Second Commonwealth and thereafter, the name "Gebal" was applied most frequently to a region in the land of Edom called in the Greek sources Γοβολῖτις or Γεβαληνή. Josephus, too, states that the children of Esau dwelt in the part of Idumaea called Γοβολῖτις (*Antiq.* II.i, 2).'

Another example is cited by Avigad and Yadin at p. 35: 'the King of Zeboiim (Gen. xiv.2, 8) is called *shmy'bd*, a form close to the Samaritan version.' (Where in the Samaritan or other translations do we find the words 'and in the thirteenth year they rebelled against him' (line 27)?) Cf. Avigad and Yadin, loc. cit.

[2] For a similar contact between Targum tradition and New Testament, see my *Aramaic Approach to the Gospels and Acts*, 2nd edn., p. 244.

[3] A.V. 'After these things the word of the Lord came unto Abram in a vision.'

identical formula can scarcely be coincidence. If we ask, where did Stephen (or Luke) obtain this formula, the answer can only be in the familiar formula of the Aramaic Targum of the period, here preserved, in written form, in the new scroll.

Some general features of the new version resemble the older forms of Palestinian Pentateuch Targum, as preserved in the Geniza texts or the Fragment Targum. If occasionally (as at Gen. xiv) it follows the Hebrew closely, it is for the most part a free paraphrase, with long expansions and additions, such as the description of Sarah's beauty at col. xx or the parable of the Palm and the Cedar on col. xix.[1] Similar poetic passages are found in the old Palestinian Pentateuch Targum.

In what period are we to set this early 'Targum'? If we accept the general conclusions of the archaeologists, the scroll itself must have been written before A.D. 70. Affinities with the apocrypha and the pseudepigrapha (especially the Book of Jubilees) support this early dating. Before a sufficient number of characteristic Aramaic idioms of a particular period can be adduced to identify the period of the scroll by linguistic criteria, we shall have to await publication of the whole text. The published folios, however, already yield one important philological fact: the scroll makes use of the Aramaic adverb 'edain, b'edain (for example, col. xxii, lines 2, 18, 20), found no less than twenty-six times in Daniel alone, but *never* in Targumic Aramaic. In several other cases we meet with non-Targumic usage, for example, ḥalta (col.

---

[1] Both poems are of some literary merit. The second (in Avigad and Yadin's English version) reads:

> And I, Abram, dreamed a dream . . .
>> and lo! I saw in my dream one cedar tree
>> and one palm
> . . . And men came and sought to cut down
>> and uproot the cedar and to leave the palm
>> by itself.
> And the palm cried out and said, 'Cut not
>> down the cedar . . .'.
> And for the sake of the palm the cedar was saved.

(The cedar is Abraham, the palm Sarah, through whose offer of herself, Abraham was saved in Egypt.)

These are the closest literary parallels we possess in Aramaic to the original (poetic) parables and poems of Jesus (for their date see the next paragraph).

See further *An Aramaic Approach to the Gospels and Acts²*, p. 240ff., Appendix D, *The Aramaic Liturgical Poetry of the Jews*.

xxii, line 4) in the sense of a 'valley'; Targ. *ḥalala* means a 'cavern'; Syriac *ḥelta*, the 'sheath' of a sword. The verb *'ethḥlem* (line 5) in the meaning 'grow strong' is attested in Syriac, but not in Targumic Aramaic. Linguistically the scroll would seem, therefore, to belong to the age of the 'Old Aramaic'.

The new scroll is almost certainly our oldest written Palestinian Pentateuch Targum, probably dating to the first century B.C. Both from a linguistic and literary point of view, it is an invaluable witness to the Aramaic language and literature of the time of Christ. Codex Neofiti I[1] and this new text from Qumran have supplied us with new linguistic material of the greatest importance for the study of first-century Palestinian Aramaic.

[1] See *NTS*, 3, 306ff.

# THE QUMRAN CALENDAR AND THE LAST SUPPER

Mlle A. Jaubert has recently developed a suggestion of Père D. Barthélemy that the Qumran sectarians or Essenes followed the calendar of the Book of Jubilees, representing the priestly calendrical tradition of Israel.[1]  Mlle Jaubert is now supported by Père J. T. Milik, who claims that this hypothesis is confirmed by the number of scrolls dealing with calendar questions from Cave 4.  Milik adds that, in this respect, Qumran sectarians followed the same calendrical system as the Boethusian Sadducees.[2]

According to this sectarian calendar (it is further claimed) the date of the great festivals are not movable (as in the Pharisaic calendar) but immovably fixed: the Day of Pentecost, for example, always falls on a Sunday and the 1st and 15th Nisan always on a Wednesday.  Thus, according to this calendar, 14th-15th Nisan, in the year of the Crucifixion, must have fallen on Tuesday-Wednesday of Holy Week, which, according to the *Didascalia* and Epiphanius, was the night of the Arrest and the Last Supper of Jesus.[3]

A note of caution has been struck with regard to these ingenious, but not always verifiable, identifications, in an important article by the late Professor Julian Obermann, entitled 'Calendric Elements in the Dead Sea Scrolls'.[4] Obermann was not convinced that the Calendar of Qumran could in fact be conclusively identified with that of Jubilees.

Nevertheless, on the general question of the existence and observance of such a type of sectarian calendar in the time of Christ there can be no doubt; and it is certain too that it was a calendar differing fundamentally from the official Pharisaic-Sadducaean system of calculations in current

---

[1] 'Le Calendrier des Jubilés et les jours liturgiques de la semaine', in *VT*, 7, 35ff.

[2] *Dix Ans de Découvertes dans le Désert de Juda*, Paris, 1957, p. 70ff., Eng. edn., p. 107ff.

[3] A. Jaubert, 'La Date de la dernière Cène', *RHR*, 146, 1954, 140ff.

[4] *JBL*, 75, 1956, 285ff.; cf. Milik, op. cit. p. 70.

use. In Plate VI of the *Manual of Discipline*, dealing with the admission of new members to the community, catechumens or converts are exhorted 'not to depart as regards their [calendar] periods from any of God's commandments', and this is explained as meaning that they are neither 'to advance their seasons nor to retard any of their festivals'.[1]

The meaning of this injunction becomes evident in the light of Pharisaic calendar references and innovations vis-à-vis the older priestly tradition. Thus the Pharisees interpreted Lev. xxiii.11, 15, 'the morrow after the Sabbath' to mean 16th Nisan, following the Passover Festival Day (or Sabbath) 15th Nisan; Pentecost, fifty days later, always fell on 6th Sivan, without regard to the day of the week. The Sadducees appear to have contended that both the Omer and Pentecost should be observed on the day following a weekly sabbath, and, therefore must always fall on a Sunday.[2]

Such a difference meant that the Pharisaic Pentecost (and the Waving of the Omer) generally always fell in advance of the time observed by the Sadducees.[3] Similarly the Pharisees might postpone certain festivals for reasons of expediency, one well-known device being that of intercalation.

The warnings of the *Manual of Discipline*, therefore, about advancing and retarding festival dates, are manifestly aimed at just such Pharisaic practices.

Was there, then, a dispute about the date of the Passover in the year of the Crucifixion, one party dating the first Day of the feast on the Friday, another earlier in the week? The theory is one that has been advanced more than once to account for the divergences between the Synoptic and Johannine chronologies,[4] but so far no evidence has been forthcoming to substantiate it.[5] Some kind of substantiation may now be held to be forthcoming from Qumran; for we can be certain that the Qumran sectarians or Essenes, an important and numerous minority in the Palestinian scene of the first

---

[1] See Obermann, op. cit. p. 292ff.
[2] See R. H. Charles, *Apocrypha and Pseudepigrapha of the Old Testament*, Vol. II, p. 35ff.
[3] Cf. Obermann, loc. cit.
[4] Cf. J. Jeremias, *Die Abendmahlsworte Jesu*, Göttingen, 1949, p. 14. (English translation by A. Ehrhardt, *The Eucharistic Words of Jesus*, p. 9ff.)
[5] ibid. p. 15.

century, did celebrate Passover in the year of the Crucifixion at a different time from the official time promulgated by the Jerusalem Temple authorities, which were dominated by Pharisaic influence and interests.  Moreover, if the sectarian dating was the old priestly one, and, as Père Milik contends, Essenes and Sadducaeans were agreed in such calendrical matters, then the non-Pharisaic date may have been more widely observed, especially outside Jerusalem.  Some liberty was allowed about the dates of celebration in the Diaspora,[1] and there appear to have been special regulations for Galilee,[2] though it is unlikely that any other law ran in Jerusalem than the Pharisaic—except perhaps in secret.

We do not require to assume that Jesus belonged to any sectarian group, even if he and his disciples actually did celebrate a Passover earlier in the week, since it may have been the Passover of the old calendar which was, in any case, being celebrated outside Jerusalem.  If this was to be the last Passover of all, the consummation of Israel's Deliverance in a new Exodus, Jesus might naturally choose what may have been widely and popularly held to be the old 'Mosaic' season.  Was it, in fact, an *illegal* Passover—so far as the date and place were concerned—which Jesus and His disciples celebrated in Holy Week?  Mark xiv.12ff, emphasizes the secret nature of the preparations for it.  The meal in John, falling before the official Passover, does show certain paschal features.[3]  Was it the illegality of the transformed rite, a new kind of Passover, abrogating by transcending the old Mosaic ordinance, and set at an illegal season (the old Calendar) which gave Judas his final opportunity to betray Christ?  In carrying off the sop, he took evidence with him to the priests and Pharisees that an illegal feast had been celebrated.  In that case, Jesus was challenging Pharisaic Law in its stronghold, Jerusalem itself.

[1] Josephus, *Antiq.* III.x.5, cf. II.xv.1.
[2] Bab. Talmud, *Pes.* iv.5ff. (cf. Jeremias, op. cit. p. 15).
[3] Cf. C. K. Barrett, *The Gospel according to St John*, S.P.C.K., 1955, p. 373ff.

# Indexes

## I. INDEX NOMINUM

## II. INDEX RERUM

## III. INDEX LOCORUM

The numbers in italic type indicate the pages of this book

### OLD TESTAMENT

### APOCRYPHA AND PSEUDEPIGRAPHA

### NEW TESTAMENT